|  |  |  |
|---|---|---|
|  |  |  |
|  |  |  |
|  |  |  |
|  |  |  |
|  |  |  |
|  |  |  |
|  |  |  |
|  |  |  |

|  |  |  |
|---|---|---|
|  |  |  |
|  |  |  |
|  |  |  |
|  |  |  |
|  |  |  |
|  |  |  |
|  |  |  |
|  |  |  |
|  |  |  |

# Mindful of Words

# Solving Problems in the Teaching of Literacy

*Cathy Collins Block, Series Editor*

# Mindful of Words

Spelling and Vocabulary
Explorations 4–8

Kathy Ganske

THE GUILFORD PRESS
New York    London

*A word is not a crystal, transparent and unchanged; it is the skin
of a living thought and may vary greatly in color and content
according to the circumstances and the time in which it is used.*

—Oliver Wendell Holmes, Jr.

**Library of Congress Cataloging-in-Publication Data**

Ganske, Kathy.
    Mindful of words : spelling and vocabulary explorations 4–8 / by Kathy Ganske.
        p. cm. — (Solving problems in the teaching of literacy)
    Includes bibliographical references and index.
    ISBN: 978-1-59385-822-3 (pbk. : alk. paper)
    1. English language—Orthography and spelling—Study and teaching.
  2. Vocabulary—Study and teaching.  I. Title.
    LB1574.G35 2008
    372.63'2—dc22
                                                        2008002966

# About the Author

**Kathy Ganske, PhD,** is an Associate Professor of Literacy in the Graduate Teacher Education Program at Oberlin College. She is a former classroom teacher and a popular speaker. Her books include *Word Journeys: Assessment-Guided Phonics, Spelling, and Vocabulary Instruction* (Guilford, 2000), *Word Sorts and More: Sound, Pattern, and Meaning Explorations K–3* (Guilford, 2006), and, with Dorothy S. Strickland and Joanne K. Monroe, *Supporting Struggling Readers and Writers: Strategies for Classroom Intervention 3–6* (International Reading Association and Stenhouse, 2002).

# Preface

I have written *Mindful of Words: Spelling and Vocabulary Explorations 4–8* as a practical resource and guide for classroom teachers and others to engage students in upper-level word study activities that are challenging, interactive, and inquiry based. The work is grounded in research on developmental spelling and vocabulary learning, with careful consideration given to motivation and intellectual stimulation as well as to meeting the different needs of students and teachers. In addition to furthering students' spelling and vocabulary knowledge, I hope the explorations will develop an enduring interest in savoring, puzzling over, and coming to know the language we call English, in students and teachers alike. *Mindful of Words* may supplement or complement an existing reading, spelling, vocabulary, or writing program, as well as serve as an adjunct to a resource such as *Word Journeys: Assessment-Guided Phonics, Spelling, and Vocabulary Instruction* (Ganske, 2000). Although they are separate, stand-alone works, *Mindful of Words* picks up where *Word Sorts and More: Sound, Pattern, and Meaning Explorations K–3* (Ganske, 2006) ends. The latter book covers the early spelling phases—emergent, letter name, and within word pattern—whereas this book addresses the needs of the more mature spellers at the syllable juncture and derivational constancy stages. It is divided into three parts.

Part 1, "Setting the Stage," presents background information relevant to the rest of the book. I discuss the book's grounding in research, define *word study* in terms of elements I believe are important for effective instruction, briefly outline historical influences on the English spelling system, describe considerations for developing students' spelling and vocabulary knowledge, and explain various components that, unless otherwise noted, are common to each of the word studies in Parts 2 and 3. For example, each sort includes a template of 21–24 reproducible words and an answer key. Answer keys identify the aim of the sorting activity—sort by sound, by pattern, by pattern and sound, by meaning, and so forth. Templates include bolded category headers at the top to guide teaching and learning; key words follow the headers. Headers may be removed before photocopying for a greater challenge to the students. Descriptions of six additional components follow:

- "What Is Known" and "What Is New" sections for each feature or sort highlight prior knowledge students are assumed to have and detail new concepts being introduced so teachers may use the sorts out of order, if desired.
- "Considerations" offer guidance and suggestions for teaching the sort.

- "Talking Points" summarize principles/rules related to spelling features targeted in the sort; they are included with all but the root-focused sorts in Part 3.
- "Integrating Idioms" sections present one of the sort words (or, in a few instances, a related word) in an idiomatic phrase. The word's literal and figurative meanings are briefly discussed. These sections are included throughout the word studies in Part 2 and phased out in Part 3.
- "Did You Know?" sections aim primarily to excite students' (and teachers') interest and appreciation for words. The history of one of the sort words (or a related word) is presented for each of the word studies in Parts 2 and 3.
- "Literature Links," included for numerous word studies, suggests relevant books.

Part 1 closes with the section "Teacher to Teacher," in which seven classroom teachers from grade 4 through middle school provide glimpses of upper-level word study in their classrooms. They share a variety of ideas about assessment, classroom management, motivation, teaching techniques, and activities. The section ends with a principal's recounting of the journey to upper-level word study in her school.

Part 2, "Word Study for Syllable Juncture Spellers," focuses on instructional activities for students with well-developed understandings of single-syllable words, who are ready to explore longer and more complex words and the spelling issues they bring. Nearly all of the targeted words in Part 2 are two-syllable words. This length provides opportunities for students to examine many new spelling issues but without the potential compounded difficulties presented by the three-, four-, and five-syllable words that characterize Part 3. At this stage students examine compound words, inflectional endings and other affixation, open and closed syllables, syllable stress, vowel patterns in stressed and unstressed syllables, and confusing consonant patterns. Sixty-three categorization activities are included in this part, including card games to encourage repeated reinforcement of homophones and homographs. Many students in grades 4–6 will be ready for the challenges of the syllable juncture stage, and, as is pointed out in Part 1, some older and younger students may also benefit from these studies. Informal assessment and observation should guide teachers' decision making.

Part 3, "Word Study for Derivational Constancy Spellers," explores families of sophisticated words of relatively low frequency. Students learn to use their knowledge of one word to spell other words in the family, and learn that although pronunciation may differ from one related word to another, the spelling tends to remain constant as a visible reminder of the family or meaning relationship (e.g., *geometry* becomes *geometric* rather than *geametric*, as the sound might suggest, because it is in the family of words derived from the Greek *geo-*, or earth). This part introduces students to several new concepts. They learn to add inflected endings to polysyllabic base words; advance their knowledge of other affixation, including the assimilation of prefixes; and understand the concepts of consonant and vowel alternations. In addition, substantial attention is given to developing students' knowledge of Greek and Latin prefixes and roots as an aid not only to spelling low-frequency words but to understanding their meanings as well. Fifty-eight word explorations are included in this part; 34 of these target Greek and Latin elements; each of the latter explorations is focused on a particular theme, as in body language, ruling and governing, and so forth.

The appendices provide support and extension materials, including lists of 100+ important vocabulary words for social studies, science, and math, and charts for recording student performance on any of the more than 120 word studies.

The stories and histories presented in the "Did You Know?" sections were garnered from a variety of sources, with a strong effort made to find the information in multiple texts and/or websites; references are cited if only one source was found. Websites such as Wikipedia (*www.en.wikipedia.*

*org*), an online encyclopedia, and Answer.com, an online dictionary, provided a wealth of information and leads to other online resources. Three valuable texts were *Chambers Dictionary of Etymology*, *Merriam-Webster New Book of Word Histories*, and the *American Heritage Dictionary*, which includes a word history every few pages in both its college edition (2004) and the larger edition (1996). The etymology sections of both of these dictionaries were used, as well as the online *Oxford English Dictionary*. Checks on word frequency were made with *The Educator's Word Frequency Guide* (Zeno, Ivens, Millard, & Duvvuri, 1995).

# Acknowledgments

I would like to thank the teachers and principal in the "Teacher to Teacher" section, who so generously shared their expertise and time. I would also like to thank Chris Jennison, Publisher; Craig Thomas, Editor; Anna Brackett, Editorial Project Manager; Paul Gordon, Art Director; and the rest of The Guilford Press staff for their insights and careful attention during the production process. Finally, special thanks to my husband, family, friends, and colleagues for the generous support and encouragement they have provided along the way.

I wish the reader many thought-provoking and invigorating investigations into the realm of upper-level word study. As Aristophanes noted, "By words the mind is winged."

# Contents

# List
# of Reproducible Pages

## Part 3. Word Study for Derivational Constancy Spellers

# Appendices

# Part 1

# Setting the Stage

## Background

Although research regarding the value of spelling instruction for young children is well established (National Institute of Child Health and Human Development, 2000; Snow, Burns, & Griffin, 1998), for older students it is scarce. Nonetheless, the very nature of the English spelling system provides a basis for trusting in the value of devoting a small amount of time to appropriate upper-level word study. Such instruction has the potential to significantly benefit students by supporting their vocabulary and spelling development and increasing their ability to use the words that are studied (Adams, 2004; Moats, 2005/2006). Students with more developed orthographic or spelling knowledge may develop stronger vocabularies over time than those with more limited understandings (Ehri & Rosenthal, 2007).

In contrast to the early stages of spelling development, in which students learn how consonant and vowel patterns work in single-syllable words (see *Word Sorts and More: Sound, Pattern, and Meaning Explorations K–3* [Ganske, 2006]), the upper stages explored in *Mindful of Words* focus on polysyllabic words. Here students extend their word knowledge through the study of more sophisticated sound and pattern relationships, including open and closed syllables, doubling, and syllable stress. Given the essentially morphological base of English (Chomsky & Halle, 1968), it is not surprising that students also examine the pattern–meaning connections evident in families of related words (Templeton, 1983), as well as explore the meanings of prefixes, suffixes, and roots and how they combine. The origins or histories of words and the development of English as a language, areas often neglected in upper-level word study, are also integrated into this volume and have the potential to fuel children's interest in word learning. Discovering that words have their own stories (for instance, that *school* originally meant "leisure," that *Superman* might have been called *Overman*, or how *egregious*, which once meant "outstanding," came to mean the exact opposite, "offensive") adds a whole new dimension to students' perception of just what a word is and can ignite an abiding curiosity and appreciation for language.

Despite the potential benefits of upper-level word study, in my work with teachers I frequently hear concerns expressed by those who teach students at the upper stages of spelling development—syllable juncture and derivational constancy. Some question whether they know enough to teach others about the nature and structure of the English spelling system at these levels. Others worry about lack of time or materials. Curricular demands can indeed fill the school day, causing time to be a limited resource. Being able to allocate time for read-alouds, independent reading, and even word study in the upper grades can require creative problem solving, but it is well worth the effort. My hopes in writing this book are twofold: to provide materials to make upper-level word study instruction easier for teachers and to cultivate students' and teachers' interest and curiosity in learning about words. After all, words are central to our everyday lives: We read words, we write words, we talk with words, we think with words, and, as writer Aldous Huxley put it, "words form the thread on which we string our experiences." We have every reason to be *Mindful of Words*.

# The Context: What Is Word Study?

Use of the phrase *word study* has become prevalent in recent years, and with its widespread use have come varying applications of the term. When someone says, "We just finished word study," it is impossible to know what that really means other than that instruction related to some type of word learning occurred. Some, including this author, have long regarded word study as encompassing phonics, spelling, and vocabulary instruction, with children's orthographic or spelling knowledge of central importance in determining timely instruction and with word sorting as a key activity (e.g., Bear, Invernizzi, Templeton, & Johnston, 2000; Ganske, 2000; Henderson, 1990). As children move into more sophisticated word studies, spelling and vocabulary development receive increasing attention. I believe that several traits help to describe effective word study across the grades. They are summarized in the following mnemonic—THAT'S Word Study:

T = Thinking
H = Humor
A = Appropriate instruction
T = Talk
S = Systematic approach and some sorting

## *Thinking*

During word study, students actively engage in thinking and questioning, as they increase their awareness of how words are spelled and what they mean. They look for common characteristics to help them generalize understandings to other words. Oddballs (words that do not fit the pattern, sound, or meaning focus of a particular sort) can often be used to encourage students to think, as well as to alert teachers to students who are not thinking but simply acting on "automatic pilot," that is, taking their cues from one aspect of the word while ignoring others. The amount of teacher guidance can also affect students' thinking. With too much teacher direction and too little incentive to problem-solve, students are likely to become disengaged; with too little guidance, they may become frustrated. When the amount of support is appropriate, students should be actively involved and conjecturing about the words.

Each of the word studies in *Mindful of Words* includes a "Considerations" section with suggestions for using the accompanying sort. The suggestions, which tend to target the needs of typical spellers at that spelling stage, are just starting points. Depending on the level of students' engagement and motivation, the suggestions may be adjusted for more or less teacher direction. For example, one group of students may need considerable support, so the teacher walks them through the sort by modeling the placement of several word cards and by thinking aloud to reveal the category traits. By contrast, a teacher may simply ask a group of students who need very little guidance to sort the words into categories, using key words and/or category headers as guides. For this type of *closed sort*, students are sometimes told to categorize the words in a particular way, such as with sound and pattern or pattern and meaning in mind. There may be times when an even less structured approach, such as *open sorting*, is desirable. No category headers or key words are used for this activity. Instead students work alone or with a partner to determine and define their own categories for the sort; as a result, responses may vary. To facilitate word sort introductions, each template of words includes key words and bolded category headers. In order to accommodate flexible use, the key words are not bolded; however, for ease of identification they are placed at the top of the template. When desired, they may be underlined.

## Humor

Wit can defuse tensions and build students' confidence and risk taking (Cary, 2000); it may come as little surprise, then, that one of the characteristics of effective teachers is a sense of humor (Block & Mangieri, 2003; McDermott & Rothenberg, 1999). Humor is a natural partner for word study, because English has given rise to many plays on words—idioms, puns, oxymora (phrases that use contradictory words), and so forth—that tend to surprise and amuse us, as, for example:

> *The children relished the thought of hot dogs for lunch.* (pun)
> *A bicycle can't stand alone; it's two tired.* (pun)
> *A thief fell in wet cement and broke his leg; now he's a hardened criminal.* (pun)
> *I can give you a definite maybe that we'll be there.* (oxymoron)
> *That picture is pretty ugly.* (oxymoron)
> *I know you can't find the paper, but don't come unglued.* (idiom)
> *He put his foot in his mouth when he said he'd be there at 5:00 A.M.* (idiom)

Although use of figurative language can add levity to the daily routine, twists of phrases such as those just described can be confusing, especially to students who are learning English, so it is important to discuss both the literal and nonliteral senses of the expressions. Each of the word studies in Part 2 of *Mindful of Words* includes an "Integrating Idioms" section, in which an idiom is presented and discussed; this feature is gradually phased out in Part 3.

## Appropriate Instruction

Spelling knowledge develops from straightforward, letter–sound correspondences to increasingly more abstract pattern–sound relationships and eventually to complex interactions involving sounds, patterns, and meaning, as well as relationships involving combinations of meaning elements. Because the sophistication of students' spelling knowledge is likely to differ from student to student within a given class, observation and informal assessment, such as the Developmental Spelling Analysis (DSA; Ganske, 2000), are used to determine appropriate instruction. Although syllable juncture spellers tend to be students in grades 4 through 6, some students at these grade levels may still be grappling with issues from earlier stages (within word pattern or even letter name), whereas others may be ready to take on the challenges of the final, derivational constancy stage (Ganske, 1999). The same can be said for students in grades 7 and 8; although most are likely ready to explore derivational constancy issues, some may still be solidifying understandings from an earlier stage. In addition, certain students in earlier grades may be ready for some of the more sophisticated word studies presented at these advanced stages. Assessment helps to ensure that word study instruction is timely. Higher levels of concern are the focus of *Mindful of Words*; more fundamental issues are addressed in *Word Sorts and More* (Ganske, 2006).

## Talk

As students in the middle grades consider how categories of words are alike and different, as they share their thinking about how words work and ponder the meanings of idioms and the origins of words, talk becomes a vehicle for them to clarify and expand their ideas. Interacting with and learning from others can be motivating to students in the upper grades (Oldfather, 1995). Exchanges among students also afford teachers opportunities to gain insights about students' understandings as they listen to, observe, and interact with them. Insights such as these can make it easier to tailor instruction to better meet the needs of individual students. Each of the word studies in this book, with the exception of those focused on Greek and Latin roots, includes "Talking Points" that highlight spelling generalizations and other information relevant to the features being studied. As students discuss their understandings, they may generate similar or other talking points. Any generalizations not raised by the students can be added to the discussion before the session ends.

## Systematic Approach and Some Sorting

In this book *systematic* refers to instruction that builds on what students already know and that is preplanned and purposeful. Decision making is not lockstep but instead is guided by assessment data and ongoing observations of students' performance. Teachers focus instruction on features that students need to understand, rather than feeling obligated to have students complete all of the word studies. As each new spelling feature is introduced in *Mindful of Words*, assumptions regarding "What Is Known" and "What Is New" to learners are discussed. Students who have previously been engaged in developmentally appropriate word study are likely to have the background indicated. When this is not the case, or when the sorts are used out of order, scaffolding may be needed.

Sorting activities play a strong role in *Mindful of Words*. Categorizing is one of our most basic cognitive abilities (Bruner, Goodnow, & Austin, 1956). We use it to develop concepts and to order the world in which we live. In fact, as you begin to think about it, there is very little we do not categorize; we categorize animals, plants, books, architectural styles, furniture types, clothing makers and styles, automobiles, foods, age groups of people, hair types . . . and the list goes on. Categorizing helps us to understand new information by comparing the new to the known and to retrieve information in an efficient manner. As we consider the role of categorizing in learning about words, we need to consider that English is a complex language, with borrowings from many other languages. By categorizing words according to their features, students are able to notice similarities and differences within and across the categories that help them to form generalizations about how the words work. Given the approximately 90,000 different words that students in grades 3–9 face in their school reading material, being able to generalize is essential if word learning is to be efficient.

# A Word about History

Many of the complexities involved in English spelling are the result of the influences of other languages, primarily Anglo-Saxon English (also known as Old English), a form of French, Greek, and Latin. For example, consider the letter *c* and the /k/ sound: The hard *c* in *cat* is of Old English origin, whereas the soft *c*, as in *cent*, is from Old French (though the French got the word from Latin). The French gave us /k/ spelled as *que*, as in the final position in *antique* and *boutique*, and from the Greeks we got /k/ spelled with *ch*, as in *chorus* and *chronicle*.

Old English was the language of England from the 6th century to the middle of the 11th. The letter–sound correspondences of Old English are remarkably regular. In fact, young children who tend to rely on sound when spelling words have been said to spell like the Saxons of England (Henderson, 1981), as in *wif* for *wife* and *hus* for *house*. Old English gave us many of our most common words. In fact, the 100 most frequently occurring words in English all have an Anglo-Saxon origin (Moats, 2005/2006).

With the Norman Conquest in 1066 came a tremendous influx of French words into the language. Over time there was a merging of Old English and Norman French into what is now called Middle English. New spelling complexities in the form of patterns resulted from the amalgamation of the languages; among them the existence of both hard and soft *c* and *g*; many long vowel patterns, such as the *ea* vowel team with its long and short pronunciations, and abstract vowels such as the *ou* and *oy* in *country* and *royal*.

During the Renaissance of the 16th century, many words of Greek and Latin origin were added to the language as interest in the classics revived and explorations and discoveries were made that led to a need for naming. Because many words with Greek and Latin roots, prefixes, and suffixes were coined or borrowed during this time, today we have lots of families of words that relate in spelling, as well as meaning. It is this spelling–meaning connection that can help students to spell words that on the surface (at the level of pronunciations) appear unrelated, as in *sign*, *signature*, and *resignation*. Moreover, awareness of morphological relationships may help students to infer meanings of new words, as, for example, deducing what *telepathy* means on the basis of understanding **tele**graph and sym**pathy** (Adams, 2004).

Since the Renaissance, words have continued to be borrowed from other languages. Some examples and their languages of origin are: African, *chimpanzee* and *kwanza*; aboriginal Australian, *kangaroo* and *boomerang*; American Indian, *chocolate* and *tepee*; Arabic, *coffee* and *monsoon*; Celtic, *heather* and *plaid*; Chinese, *tea* and *mandarin*; Dutch, *waffle* and *cruise*; French, *à la mode* and *bureau*; German, *hamburger* and *dachshund*; Greek, *church* and *tantalize*; Hebrew, *kosher* and *Sabbath*; Sanskrit, *pepper* and *yoga*; Italian, *piano* and *spaghetti*; Japanese, *haiku* and *kimono*; Russian, *mammoth* and *czar*; Scandinavian, *ski* and *egg*; and Spanish, *patio* and *vanilla*. With some initial guidance in interpreting the etymological information that is part of a word's entry in an unabridged dictionary, students can easily find additional words from other languages. For example, here is the etymology for *stomach* from *The American Heritage College Dictionary* (2004):

[ME < OFr. *stomaque, estomac* < *Lat. stomachus* < *Gk. stomakhos*, gullet < *stoma*, mouth.]

We can interpret the information as follows: The word is most recently derived from Middle English, which borrowed the word from the Old French words *stomaque* and *estomac*. These had been borrowed from the Latin word *stomachus*, which in turn came from the Greek word *stomakhos*, meaning "gullet," and referring to our throat. This word had evolved from another Greek word, *stoma*, meaning "mouth." Although exploring etymologies may seem difficult, with a list of abbreviations for the language names (which the dictionary provides) and understanding that the "<" symbol means "derived from," it is actually quite easy. You can often skim most of the history and get to the origin of the word, which for the preceding example is *stoma*, meaning "mouth." Students might then speculate how a word meaning "mouth" came to refer to the place where food is digested.

As students explore the etymologies of words, you might also ask them to consider just what *language* is and to think about or research its beginnings. In an effort to encourage students' interest in word learning and their appreciation for language, each of the word studies in Parts 2 and 3 includes a "Did You Know?" section in which the story of a word or its history is presented. Besides arousing interest, this type of activity provides rich instruction for fostering vocabulary knowledge, instruction that goes beyond definitions and encourages students to think about words and to form associations with them (Beck, McKeown, & Kucan, 2002). The "Did You Know?" sections in *Mind-*

*ful of Words* are written with a student audience in mind so that they may be read aloud to students, if desired. Words thought to be of interest to students were chosen for inclusion.

# Teaching Considerations

## Word Sorts

Although certain activities will tend to work better than others for particular word sorts, a basic repertoire of possibilities will provide students and teachers with flexibility and choice. For instance, in addition to the guided word introductions and closed and open sorts previously mentioned, students might at times be asked to complete a *blind sort*, namely to categorize words with a partner but without looking at the words. After displaying the key words for reference, one partner reads the remaining words to the other, who determines their placement. This type of categorization activity works well when there are contrasting sounds in the sort and highly visual patterns, such as with open and closed syllables (*meter* and *matter*). The format encourages students to think about sound, as well as pattern. Because groups of words can be sorted in multiple ways, answer keys are labeled to show what type of sort it is; for example, *Sorting by Sound and Pattern* or *Sorting by Pattern and Meaning*.

Another form of sorting practice, *speed sorts*, encourages automatic recall of patterns being studied. With this type of reinforcement, students categorize the words consecutive times, striving to decrease their sorting time while increasing or maintaining their accuracy. A partner format and a stopwatch for checking the time it takes to complete the categorizing work well. Sometimes students set personal goals and graph their results.

*Word hunting* is another activity that is often used in upper-level word study. Because students must apply their understandings as they search for other words with the features they are studying, word hunts are carried out after students have considerable familiarity with the patterns. Many of the word studies in Part 2 and some of those in Part 3 lend themselves to word hunting because the patterns are common to many words. When related words are involved, as in consonant alternations, students should be encouraged to generate a related word after locating either a base word or its derived form. For example, students might find *disrupt* and generate the related word *disruption*, or vice versa. The same approach works well for word hunts involving homophones. For certain studies, such as when Greek and Latin roots are explored, word hunting may not be feasible, as the roots may occur with too little frequency. Instead, groups of students might try to brainstorm other words with the roots or search in dictionaries for further examples.

Sorts and word hunt results can be recorded in a journal, along with personal reflections and other information, such as described in the "Teacher to Teacher" section in this chapter. In small groups or with a partner, students might also generate synonyms or antonyms for some of the words, explore etymologies and word meanings with an unabridged dictionary, and record questions and talking points that arise from their explorations of words. As they study roots, they might coin new words with the roots, as described in *Word Journeys* (Ganske, 2000, Chapter 7).

In general, students are likely to work with a set of words for a week, though this may take more or less time depending on how quickly they grasp the content of the sort. In the case of scheduling difficulties, the work may be spread out over a somewhat longer period. Teachers should be directly involved when students are first introduced to a set of words so they can monitor students' understandings and troubleshoot problems, if not actually guide them through the sort. Some teachers prefer to introduce words to each group on the same day, whereas others find it more workable to stagger introductions across multiple days. Once students have a clear idea of the categories and what is being focused on, follow-up activities may be carried out with a partner, in a small group, or independently, using a notebook, with teachers monitoring the work but not working directly with the students.

Performance with a set of words may be gauged by the use of observation and anecdotal notes; by word study journal or notebook work, including reflections; and by informal assessments over 10–15 of the words. The last may be dictated by the teacher, completed with partners, or carried out at listening stations with prerecorded quiz words. Two popular quiz formats include a traditional dictation and a dictation that requires students to categorize, as well as spell, the words (in other words, a blind written sort). Sometimes a sentence dictation is incorporated that includes review words. I am often asked about the use of transfer words in quiz dictations. Transfer words—words not studied but that include the pattern—are fine to include, with this caveat: Many words have alternate spelling patterns for the same sound; if a student does not have prior knowledge of the word, an alternative spelling that is legitimate though incorrect may be used, as, for instance, the spelling of *remoat* for *remote*. Some credit should be allowed in such cases, or else transfer words should not be used when a sound can be spelled several ways, unless meaning makes clear which is the correct one. For convenience in keeping track of students' performance and completion of sorts, Performance Records are included in Appendix A.

## Vocabulary Knowledge

As students work with words, they not only examine the sound, pattern, and meaning relationships of their spellings but also come to understand and use the words. This is important, considering the advantage that students who have well-developed vocabulary knowledge have over peers who do not have this knowledge in comprehending what they read (Stanovich, 2000). For instance, try comprehending the following well-known piece of literature in its "weighty-word" format:

> Two juvenescent members of the Homo sapiens species hied to the apex of a well-defined natural mass, which deviated considerably from the horizontal. Their categorical intention was to acquire an aqueous substance for a cylindrical vessel in their possession. However, the juvenescent male precipitously pitched to a supine position with a consequent cranial fissure, and an ensuing vertiginous plummet by the juvenescent female conveyed her to a state of proximity.

Words like *juvenescent, Homo sapiens, hied, apex, precipitously, supine, cranial,* and *vertiginous*, though perhaps heard before, may not be well enough known to assist readers in identifying the passage as that of the Mother Goose rhyme: *Jack and Jill went up a hill to fetch a pail of water; Jack fell down and broke his crown, and Jill came tumbling after.* Thinking of known words that are derived from the same root, as perhaps *juvenile, aquarium, precipice, cranium,* and *vertigo* can provide clues to the meanings of words in the passage and thus aid in deciphering the gist of the paragraph. As students move through the upper grades they are likely to encounter many unfamiliar words; morphology can be of benefit in understanding them. We need only consider the following estimate to realize the value of morphology in developing students' vocabulary knowledge: About 60% of the unfamiliar words that students encounter in their reading can be analyzed into parts—base words, roots, prefixes, and suffixes—that can be used to help figure out their meanings (Nagy & Scott, 2000). The importance of morphology in understanding and using words is reflected in *Mindful of Words.* Part 2 includes 15 word studies concerned with the use of prefixes or suffixes and 11 involving compound words; in Part 3, 46 of the word studies focus on prefixes, suffixes, and/or roots.

In addition to the emphasis on morphology, each of the word sorts provides an opportunity to expand students' vocabulary knowledge through discussion of the meanings of some of the less familiar words. Words that lend themselves to focused talk include those whose meanings are unknown to students, words that students may confuse with other words, and words with multiple meanings, some of which students may know and others they may not. For many of the word sorts, suggestions of words to consider are offered but not with the expectation that all be highlighted. In fact, it may be that students would benefit from discussion of words other than those listed. Discussion might include talk about word meanings; generation of sentences with the words; brainstorming antonyms or synonyms for the words; creating word webs; developing "Would You?" riddles, as described in Part 2, Sorts 60 and 62; and so forth. For some of the Greek and Latin root sorts in Part 3, as well as word sorts that include several unfamiliar words, you might introduce the words by asking students to evaluate how well they know them. Begin by asking students to take an 8.5- × 11-inch piece of paper and fold it in half along the width and then repeat the process, so that when the paper is unfolded, four rectangular boxes are revealed. Ask students to label each box as shown (adapted from Blachowicz, 1986; Dale, 1965; Allen, 1999). Then ask them to categorize the sort words according to their level of understanding by writing each word in an appropriate box. As an alternative, provide students with the category headers and ask them to complete the categorizing with their word cards. Discuss the results. The same process could be used as a check on understanding after the words have been explored, with the possible addition that students be asked to provide an oral or written sentence for some of the words listed under *Could use or define the word*.

| Don't know it | Have seen or heard but don't know meaning |
|---|---|
| Think I know the meaning | Could use or define the word |

Certain unfamiliar words from word study or from classroom conversations, read-alouds, or content-area reading (such as those from Appendices B–D), may be deemed worthy of students *owning*; in other words, not only do they understand the words but also they are able to use them. For this to happen, students will likely need 7 to 10 meaningful encounters with the words. A "Teacher's Word Wall" (Ganske, 2006) can help to make this happen. The word wall reminds busy teachers of the need to bring targeted words into classroom conversation and activities. A few words of interest (10 is a good maximum to ensure prominent visibility) are posted on a wall facing a common teaching location within the classroom. The words are written on sentence strips or large note cards so they can be seen from anywhere in the classroom. As students begin using the words, new words can replace the known.

In the final section of this part, seven teachers from fourth grade through middle school offer suggestions for successful and engaging word study with older students. In addition, because administrators play a crucial role in effective teaching and learning (Copland, 2004; Cotton, 2003), the section ends with the vignette of a principal, who shares the story of how word study was started in her school.

# Teacher to Teacher: Tips from Teachers for Teachers

## Jennifer Clipper Greenwald, Fourth-Grade Teacher, North Brunswick Township Schools, New Jersey

As a fourth-grade teacher, Jenny is always looking for ways to make the most of her time and energy with word study. She offers two tips to help maximize time and students' learning.

### Developmental Spelling Analysis Assessment

One of my colleagues suggested writing the letters of the features on the DSA (Ganske, 2000) answer sheet form ahead of time. I made a master by copying the DSA answer page and writing the letter of each word's feature at the end of the answer line (as shown). In the white space at the bottom of the answer sheet, I also added a row of boxes with the feature letters, so I could record the results.

**ANSWER SHEET: FORM A**          Name: _____

Stage: _____ SJ _____          Date: _____

1. _____ N

2. _____ K

3. _____ L

4. _____ M

5. _____ L

And so on . . .          Stage score: _____

Feature scores:

| K | L | M | N | O |
|---|---|---|---|---|
|   |   |   |   |   |

The altered format and the following approach saves me much time in correcting the assessments. I simply circle the feature letter if the feature is wrong, and I circle the word if the feature is correct but the word is wrong. When calculating the feature scores, I count the number of times a particular letter is *not* circled (e.g., if I circled three of the *K*'s because the student missed the feature in three words, then two of the 5 words targeting this feature had a correct feature, and the score recorded for *K* is 2. For the number of correctly spelled words or stage score, I count how many words have no markings at all.

## Word Lists

When making my word lists, I make a master list for myself that includes all of the groups' words. I set up the master list in Microsoft Word by typing the individual lists of words and organizing them by stage, feature, and sort. To create the student lists, I simply highlight a particular list, go to the Table toolbar, and select the following: first Table, then Convert, and finally Text to Table. I then change the sizes of the table and font to allow space on each card for students to write definitions, parts of speech, synonyms and/or antonyms, and any other information that may be helpful. When I introduce or review the words with students during our group work, students use this set of word cards to take notes. I have found that having the additional information easily accessible on their cards helps students retain it better.

## Kristin Capel, Fifth-Grade Teacher, Solon Schools, Ohio

Kristin began using word study as a third-grade teacher. In her current work with older students, she maintains students' interest by varying her approach. Here are some of her ideas.

### The Looping Game and Getting Started

Before I begin small-group instruction based on informal spelling inventory results, I establish routines and expectations for each of the sorting activities I will be using within the classroom by engaging students in whole-class sorts. I focus on a feature that is problematic for all students and required by Ohio state standards—for example, homophones. Even if students are usually pretty fluent spellers, this is one feature on which they falter. At the beginning of the year I use one-syllable homophones to review patterns from the within word pattern stage. One of the activities I use is a looping game. I prepare a set of note cards; on one side I record a homophone and on the other a sentence that reveals the meaning of another homophone. I continue the process, making sure to begin the second card with the word that matches the meaning on the first card. For the example shown, the second card would begin with *knight*. The meaning on the back of this card would match the word on the third card, and so on. The final card includes the meaning for the first word, in the example, *isle*. Every student is given one of these cards. Player 1's card might look like this:

(front)

(back)

The game begins with Player 1 saying "Who has *a man in shining armor?*" Player 2, the person with the corresponding word, replies "I have *knight,* k-n-i-g-h-t" and then asks about the definition on the back, as, for example, "Who has *7 days make up a. . . .*" If completed correctly, the loop will end with the last player saying the definition for Player 1's word, as "Who has *another name for an island?*" and Player 1 responding with "I have *isle,* i-s-l-e." The students love this activity. It encourages listening and gets them to focus on the meaning and spelling of homophones. It could easily be used with other concepts, as well.

## 3-S Activity

Once I begin meeting with word study groups I have a few things I do to make management easier. We typically work with a set of words for a 2-week interval due to scheduling issues. Although I meet with groups initially to guide students through the new sort and to help them identify generalizations about the patterns that will assist their spelling, for ease of scheduling I plan notebook activities for follow-up practice. This allows me to keep a check on students' progress and any difficulties they may have. Because many of the students have been engaged in word study since kindergarten; I have found that they need some fresh approaches to the follow-up practice, activities that offer a twist to just re-sorting their words. I have also found that in fifth grade, my students' success rate comes more from multiple opportunities to write the words in some type of format than from manipulating the word cards. I still give students the option of physically sorting the cards but hold them accountable for completing written word sorts in their word study notebooks. The day I introduce a sort, I follow up by asking students to return to their seats and complete what I call the 3-S Activity, in which they Say the words, Spell the words, and Sort the words. First they look at their word and say it. Then they spell the word by either whispering or spelling it in their head. Finally they write the word in their journals in the columns in which they belong. After completing the written sort, they write down the gist of that sort. What did they learn that would help them to spell other words with the same pattern?

## Home-Communication Activity

Another routine notebook assignment is the Home-Communication Activity. Parents in our district are very involved and really want to know what we are working on. To keep them informed about each cycle of words, students write a note to their parents that includes a sampling of six words from their current sort. They explain the gist of the sort to their parents and also provide a sampling of a few brainstormed nonsort words that fit the pattern. The communication goes home, and parents sign and return it to verify their receipt of it.

## Cloze Sentences

Sometimes I also ask students to write sentences for their words, but they do them as cloze sentences. I show them how to do this with repeated modeling. Once words are learned, the students create a word bank with 5–10 of their words; then they create sentences for some of the words, blanking out the spelling word and making sure that their sentences meet a critical requirement: The sentence has to be one of description. It can't be vague so that just about any word could complete it, as, for example, *It is* _____ (*cold*). They have to really describe *cold* so that someone else is able to know what word would fit in the blank. This is really difficult for them at first, but it helps them to become more aware of meaning, which is useful for their later studies of more advanced words. When there's time, students can trade papers and fill in the answers to each other's sentences.

## Writing Definitions

I suggest using this activity only occasionally, but I do find it useful because our achievement tests require students to choose the correct word and its meaning from a list of possibilities. In their notebooks, students write a sentence for one of their words and then turn to the dictionary to see if they can pick out the meaning that matches the way they used the word. Once they find it, they rewrite the definition in their own words below the sentence, using 5 or fewer words.

## Jennifer Herrick, Fifth-Grade Teacher, North Brunswick Township Schools, New Jersey

As a veteran teacher, Jennifer knows that motivation is a key to older students' learning. She offers suggestions for keeping students engaged in their word studies and for furthering their vocabulary development.

## Weekend Word Warriors

To keep students learning out of school as well as in, I invite them to listen and look for interesting words over the weekend. The words may be new to them, fun to say, annoying or confusing, or fascinating for some other reason. On Monday mornings we take a few minutes to talk about the words students heard over the weekend. Sometimes we dissect a word and break it down into spelling and/or meaning units. We also try to guess the meaning, spell the word, or talk about the experience that brought the word to attention. Then we add it to our "Words We Found" list that is displayed in the classroom.

## Be the Computer

For this activity, I distribute a paragraph containing intentionally misspelled words and grammatical errors. I then ask students to "Be the Computer" by underlining misspellings in red and grammar, capitalization, or punctuation mistakes in green, just as most computer word processing programs do. (Colored pencils work well.) Students gain editing practice, and follow-up discussion provides an avenue for reviewing some of the issues raised as errors.

---

Name: _____     Date: _____

### YOU ARE THE COMPUTER

You're going to do the job of a computer. It is your job to show where the mistakes are in this paragraph below. Place a **green** line under any words or phrases that have grammar mistakes. Place a **red** line under any spelling errors. Then go through and correct all the mistakes.

My dogs name is doodle. he isnt a very frendly dog. Whenever I take him for walk, he likes too bark at other dog. Sometime it annoying. once we saw a cat and He chased it up a tree Were taking him to school to learn how to behave

*Sorting Variation*

Practice sorting is an important component of a word study routine because it helps students' recall of the patterns to become automatic. To vary the sorting practice, I provide each student with a laminated blank word card template on card stock paper. You can create your own template or photocopy one (see, for example, the one in Appendix E). I allow students to use a dry-erase marker to sort their words on the blank template. When there are more categories than columns for the words, I have them use the lower part of a column as a separate category, suggest that they turn the paper into a horizontal position, or distribute another page. Students find this activity a fun substitute for paper and pencil.

*$.50 Word Box*

I use this activity to reinforce new vocabulary. Begin by photocopying a half-dollar coin manipulative or a reproducible. On the back, write a really interesting, long, or unusual word. You'll need enough words to fill a small box or manila envelope. Choose words to which students previously have been exposed (e.g., from a science textbook or other content area [such as Appendices B–D], Weekend Word Warrior game, current events, etc.). Once you have enough, as part of a whole-group activity, invite students to blindly pick a word out of the container. If they're able to use it correctly in a sentence, they earn $.50 and get to keep the "coin." The coins can be saved, and when a certain goal is achieved, they can be "spent" for something special, such as extra computer or library time.

## Marianne Larson, Fifth-Grade Teacher, Warren Township Public Schools, New Jersey

Marianne taught an earlier grade (second) before moving into fifth grade 3 years ago. With the move to fifth grade Marianne found that she not only needed to learn more advanced spelling concepts but that she also had to create a learning environment appropriate for older students. In the process, Marianne added several new activities to her routine to challenge and engage her students. Description of a favorite follows:

*Flap Books*

To encourage vocabulary development as well as spelling knowledge, one of the writing activities I use with students is a foldable flap book, such as the one shown. To make the flap book students begin with a piece of paper at least 8.5 × 11 inches and follow these directions:

- Fold the paper lengthwise (vertically). The result will resemble a skinny book.
- Fold this long rectangle in half by bringing the top down to meet the bottom.
- Repeat the previous step two more times, until you have made four folds. You should end up with a small rectangle, much wider than it is high.
- Unfold the paper until you are back to where you were after the first fold. The "cover" of the skinny book should now show creases across it that create eight rectangles.
- Cut the creases on the "cover" of the book, but only on the cover, making eight flaps. You should be able to lift the flap and see the inside of the back cover underneath.
- There are many ways a flap book can be used at this point, including for science, social studies, and math. For word study, I have the students pick eight words that they feel they need to explore more in terms of definition and usage. They write one word on each flap of the

cover. On the back side of the flap they write a definition for the word, and on the rectangle underneath the flap, they write a sentence using the word according to their recorded definition. (See the accompanying figure.)

| barren |
| brighten |
| poison |
| falcon |
| rotten |
| sharpen |
| wooden |

| A large ocean fish that can be eaten | Salmon is the best ocean fish for eating. |

## Colleen Vay and Erin Greco, Sixth-Grade Teachers, West Irondequoit Community School District, New York

Colleen's and Erin's sixth-grade students are eager to learn about the more sophisticated aspects of our English spelling, so they set up routines and resources in the beginning of the year that will facilitate this process. They discuss a key ingredient for success—the word study journal.

### Introducing the Journal

Students use a word study journal or notebook as a reference, a place of reflection, and an instructional tool throughout the year. The journal is on the students' supply list and comes in the first day of school. It is a 100-page spiral notebook, not a composition book. We help the students to set up their journals in two parts: a reference section (the last 20 pages) and an introduction/work section (the first 80 pages). For homework the first week of school, students are asked to number the pages for future reference. The first page is an explanation of word study. Each stage is defined, and an example is given. The class discusses the whole meaning of word study. At the end, students reflect in their journals on the personal implications of this type of study and set a goal for the upcoming year.

### Reflection: A Critical Element

We again ask students to write a reflection after we have gathered information about their spelling knowledge through an informal spelling assessment, such as the DSA. They reflect on what they have previously learned about words, their patterns, and exceptions. As time goes on, students continue to reflect in their journals, sharing their thinking about the features we are studying and any generalizations they develop about how the features work (see the sampling of student reflections included at the end of this vignette). We have found the reflection piece to be very powerful in students' retention of the features. They not only reflect in a written form but also are given a chance to discuss their reflections with others in their group. The word study lessons are very meaningful to students, as they talk about their progress, experiment with words in their writing, and develop understanding of the written words that they are reading.

## *The Reference Section*

The last 20 pages of the journal are used to describe activities from professional resources. We provide students with half-page copies of directions for the activities; they add these to their journals and use the other half-page to practice the activity for future reference. Also, the different types of sorts are defined and examples given. When students are assigned to do homework, there is less confusion than there was before notebooks were used, and parents are able to assist if needed. For example, word hunts are a frequent form of homework. Students are either hunting for words in their current reading or in their own writing. When word hunting, students date the page in their journal, write down the feature being studied, and record the title of the literature work they are using. They organize the feature words they find by category, document how the word is used, and note the meaning of the word, as shown in the sample template here. We model this together as a whole class first and then give students the opportunity to try it individually. At the end of the activity, everyone reflects on what they learned about that feature. With the pages numbered, students in the same group can find their place very quickly, instead of fumbling through the whole notebook.

## WORD HUNT TEMPLATE

Feature: _____     Date: _____

Title of Literature: _____

| Feature word | Part of speech | Definition |
|---|---|---|
|  |  |  |
|  |  |  |
|  |  |  |
|  |  |  |

Reflection — What have you learned about this feature from this reading?

## *Monitoring Student Progress*

Teachers can monitor student progress very easily by collecting the journals, which not only include all of their work but also a record of their thinking. Assessments are completed in the journal, so students can monitor their own progress and go back to features for clarification. The journal helps students manage their own learning, creates a tool they can use in the future, documents a year's worth of progress, and informs our teaching so that we can differentiate lessons based on what the students need.

## Final Thoughts

The word study journal has provided us with a consistent routine for students to work within. While the teacher is working with a small group on a specific feature, individual students can be working independently, completing a word sort, documenting features in a word hunt, or reflecting with a partner about the current feature and word meanings. For upper elementary teachers, time is an important consideration when it comes to word study. How can we fit it in to our daily instruction? By having a consistent routine and reference materials in the students' hands and by involving students in the process, we have made word study a strong part of our curriculum. The best part about all of this is that students see the connection between their effort and their success. They get it!

### A Sampling of Student Reflections

4/06 I keep misspelling words that end with ion. I am still confusion tion, sion, and ion. There are so many words in this feature. Tonight I am going to look at the newspaper for homework and see what I can find. I hope it helps me with this.

11/06 Today's word hunt was easy for me. I found a lot of homophones in Tuck Everlasting. Then I went to my reading journal to hunt for homophones. I am writing them wrong. I used there instead of their 5 times. In my group discussion today, I am going to ask my partners if they are doing the same thing? Mrs. Vay says she sees this all the time in our papers. I will be more aware the next time I am writing homophones to use the correct one.

10/06 Short and long vowel sounds are easy when we are discussing them with Mrs. Vay. Sometimes I forget to put the e on the end of the word. That makes a big mistake. It changes the meaning of the word I want to write.

## Tiffany Worden, Middle School Teacher, Montgomery Township School District, New Jersey

As a middle school language arts teacher who knows the importance of motivation, one of Tiffany's goals is to pique students' interest in language. In her experience there is no better way to accomplish this than to launch word study with idioms and follow up with homophones. Once she has aroused the interest of her students, she moves on to explorations of Greek and Latin roots in order to develop their vocabulary and spelling knowledge.

### Idioms

I begin by asking students to brainstorm familiar expressions to activate their prior knowledge of idioms. As students list common phrases such as *raining cats and dogs*, *under the weather*, and *couch potato*, they are eager to understand what they mean and how they came to be. I explain that each word—or in this case phrase—in our language has a story behind it, an etymology that tells about its origin and how it developed through the centuries. I send partners off to our idiom dictionaries, such as the *Scholastic Dictionary of Idioms* by Marvin Terban, to become familiar with some idioms and their etymologies (see the Idiom Scavenger Hunt on the next page). The room is lively as students make connections and excitedly read the stories behind these everyday phrases. For the next week during our word study time, students use the idiom dictionaries to research an additional three to five idioms they find interesting. At the end of the week, students synthesize and share their knowledge through a small project of their choosing. They might:

- Write a journal entry from an idiom's perspective.
- Write a poem or story.
- Compose a song or rap about idioms.
- Create a small crossword puzzle using idioms.
- Develop a PowerPoint presentation.
- Illustrate an idiom.
- Create a poster with the word, etymology, and an illustration displayed (see example).
- Prepare a short skit about an idiom.

I encourage students to come up with their own ideas and to confer with me about them. Students share their final idiom project through a *gallery walk* (Rutherford, 2002). In a gallery walk, students leave their projects on their desks and walk around the room, learning about new idioms from their classmates' projects.

It is important for students to understand how the idioms they have researched and integrated into projects relate to their reading and writing. We talk about how recognizing idioms as expressions and not literal sayings makes it easier to comprehend texts. I also explain how idioms are

BAKERS DOZEN

**THIRTEEN**

In 1266, England made a rule that bakers had to give a certain amount of goods to the customers, so in order to meet the amount, bakers would give one extra to a dozen.

Name: _____ Date: _____ Period: _____

# IDIOM SCAVENGER HUNT

**Directions:** Working with a partner at your table, use an idiom dictionary to find the meaning and story behind the following idioms.

**I'll give you the definition; you find the idiom:**

1. Sometimes we describe a person who spends lots of time watching television as a _____
   _____ .

2. Manuel, from Gary Soto's short story "La Bamba," loves the attention he gets from the talent show. He loves to be in the _____ .

3. An idiom we use to say "Have a good night's rest" is _____
   _____ .

**I'll give you the story behind the expression; you find the idiom:**

1. In thirteenth-century England, bakers began including 13 baked goods instead of 12. We call this a _____ .

2. When there was a storm at sea, sailors would go below deck. They were under the
   _____ .

**I'll give you the idiom; you find its meaning and the story behind it:**

| Idiom | What does it mean today? | What is the story behind this idiom? |
|---|---|---|
| Let the cat out of the bag | | |
| Once in a blue moon | | |

mostly used in speech. Writers usually choose to omit idioms from formal writing. We discuss times when writers may use idioms, such as within dialogue to develop a character. This new knowledge helps students to make choices about using idioms in their own writing.

## Homophones

As in idiom study, homophones ignite students' enthusiasm for words. Before creating the following homophone activities, I review my students' writing and select three to four sets of homophones that students will benefit from studying. After introducing homophones and briefly reviewing the meanings of each set of words, students interact with the homophones at learning stations over the course of several days. They:

- Use computers to explore homophone-related websites (this includes listening and watching the song "Homophones" at the PBS kids' website, *pbskids.org/lions/videos/homophones.html*).
- Work with a partner to match homophones to sentences. The sentences are written on colorful strips of paper called sentence strips. In each sentence a homophone is omitted; students must choose the word card that matches and insert it into the sentence, explaining their thinking to each other.
- Illustrate the meanings of homophone pairs, act out the meanings, or use the pair in a sentence.
- Scan their books, searching for homophone examples. When students find *their* or *too*, for example, they record the sentence on a note card and post it on our bulletin board.

It is important for students to use their new knowledge of homophones in authentic writing activities, so I add the homophone sets to peer-editing sheets and to the editing section of our rubrics. This encourages students to look for these homophones as they edit their papers and carefully consider whether the words are being used correctly.

## Root Study

When we study word roots as a means for developing vocabulary, I choose two roots to study together, with approximately six spelling words that contain either root. I want the roots and spelling words to be ones that students will use in authentic reading and writing tasks. The best way I have to ensure this is to connect our root study to the content area classes. For example, my students study astronomy in science. Over the course of that science unit, students read and write many words containing the roots *astr* ("star") and *geo* ("earth"). Therefore, during this time, we study *astr* and *geo* in language arts class, and the words I choose include *astronomy, astronaut, astronomical unit*, as well as *geocentric* from science and *geography* and *geometry* from social studies and math.

I introduce the words with a word web. I draw a circle with the root in the middle, and students brainstorm any words branching from that root. This task activates students' prior knowledge of words containing the root, and they enjoy deducing the root's meaning based on our word web. Over the course of the week, students complete various activities to build their vocabulary and spelling skills and to make connections to their reading. For each set of words, I create a packet with directions for the various activities. Activities may include sorting the words, illustrating the roots, identifying each spelling word's root by circling it, searching for additional words with the roots, unscrambling spellings, alphabetizing the words, and completing a crossword puzzle (a free crossword puzzle maker can be found at the Discovery School's website: *www.puzzle-maker.com*).

*Mary Lou Cebula, EdD, Principal,*
*Warren Township Public Schools, New Jersey*

The birth of a differentiated spelling program in my school began the way educational leaders envision, but rarely witness—with the teachers. The school year was ending. Teachers were packing up their classrooms and planning summer vacations. Everyone, that is, except my third-grade teachers. They were standing at my office door with a proposal. When the teachers entered my office and asked to speak to me, I thought it must be serious for them to come together. I was outnumbered but respected them and their dedication to their students.

They described their frustration with the traditional one-size-fits-all approach to spelling and its inability to meet students' needs. After describing the problem they suggested a solution—differentiated word study. The teachers had researched other ways of teaching spelling, read professional books on the topic, and visited teachers from another district that implemented word study. They proposed to pilot the approach the following year and expressed a willingness to prepare for the venture over the summer. Fascinated by their enthusiasm and intrigued by the possibilities for students' learning, I agreed to their request. At the end of the next school year, when we discussed the project, the teachers asked to continue word study and expressed an interest in the possibility of expanding its implementation to fourth grade so that their students could continue to benefit from the approach.

After receiving permission from the superintendent of schools to continue the word study pilot program, I asked teachers in second and fourth grades to pilot word study with their students. An interesting development occurred: By the middle of the school year, all the second-grade teachers were experimenting with word study, meeting with the third-grade teachers, and observing them implementing word study; but in fourth grade, the pilot was less successful. I knew more support was needed for the staff, so I provided professional development for all second- through fourth-grade teachers, including time to observe colleagues, professional books, and the opportunity to take a 1-hour graduate summer course. The six of us who took the class came away not only with ideas for implementing word study but also with the knowledge that word study is not just about spelling but about our language and the importance of vocabulary development. Over the summer we developed word sorts to share with other staff members.

With the support and encouragement of the teachers who had piloted word study, we began the school year with a plan for full implementation of word study in second through fifth grades. The third-grade team, a second-grade teacher who had attended the summer word study course, and I designed 10 one-hour training sessions for our staff members and any other teachers in the district who were interested. Twenty-five teachers volunteered to attend the after-school classes. Word study had started with a group of interested classroom teachers but quickly gained everyone's attention. As an administrator, I could hardly contain how proud I felt that the staff was committed to practices that required more time and effort than their previous one-size-fits-all approach. The needs of their students and the positive results they saw in the students' daily writing were the driving forces.

We continue to provide support for word study. Teachers still observe each other on a regular basis, a word study refresher class is held in the fall for interested staff members, new teachers receive training at the beginning of the school year, new word sorts are created as needed, and teachers meet together to share students' DSA results and to provide information so the next year's teacher can continue the flow of instruction at the child's level. Grade-level teachers meet at the beginning of the year to discuss assessments and determine spelling groups. The lines of communication move at and across grades.

How did parents react to this sudden shift from a traditional spelling list to a word sort? Once again, communication played a major role in making word study accepted. We invited parents to attend an information session on word study. Two teachers (grades 5 and 3) and I had prepared a PowerPoint presentation for district administrators. We revised this for parents, tracing the how, what, and why of word study. We included pictures of their children engaged in word sort activities and teachers conducting a word walk. Parents were able to see the program in action and develop a better understanding of the benefits of word study. Except for an occasional parent questioning the current small-group placement of his or her child, the program has been warmly received and supported.

Word study is now an integral component of our balanced literacy program in kindergarten through grade 5. Several teachers in the middle school have attended the training sessions offered in the district and have begun experimenting with word study in their classrooms. The teachers deserve all the credit for introducing word study and displaying the leadership that brought the program to our school district. My role was to learn all I could about word study and to provide the resources and encouragement to help the implementation succeed. As I travel around the school and wander into the classrooms, I witness students talking and interacting with words with an enthusiasm and knowledge I never observed with our former approach. It's a wonderful sight to behold.

# Part 2

# Word Study for Syllable Juncture Spellers

Syllable juncture spellers are likely to be students in the upper elementary grades or middle school who are well on their way to becoming proficient readers. They know how to spell many words, and most have solid understandings of how basic consonant and vowel patterns work in single-syllable words. At the syllable juncture stage (also known as syllables and affixes stage), students learn to negotiate the patterns and structures of polysyllabic words. As they closely examine the longer words that characterize this stage, several new spelling issues surface. Not only must they learn to apply their knowledge of consonant and vowel patterns to the context of polysyllabic words and learn a few new patterns in the process, but they must also acquire a working knowledge of other aspects of spelling, in particular, the doubling principle and syllable stress or accent. *To double or not to double*, that is the question—at least for many syllable juncture spellers. Doubling in the middle of words is one cause for deliberation (*His shirt was in tatters* [not *taters*] *after going through the thorn bushes*), and the other is before an inflected ending (*I am starring* [not *staring*] *in the movie.*) Students must also grapple with syllable stress. In longer words, one syllable is usually accented or stressed, whereas another is unstressed. Although sound provides a clue to spelling stressed syllables, it does not when the syllable is unstressed, making unstressed syllables more challenging to spell. Vocabulary knowledge becomes increasingly important for students at this stage, as they are faced with understanding the sophisticated words encountered in upper-grade reading material and the need to respond to such material in writing. The study of prefixes and suffixes and how they affix to other word parts, known as *morphology*, is a critical component of upper-level word study, one that receives considerable attention at this stage and even more at the next.

## Introducing Compound Words

Many students will already be familiar with the concept of a compound word as two words put together to form a new word. (Compounds are introduced in the "Additional Sorts" section of *Word Sorts and More*; Ganske, 2006.) A brief study of compounds was chosen to introduce the syllable juncture stage for several reasons. This stage focuses on words of more than one syllable and on the patterns of consonants and vowels within and across those syllables. Not only do the separate words in compounds clearly reveal the syllables, but they also enable students to see that although there are more letters in the words, many of the patterns are familiar. For example, the sort that follows includes numerous previously studied patterns, including several blends and digraphs, all five short vowels, several long vowel patterns, numerous *r*-controlled patterns, and some abstract vowels. Finally, in addition to expanding students' pattern knowledge, the word studies at this stage begin to develop their awareness of meaning connections, which will form the heart of word study at the derivational constancy stage, and meaning is the essence of compound words. Note that 10 additional compound sorts, including two that focus on hyphenated compounds, are included in the "Additional Sorts" section of this part. Most may be used at any time during syllable juncture studies; those dealing with hyphenated compounds should be reserved for the latter part of this stage. The compound sorts might serve as a break from other word studies, as well as an alternative when schedules are not routine or when the class has a substitute teacher.

## SORT 1. Introducing Compound Words

### Sorting by Pattern/Meaning

| book | back | ear | hair | way |
|------|------|-----|------|-----|
| **bookmark** | **backpack** | **earplug** | **haircut** | **doorway** |
| bookshelf | backbone | earache | hairbrush | driveway |
| bookworm | backfire | eardrum | hairline | freeway |
| cookbook | background | earring | hairpin | halfway |
| | backtrack | earshot | | hallway |
| | | | | stairway |

*Considerations:* Ask students to examine and sort their words into groups. Discuss the results and their rationales for grouping certain words together. One of the outcomes will likely be a sort similar to the preceding. Turn their attention to it and discuss the word meanings, being sure to encourage connections with the two smaller words that compose the compound. For example, an ache in your ear is an *earache*; the line formed by the growth of hair on your head is your *hairline*, and so forth. This is an opportune time to discuss multiple meanings of any words, as in the phrase *a hairline crack* or a fracture in a bone. The meaning connection for *earshot* is less obvious than for most of the words; it refers to the range in which you can hear a sound unaided; if you are *out of earshot*, you are too far away to hear it. Ask students to speculate on the meaning connection to *shot* and share their thinking. Perhaps the range was originally determined by a gunshot. With *earring*, draw students' attention to the double *r* and remind them of the importance of thinking carefully about the words that make up a compound when spelling; spellings that may not "look right" can be right because the spelling maintains meaning. Finally, point out the various familiar patterns within the syllables and the ease with which syllables can be identified in compound words.

### Talking Points

- Compound words are made up of two or more smaller words that affect the word's meaning.
- It is important to remember that meaning is key when spelling compounds, because double letters that may not look right can occur where the syllables (words) come together, as in *earring*.

*Integrating Idioms:* "Mom said I don't have to give in to my sister, but I have to **meet her half-way**." (A compromise. If instead of making someone come to you, you walked half the distance to that person, you would be showing a willingness to reach out to her and consider her point of view.)

*Did You Know?* **Book**, developed from *boc*, an Old English word for "writing tablet." *Beech* shares the same ancestry, probably because early inscriptions were made on tablets made from this wood. *Library* also derives from a word meaning "book"; however, because its roots are Latin, the spelling *liber* is not the same. Libraries have existed for a long time. Books in the first known library, which existed more than 4,000 years ago in Babylonia, were clay tablets rather than wood. The first public library in the United States opened in Boston in mid-1600. The world's largest library began as a library for the Congress of the United States and eventually became a national library. The Library of Congress is located in Washington, D.C. Its original 1801 collection included 740 volumes and 3 maps. Today the library has over 35 acres of floor space and about 530 miles of bookshelves! It includes about 18 million books and 4½ million maps (as well as music, photographs, manuscripts, and other media)—more than 130 million items in all! How did the collection become so big? According to law, two copies of every book that is copyrighted must be given to the library. It is truly a bookworm's paradise! Do you have a classroom, school, or home library? If so, what is it like?

| book | back | ear | hair | way |
|------|------|-----|------|-----|

| | | |
|---|---|---|
| bookmark | backpack | earplug |
| haircut | doorway | hairpin |
| stairway | backfire | earring |
| earshot | halfway | bookshelf |
| background | cookbook | hallway |
| earache | driveway | backtrack |
| bookworm | hairbrush | eardrum |
| hairline | backbone | freeway |

# Inflectional Endings

Sometimes people are unsure as to just what an *inflectional ending* is. The phrase refers to "a suffix that expresses plurality or possession when added to a noun, tense when added to a verb, and comparison when added to an adjective and some adverbs" (Harris & Hodges, 1995, *The Literacy Dictionary*, p. 116). This section examines three of these issues: adding *-ing* or *-ed* to base words, forming plurals, and creating comparative adjectives, with greatest attention given to adding *-ed* or *-ing* to base words where no change, *e*-drop, or doubling is required.

## Adding -ed and -ing with No Change, E-Drop, and Doubling (DSA Feature K)

The sorts in the first part of this section address *-ed* and *-ing* inflected endings. Knowing how to correctly add these suffixes is critical for students, considering that more than one out of every three words with a suffix ends in *-ed* or *-ing* (Blevins, 2001). How the past tense and participle are formed depends on the base or root word. For example, we (1) add *-ed* or *-ing* to words that end in a VVC pattern, namely that end with a single consonant preceded by two vowels, as in *mailed* and *peeking*; (2) drop the final *-e* of words with a VCe pattern, then add *-ed* or *-ing*, as in *taped* and *shaking*; and (3) double the final consonant and then add *-ed* or *-ing* to words with a VC pattern, namely words that end with a single consonant and include a single vowel, as in *dotted* and *pinning*. A few words alter the spelling instead of adding an ending (e.g., *sleep/slept* and *say/said*) or follow other considerations for adding an inflectional ending (see Sort 2). Because base words are the building blocks for inflections, it is important that students know how to spell them. This is easily verified through discussion or by asking students to underline or record the spelling of the base words on their word cards. Following is a collection of sorts to teach this feature; choose those that seem most appropriate for your students' needs.

*What Is Known:* Vowel patterns in single-syllable words; *Word Sorts and More* introduced students to the *e*-drop principle used when adding *-ed*. This principle is reviewed here.

*What Is New:* Learning to form inflections with *-ed* and *-ing*, especially those involving doubling of the final consonant.

---

**SORT 2.** Adding *-ing* to Words with No Change and *E*-Drop

|  | Sorting by Pattern | |
| --- | --- | --- |
| **No Change** | | **E-Drop** |
| VCC | VVC | VCe |
| **asking** | **mailing** | **shaking** |
| blinking | cleaning | chasing |
| fishing | keeping | living |
| guessing | floating | making |
| jumping | shouting | riding |
| limping | snooping | saving |
| smelling | speaking | smiling |
|  |  | using |
|  |  | voting |
|  |  | writing |

*Considerations:* Explain to students that for this sort they will be exploring various ways of adding *-ing*. Discuss any unfamiliar meanings. Begin the exploration by asking students to underline or record the name of the base word on each card. Then ask them to consider possible groupings for the words by examining patterns that may reveal how the *-ing* ending was added. Students may need prompting to subdivide the no-change list. Also, some students may regard *living* as an oddball because it does not have a long-vowel sound. Remind them that the focus is on pattern rather than sound. Once the activity is completed, invite students to explain how the three categories are alike and how they are different. Some words with two vowels also end with two consonants; inflections for these are formed by just adding the ending, as in *coaching*, *touched*, and *pointing*. The same is true for words that end in VV, such as *chewing*, *played*, *snowing*, *seeing*, and so forth.

### Talking Points

- Drop the final *-e* of a base word before adding *-ing*, as in *smiling*.
- Simply add *-ing* to one-syllable words that include a team of vowels or that end in two or more consonants, as in *cleaning* and *fishing*.

*Integrating Idioms:* "Ignore my sister if she comes dancing in here; she just got a new haircut, and she'll be **fishing for a compliment**." (Hoping someone will say something nice. Just as a person who goes fishing tries various approaches to catch a fish, the sister will probably act or talk in certain ways to attract attention to her haircut.)

*Did You Know?* When we think of someone **snooping** around, we usually think of a detective or perhaps a thief. However, the original Dutch root of the word, *snoepen*, had more to do with our own habits of raiding the cookie jar or breaking a diet by secretly indulging in an ice cream cone; the Dutch word meant to "eat snacks and sweets on the sly."

---

## SORT 3. Adding *-ed* to Words with No Change and *E*-Drop

### Sorting by Pattern (and thinking about meaning—the base word)

| No Change | | *E*-Drop | |
| --- | --- | --- | --- |
| VCC | VVC | VCe | Oddball |
| **lifted** | **gained** | **liked** | **?** |
| combed | aimed | choked | knew |
| dressed | braided | named | popped |
| marked | healed | placed | slept |
| pulled | leaned | raced | |
| pushed | pouted | waved | |
| stacked | | wiped | |

*Considerations:* The same considerations described for adding *-ing* apply when adding *-ed*. A process similar to the one used for the previous sort may be used here. Note that this sort includes three oddballs; two of them are irregular past tense verbs. As part of the discussion, ask students to brainstorm other words with irregular past tense (e.g., *blow/blew*, *drive/drove*, *eat/ate*, *feel/felt*, *grow/grew*, *keep/kept*, *make/made*, *meet/met*, *read/read*, *ride/rode*, *shake/shook*, *speak/spoke*, *strike/struck*, *take/took*, *write/wrote*). The third oddball provides students with a glimpse of yet another way to form the past tense, namely by doubling the final consonant before adding -ed. As an extension, students might determine the past tense form of each of the following words; several are irregular: *feel/felt, read/ read, get/got, quit* (may be *quit* or *quitted*), *run/ran,* and *sit/sat.*

### Talking Points

- As with -*ing*, just add -*ed* to one-syllable words that include a team of vowels or that end in two or more consonants, as in *aimed* and *pushed.*
- Drop the final -*e* of a base word; then add -*ed*. It may seem as though *d* can just be added to words with a final -*e*, but *d* is just a letter; what's needed is the meaning unit for past tense, and that is *ed*.
- Some words form the past tense in irregular ways, as in *knew* and *slept.*

*Integrating Idioms:* "Last night was my parents' wedding anniversary, and Mom was **dressed to the nines**." (Dressed very well. In Olympic events in which judges rate contestants on their performance, if the ratings for a person's dress were straight 9s, on a 10-point scale, that would be very high.)

*Did You Know?* The sulky expression of a **pout** stems from a word meaning to "swell up" or "inflate," perhaps because a pouting person's face resembles that of someone blowing out air. Some believe it may also relate to a Flemish word for "frog." These creatures puff out their throat area before making their traditional croaking sound. Either way the look is less than complimentary and well worth avoiding. Interestingly, some pigeons are called "pouters," after their habit of puffing up their breasts as part of their mating ritual.

---

## SORT 4. Adding -*ing* to Words with No Change, *E*-Drop, and Double

| Sorting by Pattern | | |
|---|---|---|
| No Change | *E*-Drop | Double |
| VCC or VVC | VCe | VC |
| **meeting** | **hoping** | **hopping** |
| climbing | hiking | begging |
| feeling | joking | getting |
| looking | piling | quitting |
| missing | taking | rubbing |
| reading | wading | running |
| standing | | sitting |
| thinking | | skipping |
| waiting | | sobbing |

*Considerations:* As students look over their words they may notice that several contain double consonants, as did the oddball, *popped*, in Sort 3. Introduce the sort with the level of structure needed. (1) *Considerable*: Ask students to underline or write the name of the base word on each card and then sort the words under the appropriate header according to how the ending was added. Model and guide as needed. (2) *Some*: Provide the inflectional ending key words and ask students to categorize accordingly. (3) *None*: Ask students to complete an open sort. Discuss the results. English includes numerous words that end with double consonants, especially with final *f, l, s,* and *z*; such words provide an opportunity to caution students to sort words with double consonants thoughtfully, because they do not always signal an added letter, such as *missing* in this sort. Students may notice that words in the doubling column all have short vowels; if they do not, call their attention to the difference in the vowel sound of *hoping*, which relies on a single consonant, and *hopping*, which includes double consonants. It is important for students to understand that in English double consonants signal a short-vowel sound. To reinforce formation of inflected endings with no change, *e*-drop, and double, see discussion of the Reach the Peak game in Chapter 6 of *Word Journeys* (Ganske, 2000). Teaching students the 1-1-1 Check (a helpful mnemonic also explained in Chapter 6, Ganske, 2000) can make it easier for them to determine when and when not to double the final consonant of single-syllable words.

As an added challenge to this sort, write *putting* on the board, point to it, and ask students to identify the base word and to name its past tense. Their responses may be *put* and *put*, or *putt* and *putted*. Point out that although *put* and *putt* have different past tense spellings, their *ing* forms are both spelled *putting*, which are pronounced differently. Note that there are numerous words of this type, called *homographs*, that are spelled the same but pronounced differently—*read/read, bow/bow, desert/desert, record/record, present/present,* and so forth. They present special challenges during reading and require careful use of context clues to determine the appropriate pronunciation. Issues related to their spelling are explored later at this stage.

### Talking Points
- If a one-syllable word includes one vowel and ends in one consonant (VC), double the final consonant before adding *-ing*; this keeps the vowel sound short—*hopping*, not *hoping*.

***Integrating Idioms:*** "Why are you **running around like a chicken with its head cut off?**" (Acting frantic and disorganized. Amazing though it may seem, when a chicken is slaughtered, it will sometimes wander around headless before dying.)

***Did You Know?*** When we thank someone, we put a lot of **thinking** or thought into it. Perhaps it's not surprising, then, that the words *think* and *thank* share the same ancestry. When someone asks you to *put on your thinking cap* they mean to take time to consider the matter. The expression may come from the 1600s when professional men such as scholars, clergymen, and jurists who were thought to be intelligent, thinking men wore tight-fitting caps. Judges, also, wore a "considering cap" before determining a sentence, so the phrase may have originated from them.

## SORT 5. Adding *-ed* to Words with No Change, *E*-Drop, and Double

| Sorting by Pattern | | |
|---|---|---|
| No Change | *E*-Drop | Double |
| VCC or VVC | VCe | VC |
| **fooled** | **traded** | **hugged** |
| crossed | baked | bragged |
| joined | blamed | grabbed |
| melted | closed | hummed |
| needed | faced | patted |
| slumped | filed | ripped |
| spilled | taped | slammed |
| treated | | tapped |
| | | zipped |

*Considerations:* As with Sort 4, this set of words may be introduced as an open sort or a closed sort with just the headers as guides. If the latter approach is used, remind students to consider the base word carefully when categorizing the words. Though *crossed* and *spilled* may resemble the "double" words, if we remove one of the final consonants what remains is not a word—*cros* and *spil*. Including a word or two of this type helps to encourage students to consider meaning in their decision making rather than relying solely on visual cues. As with *hopped* and *hoped* in the previous sort, *taped* and *tapped* provide opportunity to discuss the effect of a doubled consonant on the vowel sound. Students might consider how words in the VCe category would be pronounced if they were written with double consonants or how words in the VC category would be read with just a single consonant. To review sounds of the *-ed* ending, extend the sort by asking students to recategorize the words according to /d/, /t/, and /id/ as follows:

Sorting by Sound

| /d/ | /t/ | /id/ |
|-----|-----|------|
| blamed | baked | melted |
| bragged | crossed | needed |
| closed | faced | patted |
| filed | ripped | traded |
| fooled | slumped | treated |
| grabbed | taped | |
| hugged | tapped | |
| hummed | zipped | |
| joined | | |
| slammed | | |
| spilled | | |

### Talking Points

- Add *-ed* to a single-syllable base word in the same way as *-ing*: If the word has one vowel and ends in one consonant (VC), maintain the short vowel sound by doubling the final consonant before adding *-ed*, as in *tapped*.

*Integrating Idioms:* "I know you lost your homework paper, but there's no point in **crying over spilled milk.**" (Regretting something you can't change. If you've tipped over a glass of milk on the table, crying about it isn't going to help. Instead, take action: clean up the mess and pour a new glass.)

*Did You Know?* We have early metalsmiths to thank for the word *fool*, which derives from a Latin word meaning "bellows" or "windbag." Rather than blowing on the fire to heat it up so he could temper his metal, a smith would use a bellows, a kind of hand-operated apparatus, to increase the draft. When a person went around talking nonsense as though he were knowledgeable, he reminded people of the bellows, a windbag full of hot empty air. Court jesters sometimes played the part of a fool in order to mimic people of the ruling class. *Foolscap*, a large-sized paper (13 × 16 inches) used for writing or printing, got its name from the watermark of a jester's cap found on the paper. (A *watermark*—see Sort 53—is a design impressed on certain kinds of paper when it is made; it becomes visible when held to the light.)

## SORT 6. Adding -ed to R-Controlled Words with No Change, E-Drop, and Double

### Sorting by Pattern

| No Change | E-Drop | Double |
|---|---|---|
| **started** | **scared** | **scarred** |
| burped | dared | barred |
| cheered | fired | blurred |
| harmed | scored | marred |
| learned | shared | slurred |
| parted | snored | starred |
| purred | stared | stirred |
| soared | stored | |
| squirmed | | |

*Considerations:* This sort provides an opportunity to review *r*-controlled vowels while reinforcing spelling with the *-ed* ending. As with the other sorts in this section, knowledge of the base word is important. This is particularly apparent in *scared* and *scarred*, *stared* and *starred*, and *purred*. The two pairs of words are often misspelled and misread by students, and the last word is likely to be missorted by students who are relying primarily on visual cues rather than on what the base word actually is. Be sure to discuss the meanings of unfamiliar words. You may want to ask students to sort the words by the rime pattern of the base word (the vowel and what follows) as an introduction to the sort or as an extension. The results follow:

### Sorting by Pattern

| VC | VCC | VVC | VCe |
|---|---|---|---|
| barred | burped | cheered | dared |
| blurred | harmed | learned | fired |
| marred | parted | soared | scared |
| scarred | purred | | scored |
| slurred | squirmed | | shared |
| starred | started | | snored |
| stirred | | | stared |
| | | | stored |

The placement of *squirmed* may prompt discussion from students who regard the *u* as part of the vowel pattern. Remind them that the vowel pattern is not *ui* but that the *u* partners with *q*, as in *quick, quiet, squirt, squint,* and so forth.

*Talking Points:* R-controlled-vowel words follow the same principles as other words when adding *-ed*.

- Drop the final *-e* of VCe words; just add *-ed* if the word ends in a VVC or VCC pattern; and double the final consonant of words with Vr to maintain the vowel sound: *He scarred his arm*, not *scared his arm*.

*Integrating Idioms:* "I **started off with a clean slate**, but I'm already in trouble." (Nothing held against him or her. The origin of this idiom is unknown. You might ask students to speculate on its origin.)

*Did You Know?* Perhaps you've gotten a **scar** before by burning yourself. It's likely that many people did in ancient Greece when open fires provided warmth and means for cooking food. The word stems from the Greek word *eskhara*, meaning "hearth" (the floor of a fireplace). As the word came to be used by the Romans and later the French, it took on the related but slightly different meaning of "scab caused by burning"; its meaning was altered again by the time we got it to indicate the mark left on the skin after a wound has healed. What might the word mean in another few hundred years?

## SORT 7. Adding *-ed* and *-ing* to Words with No Change, *E*-Drop, and Double

### Sorting by Pattern

| No Change | E-Drop | Double |
|-----------|--------|--------|
| **greeted** | **graded** | **planning** |
| bending | guided | batted |
| blushing | lined | fanning |
| boiled | owed | jogged |
| groaned | poking | letting |
| packed | rated | rotted |
| peeled | shaped | tipped |
| screamed | | tugging |
| walking | | |

*Considerations:* Review the meanings of any unfamiliar words. Be sure to check students' understanding of the base-word spelling. If students find the inclusion of both *-ed* and *-ing* words confusing, ask them to begin by sorting the words into two categories, *-ing* and *-ed*, and then re-sort the words by pattern as in Sort 6. This sort, as well as Sorts 4–5, may be introduced or extended by asking students to categorize the words according to vowel sound and/or pattern, as shown next. Students should notice that all of the short-vowel words have two consonants before the inflectional ending, either as a result of doubling or because the base word ends in two of them. By contrast, a single consonant precedes the ending of long-vowel words.

### Talking Points

- When adding either *-ed* or *-ing* to a one-syllable word, it's important to think about the base word. Drop the final *-e* of VC*e* words before adding the ending; if the word ends in a VVC or VCC pattern, just add the ending; and double the final consonant of VC words, as in *shaped*, *screamed*, *blushing*, and *tipped*.

## Sorting by Vowel Sound

| Short | Long | Other |
|---|---|---|
| batted | graded | boiled |
| bending | greeted | walking |
| blushing | groaned | |
| fanning | guided | |
| jogged | lined | |
| letting | owed | |
| packed | peeled | |
| planning | poking | |
| rotted | rated | |
| tipped | screamed | |
| tugging | shaped | |

## Sorting by Pattern

| VC | VCC | VVC | VCe |
|---|---|---|---|
| batted | bending | boiled | graded |
| fanning | blushing | greeted | guided |
| jogged | packed | groaned | lined |
| letting | walking | peeled | owed |
| planning | | screamed | poking |
| rotted | | | rated |
| tipped | | | shaped |
| tugging | | | |

*Integrating Idioms:* "**Keep your eyes peeled**; we don't want to miss them." (Keep a sharp lookout. When something is peeled, the outer covering is removed so that nothing is in the way of getting at whatever is underneath—an orange, a potato, and so forth. In other words, if you *keep your eyes peeled*, there's nothing to prevent you from seeing well.)

*Did You Know?* The *l-i-n* spelling connection between **line** and *lint*, *lingerie*, and *linoleum* is obvious, but a meaning connection among the words may seem surprising. The origin of *line* goes back to ancient times and to *linum*, the Latin word for flax, a plant used to make a kind of cloth called *linen*. Clothmaking was important, so other words stemmed from *linum*, including *lint*, bits of linen left on the loom; *lingerie*, which was made from linen; and even *linoleum* (though much later, in 1860), which was originally canvas coated with a preparation made from linseed oil, the oil of flax seeds. Many words and expressions relate to *line*, including *lineage*, *linear*, *airline*, *ocean liner*, *draw the line*, *fall in line*, *toe the line*, *out of line*, *bottom line*, *end of the line*, *hold the line*, *sign on the dotted line*, *line of thought*, and so forth.

# SORT 2  Adding -ing to Words with No Change and E-Drop

| No Change | | E-Drop |
|:---:|:---:|:---:|
| asking | mailing | shaking |
| cleaning | voting | snooping |
| living | riding | fishing |
| guessing | keeping | making |
| floating | writing | smelling |
| shouting | blinking | chasing |
| limping | using | jumping |
| smiling | speaking | saving |

# SORT 3   Adding -ed to Words with No Change and E-Drop

| No Change | | E-Drop |
|---|---|---|
| lifted | gained | liked |
| waved | slept | aimed |
| healed | pulled | wiped |
| dressed | placed | leaned |
| choked | pouted | combed |
| pushed | raced | popped |
| named | marked | knew |
| stacked | braided | ? |

# SORT 4 Adding *-ing* to Words with No Change, *E*-Drop, and Double

| No Change | E-Drop | Double |
|-----------|--------|--------|
| meeting | hoping | hopping |
| sitting | thinking | piling |
| hiking | begging | standing |
| waiting | taking | running |
| quitting | feeling | getting |
| reading | skipping | looking |
| wading | climbing | sobbing |
| missing | rubbing | joking |

# SORT 5  Adding -ed to Words with No Change, E-Drop, and Double

| No Change | E-Drop | Double |
|:---:|:---:|:---:|
| fooled | traded | hugged |
| treated | zipped | filed |
| slammed | joined | spilled |
| needed | tapped | blamed |
| taped | closed | bragged |
| grabbed | crossed | patted |
| faced | hummed | slumped |
| melted | ripped | baked |

# SORT 6 Adding *-ed* to *R*-Controlled Words with No Change, *E*-Drop, and Double

| No Change | E-Drop | Double |
|-----------|--------|--------|
| started | scared | scarred |
| shared | parted | snored |
| harmed | blurred | stared |
| scored | dared | cheered |
| stirred | learned | marred |
| starred | slurred | soared |
| purred | burped | stored |
| fired | barred | squirmed |

# SORT 7  Adding -ed and -ing to Words with No Change, E-Drop, and Double

| No Change | E-Drop | Double |
|-----------|--------|--------|
| greeted | graded | planning |
| shaped | letting | groaned |
| packed | guided | rated |
| poking | bending | jogged |
| walking | rotted | peeled |
| blushing | batted | owed |
| tipped | boiled | tugging |
| screamed | lined | fanning |

## Plurals

In the following sorts, students increase their understanding of how to form plurals. This is an important concept, as more than 30% of words with a suffix are plurals (Blevins, 2001). You may need to explain to students that plurals are formed with nouns to express *more than one*. Plurals can be formed by adding *-s* (*socks*) or *-es* (*churches*) or through spelling changes, such as changing *-y* to *i* and then adding *-es* (*fly/flies*), changing *f* to *v* and then adding *-es* or *-s* (*half/halves* and *life/lives*), or changing vowels (*foot/feet*). There are also a few unusual formations, such as adding *-en* (*ox/oxen*) or using the same word for both the singular and plural forms (*deer, moose, sheep*), as well as words that have more than one correct form (*gases* or *gasses*, *zeros* or *zeroes*, and *dwarfs* or *dwarves*). Despite the variation, understanding a few key principles about plural formation will enable students to correctly change the number of most nouns. Developing a spelling awareness that helps them to realize when they are unsure of the formation and need to check it out with an expert or the dictionary will help them to tackle the rest.

**What Is Known:** Spelling of the base words and likely the simple plural formation of adding *-s*.

**What Is New:** Forming plurals by adding *-es* and through spelling changes.

---

### SORT 8. Plurals with *-s* and *-es*

| | Sorting by Pattern | | | |
|---|---|---|---|---|
| Base + *s* | Base + *es* | | | |
| | *-ch* | *-sh* | *-s* | *-x* |
| **pieces** | **inches** | **wishes** | **classes** | **foxes** |
| bridges | branches | brushes | guesses | indexes* |
| chances | crutches | dashes | losses | sixes |
| sevens | peaches | dishes | passes | taxes |
| sponges | stitches | | | |
| voices | watches | | | |

*Also spelled *indices*.

**Considerations:** Whether or not *-es* is used to form the plural of a noun is determined by the final consonant(s) of the base word; *-ch*, *-sh*, *-s*, and *-x* (and *-z*, as in *quizzes*) require *-es*. For most words that end in other consonants or final *-e* you just add *-s*. Although students likely will be familiar with the word meanings, remind them that the words they are working with are all nouns. Many of the words in this sort can function as present-tense verbs, also; however, because plurals are the focus, it is important for students to consider the noun-related meanings.

### Talking Points

- *Plural* means "more than one."
- To form the plural add *-s* to words that end in *-e*; add *-es* to words that end in *-ch*, *-sh*, *-s*, *-x*, or *-z*.

*Integrating Idioms:* "Everyone in the class **was at sixes and sevens** after having a substitute for two weeks." (Confused and disorderly. Six is an even number and seven is an odd number, so to be at sixes and sevens is to be out of harmony.)

"His dad told him if he dropped out of school he'd be **burning his bridges behind him**." (Making a decision he can't reverse. The reference is to historical and literary figure Julius Caesar, who burned bridges behind his army at the start of a civil war, making it impossible to turn back.)

*Did You Know?* Although your experiences with **taxes** may be limited to paying a little extra for an item when you purchase it, there are many kinds of taxes—property tax, inheritance tax, sales tax, income tax, and so forth. In fact, it was a tax called the *stamp tax* that was a stimulus for the Revolutionary War. That taxes are significant to people is evident in the expression that *there is nothing as certain as death and taxes*. Though people have an aversion to taxes, the word actually comes from the Latin root for "to touch," *tangere*. Why touch? People used to pay a certain percentage on everything they owned that could be touched, in other words, their property. The origin of *task* is also related to tax; if you couldn't pay your taxes in goods, you might work off the debt by completing some sort of task.

*Index* is also related to "touch." Many people use their index finger to flip through the indexes of reference books, touching each page as they go. This second finger was called *towcher*, meaning "toucher" in Middle English, because it was so often used to touch objects. Today's name of *index* for a part of some books stems from our common use of this finger for pointing.

## SORT 9. More Plurals

### Sorting by Pattern

| -y + s | -y → i + es | -f(e) → ves | Oddballs |
|---|---|---|---|
| **turkeys** | **cities** | **lives** | **?** |
| alleys | armies | knives | deer |
| holidays | babies | leaves | geese |
| journeys | bodies | shelves | mice |
| monkeys | copies | thieves | women |
| valleys | duties | wolves | |
| | ladies | | |

*Considerations:* This sort builds on the previous sort by extending plural formation to words that require a change of spelling. Although the sort contains numerous one-syllable words, several new spelling issues are explored, making the sort more complex than it may initially seem. Because knowledge of the base word is once again very important, you may want to introduce the sort by checking students' understanding of the base words. Ask them to record the base word for each of the plurals underneath the word on the card. Discuss the spellings or misspellings and any unfamiliar words; then ask the students to look for different ways in which the plural is formed. Guide them to discover the categories listed for the sort and discuss the results. Explain to students that words sometimes have more than one acceptable spelling for the plural form, as in *hoofs* and *hooves*. When determining what to do about words that end in -y, students will need to consider the letter that precedes the *y*. If the letter is a consonant, the change to *i* should be made; if the letter is a vowel, an *-s* is all that is needed, as in *alleys* and *turkeys*. Because spelling such words can be confusing, most dictionaries include the plural spelling as part of the word's entry, whether or not a spelling change is needed. You might invite students to brainstorm or hunt for other nouns that end in *-ey* and verify the spelling of their plurals with a dictionary. Generated examples might include *chimneys, donkeys, galleys, jerseys, jockeys, monkeys, surveys, trolleys*. Both *moneys* and *monies* are correct for the word *money*, but the former is more commonly used. How can you tell which spelling is more common? Dictionaries typically list the most common form of a word first when there are several possibilities. You may also wonder why there are two spellings. Perhaps this is because the change-*y*-to-*i* principle was mistakenly applied so often by writers that the alternative spelling became common, so lexicographers—those who write dictionaries—decided to accept it. When talking about the change-*y*-to-*i* category, you might point out to students that this principle or rule applies to adding many other suffixes These changes are described in later studies. When discussing the oddball words, ask students to explain why they placed the words in this category. They should note that *deer* is both the plural and singular form of the word (as is *sheep*) and that the other words involve spelling changes. You might ask students to try to generate other examples of unusual plurals (such as *oxen, children, mice*).

## Talking Points

- Change the *-y* to an *i* and add *-es* to form the plural of words that end in consonant *-y*; just add *-s* to form the plural of words that end in vowel *-y*, as in *copies* and *monkeys*.
- Words with final *-f* or *-fe* often change to *v* or *ve* before *-s* is added to make the plural, as in *wolf/wolves*.
- Some words have irregular plural forms, and some words use the same spelling for both plural and singular forms, as in *woman/women* and *deer/deer*.
- When in doubt about the spelling of a plural, consult a dictionary.

**Integrating Idioms:** "Upon her return to the classroom, the teacher shook her head and said, 'I guess **when the cat's away the mice will play.**'" (Cause mischief when not watched. Mice must be very cautious when a cat is watching their mouse hole, but they can put down their guard when the cat is away.)

**Did You Know?** You may know that Benjamin Franklin once suggested the **turkey** for consideration as our national bird. But did you ever wonder why this bird, which is native to the New World, is called a *turkey*? After all, Turkey is a country of southwest Asia and southeast Europe, situated between the Mediterranean and Black Seas, and far from the New World. As *The Merriam-Webster New Book of Word Histories* (1991) tells the story, the bird was first domesticated by Indian tribes in Mexico and Central America. It was later exported by the Spanish conquerors and first introduced to the Mediterranean region in the early 1500s. It was immediately confused with a bird long found in the area and known by various names: *guinea fowl* or *guinea cock*, because it had originally come from the country of Guinea on the African west coast, and *turkey-cock*, because Europeans imported the bird from an area they called Turkey, which was much larger then than the country of Turkey today. At that time Turkey was considered exotic, so something out of the ordinary was often assumed to have come from there. A well-known botanist of the time even attached the name *turkey* to two New World plants. He catalogued maize as *Turkish corn* and pumpkins as *Turkish cucumbers*. It is not so surprising, then, that the New World fowl came to be associated with the Old World turkey-cock that it resembled.

# SORT 8 Plurals with -s and -es

| Base + s | | Base + es |
|---|---|---|
| pieces | inches | wishes |
| classes | foxes | passes |
| crutches | dishes | sponges |
| guesses | bridges | dashes |
| sevens | taxes | branches |
| sixes | peaches | chances |
| indexes | brushes | losses |
| stitches | voices | watches |

# SORT 9 More Plurals

| -y + s | -y → i + s | -f(e) → ves |
|--------|-----------|-------------|
| turkeys | cities | lives |
| mice | holidays | shelves |
| ladies | women | bodies |
| journeys | wolves | alleys |
| leaves | babies | geese |
| copies | armies | knives |
| monkeys | thieves | deer |
| valleys | duties | ? |

*Comparisons*

---

**SORT 10.** Adding *-er* and *-est* to Words with No Change, *E*-Drop, Double, and Change *Y* to *I*

Sorting by Pattern

| No Change | *E*-Drop | Double | Change *-y* to *i* |
|---|---|---|---|
| **cheaper** | **bravest** | **bigger** | **driest** |
| brightest | closer | hottest | busiest |
| oddest | finest | sadder | easier |
| quicker | larger | slimmer | happier |
| smaller | ripest | thinnest | prettier |
| | | | silliest |

**What Is Known:** Students know the concept of a base word and have had experience with the four category principles through their work with adding *-ed*, *-ing*, and plural endings. Also, students should be familiar with base-word spelling patterns in the first three categories. Although the polysyllabic base words in the final category are more challenging, most students at this stage will know how to spell them.

**What Is New:** Considering four options (no change, *e*-drop, double, and change *-y* to *i*) when adding an inflected ending, as well as working with comparatives and superlatives (*-er* and *-est*).

**Considerations:** This sort includes just 21 words in order to accommodate additional headers. Introduce students to comparisons by writing on the board *loud*, *louder*, and *loudest*. Explain that one of the ways we express differences when comparing two or more things is by adding *-er* or *-est* to the base word, as with the words on the board. Write *comparative* and *superlative* on the board; then say something such as:

> "*Louder* is the comparative form, and *loudest* is the superlative form. The word *comparative* tells us we're comparing two things, and just as *super* means first-rate, *superlative* means 'superior to all others' and is used when we are comparing three or more things. Although we usually show comparison by attaching the *-er* or *-est* ending, as with *louder* and *loudest*, sometimes we add a word such as *more* or *most*, as we do with *more beautiful* or *most beautiful*. Could you imagine trying to say *beautifuller* or *beautifullest*?! Certain other words use different words to show comparison. This is the case with *good*. Here *better* and *best* are the comparing words, not *gooder* and *goodest* or even *more good* and *most good*. For the set of words we're working with, we'll just be using *-er* and *-est* comparisons."

Introduce the sort by asking students to classify the words according to whether they are comparative or superlative adjectives.

## Sorting by Meaning/Pattern

| Comparative | Superlative |
|---|---|
| bigger | bravest |
| cheaper | brightest |
| closer | busiest |
| easier | driest |
| happier | finest |
| larger | hottest |
| prettier | oddest |
| quicker | ripest |
| sadder | silliest |
| slimmer | thinnest |
| smaller | |

As you go over the listing, ask students to say the other form of the adjective (i.e., *biggest* for *bigger*, *braver* for *bravest*, and so on). For a few of the words, you might ask students to brainstorm sentences that clearly show the word's comparative or superlative status (e.g., *I saw two pairs of shoes that I liked, but I bought the **cheaper** pair* or *Venus is often the **brightest** star in the night sky.*)

Let students know that for this sort they will have a chance to use understandings they have gained from their recent work with *-ed* and *-ing* endings and plurals. Ask them to identify each base word and its spelling (you might ask them to write the base word at the bottom of the word card). Place the four headers and the key words in front of the students as category headers and point out how the *-er* or *-est* ending was added to each: no change, *e*-drop, double, or change *-y* to *i*. Explain that they will be sorting the rest of the words in the same way, according to how the comparison is formed. If needed, model the placement of a few words before inviting their participation. Discuss the categories when the sorting is complete. As an extension or assessment, ask students to complete a chart for their words, similar to the one started here. Additional words could be added, if desired.

| Base word | Comparative form | Superlative form |
|---|---|---|
| big | bigger | biggest |
| brave | braver | bravest |

### Talking Points

- Add *-er* to the base word when comparing two things, and add *-est* when the comparison involves three or more things, as in *bigger brother* and *tallest girl in class*.
- Apply the *e*-drop, doubling, no-change, and *y*-to-*i* principles when adding *-er* or *-est* to base words, as in *finest, sadder, quicker, busiest*.

***Integrating Idioms:*** "My mom is always telling me that **my eyes are bigger than my stomach.**" (I take more food than I can eat. When a meal or a particular food item looks good to eat, a person may take a lot of it, and then not be able to eat it all.)

***Did You Know?*** The word **odd**(est) comes to us from Scandinavia, a region of northern Europe. In medieval times, the Old Norse word *oddi* was the name for triangle. The connection between *odd* and *triangle* stems from fact that a triangle can be thought to have a pair of angles at the bottom and an unpaired, or odd, one at the top. The same connection gives us *odd man*, an unpaired person in a game or the person who can cast a deciding vote, as well as other words and phrases. Odd numbers have no partner, an oddball stands out as though unpartnered, odd jobs are typically unrelated jobs, and if you are at odds with someone, you are certainly not working like partners.

# SORT 10

Adding *-er* and *-est* to Words with No Change, *E*-Drop, Double, and Change *Y* to *I*

| Comparative | | Superlative | |
|---|---|---|---|
| **No Change** | **E-Drop** | **Double** | **Change Y to I** |
| cheaper | bravest | | bigger |
| slimmer | larger | | busiest |
| ripest | happier | | thinnest |
| quicker | finest | | easier |
| sadder | silliest | | smaller |
| driest | brightest | | hottest |
| closer | prettier | | oddest |

# Patterns across Syllables: Other Syllable Juncture Doubling
(DSA Feature L)

This section introduces students to two key syllable patterns—open and closed syllables. In the sorts that follow, four basic vowel and consonant patterns found across the juncture of syllables are described: VCV, as in *tiger* and *lemon*; VCCV with double consonants (also called a *doublet*), as in *hello*; VCCV with different consonants, as in *forget*; and VV, as in *diet*. Other sequences of letters, such as the three consonants in *athlete*, are introduced as variations of one of these four basic syllable patterns. As we will see, in these other sequences of letters two of the letters act as a team (namely, as a consonant blend or digraph, or as a vowel digraph). This approach limits the number of patterns that students must otherwise consider as they form generalizations, and it encourages them to look for and use what they already know about patterns from the letter name and within word pattern stages. Let's look at a few examples. Consider *athlete*; the basic across-syllable pattern is VCCV, represented by *a, th, l,* and the first *e*. The *th* is a digraph, and the letters work together as a team. In *reason* the pattern is VCV: V (*ea*), C (*s*), V (*o*). What about *instead*? Which of the four basic across-syllable patterns is it, and what letters make up each element? It is a VCCV pattern, with V (*i*), C (*n*), C (*st*, a blend), and V (*ea*, a vowel team). Each team of letters acts as a unit, not as separate letters. Knowing how syllables are put together can aid students in spelling and reading polysyllabic words, especially when they also understand the key principles that govern the vowel sounds associated with open and closed syllables. *Open* syllables are those that end with a vowel rather than a consonant sound, and typically the vowel sound is long, as in *tiger, beaver,* and *diet*. *Closed* syllables are those that end with one or more consonants, as in *lemon, hello, forget, instead,* and even *trickster*.

*What Is Known:* Students who completed sorts from *Word Sorts and More* (Ganske, 2006) may have been exposed to syllable structures as part of learning to recognize polysyllabic words (see Part 1 there). For other students the concepts may be new. By this stage, all students should be familiar with long and short vowel patterns and with syllables.

*What Is New:* The concept of open and closed syllables and the patterns across syllables that signal whether the vowel sound of the first syllable is long or short.

## SORT 11. Open and Closed Syllables with VCV and VCCV (Doublet)

### Sorting by Sound and Pattern

| Open | Closed | |
|------|--------|--------|
| VCV | VCCV Doublet | Oddball |
| **diner** | **dinner** | **?** |
| crater | better | study |
| crazy | bottom | |
| duty | letter | |
| even | matter | |
| meter | penny | |
| music | ribbon | |
| paper | soccer | |
| ruler | summer | |
| student | supper | |
| super | | |
| unit | | |

*Considerations:* Clarify any unfamiliar words. In particular, a discussion of the relationship among *diner, dinner,* and *supper* may be beneficial. Some students may not be familiar with *diner* as both "a small, inexpensive place to eat" and "one who dines." You might ask students whether they call their evening meal *dinner* or *supper*. Guide them to understand dinner as the main meal of the day, whether at midday or in the evening. The other light meal is usually called *lunch* or *supper*, depending on the time of day. Then introduce the sort by saying something such as:

> "Although we've been working with polysyllabic words in our studies of *-ed, -ing,* plurals, and compounds and thinking about the way they are spelled, especially where the ending joins the base word or, in the case of compounds, where the two base words come together, we're now ready to explore other ways syllables join. All of our words this time have two syllables. To begin, I want you to sort the words into two categories according to whether the vowel sound in the *first* syllable is long, as in *paper*, or short, as in *summer*."

(Results will be the same as those shown in the sound and pattern sort, except that *study* will be placed in the "summer" category.) If necessary, model the process by categorizing a few words; then invite students to assist with those that remain. Once the sound sort is complete, ask students to examine each category for pattern similarities. Students should notice the doubled versus single consonants. Guide with questions as needed and discuss the ideas. If they do not recognize *study* as an oddball, point this out. Then move *diner* and *dinner* as key words to the top, and point out to students that in learning how syllables join, it is important to keep in mind consonant and vowel patterns, just as it was helpful to consider the pattern of the base word when adding *-ed* or *-ing*. Show students that all of the words under *diner* have a VCV pattern at the syllable juncture. (It will likely be worth the time to go through each word and point out the VCV pattern, or invite students to do so; do likewise with the VCCV doublet pattern.) Students should develop understanding that VCV patterns in the sort are associated with a long vowel sound and the VCCV pattern with a short vowel. Point out that the syllable division in words with double consonants occurs between the two consonants. By closing off the first syllable with a consonant, we make the vowel sound short. Students should acquire understandings to aid them in reading and spelling words with VCV and VCCV across-syllable patterns. You might say something like:

> "There are two strong principles that can be gleaned from today's lesson. The first relates to reading words: When double consonants occur at the juncture of two syllables, the first syllable will have a short vowel sound, as with *dinner* and other words in our second category. The second principle deals with spelling: When trying to spell words with a long vowel sound like *diner* and the others in our first category, follow the vowel with one consonant rather than two. You can see what happens if you mistakenly include two consonants: Instead of writing, 'I did a super job on my project,' you'd end up with 'a supper job,' which makes no sense. Finally, as you can see from the word *study*, which has a short vowel but just one consonant following it, there's more to learn about joining syllables in longer words. Keep your eyes peeled as you read and write, and perhaps you'll pick up some clues to help us figure that out."

Open and closed syllables and patterns at syllable junctures are discussed further in Chapter 6 of *Word Journeys* (Ganske, 2000).

### Talking Points

- An open syllable ends with a long vowel sound; it has a VCV pattern across the syllables, as in *diner*; the syllable divides after the first vowel.
- A closed syllable has a short vowel sound and ends with a consonant; it has a VCCV pattern across syllables, sometimes with double consonants, as in *dinner*. The syllable divides between the consonants.
- Being able to divide words into syllables provides readers and writers with more manageable chunks for decoding and spelling words.

**Integrating Idioms:** "I know you said you got a good deal on this skateboard, but buying it is just being **penny-wise and pound-foolish**; there is nothing wrong with the one you have." (Saving a little by spending a lot. *Pound* here refers to money, not weight. Just as the dollar is the basic monetary unit in the United States, in the United Kingdom the basic unit is called the *pound* or *pound sterling*. The idiom points out how unwise it is to think you've done well if you saved a little but spent a lot to do so.)

**Did You Know?** Perhaps you've heard someone talk about their dislike of the *dog days of* **summer**, usually referring to the hot months of July and August. People sometimes mistakenly relate the expression to the fact that during the really hot months dogs tend to do little more than lie around. Instead, the phrase comes to us by way of a star in the constellation *Canis Major*, or "Greater Dog." The ancients called this second brightest of stars (our own sun being the brightest) *Sirius*, meaning "scorching or burning," because they associated its appearance with the dry, hot days of summer.

How did **soccer**, a game known most commonly in the world as *football*, get its name? Rules of the game were first written down in 1863 in England under the name of *association football* in order to avoid confusion with other types of football, such as rugby football. The longer name of *association football* was soon shortened to **soccer**.

## SORT 12. Open and Closed Syllables with VCV and VCCV (Doublet or Different)

### Sorting by Sound and Pattern

| Open | Closed | | Oddball |
|---|---|---|---|
| VCV | VCCV Doublet | VCCV Different | |
| **open** | **funny** | **contest** | **?** |
| bacon | dizzy | insect | limit |
| focus | follow | history | |
| human | pattern | number | |
| rotate | pretty | problem | |
| tulip | spelling | sandwich | |
| | traffic | sister | |
| | yellow | winter | |

*Considerations:* This sort expands understanding of the VCCV across-syllable pattern to include different, as well as like, consonants. After reviewing any unfamiliar words, invite students to try categorizing the words based on work from the previous sort and from what they anticipate to be the focus of this lesson. When they are finished, ask them to turn to a partner and share their rationales for placing certain words together. Discuss the results as a group, including the oddball. If students do not suggest the VCCV pattern with different consonants as one of the categories, demonstrate and discuss this possibility.

### Talking Points

- The consonants in a closed VCCV pattern across syllables can be the same or different, as in *contest* and *funny*. Divide into syllables between the consonants.

*Integrating Idioms:* "I've got to show Mom and Dad my report card first, before they see my brother's; his will be **a tough act to follow**." (Hard to compete with or show to be as good. In a performance, if the person or group before you performs really well, it's difficult to be the one who follows, because the audience may think your act is not as good and will be disappointed.)

*Did You Know? Sandwich* is a word with special beginnings because it originated from a person's name, or actually his title. John Montagu was the fourth Earl of Sandwich, an area in southeast England, during the 18th century. He was a hardcore gambler who reportedly sometimes gambled around the clock (24 hours straight). Instead of stopping the game for a meal, he asked that cold beef be brought to him between toast, so that he could continue playing, and voilá, the sandwich was born. Words such as *sandwich*, which originate from the name of a person (or place), are called *eponyms*.

Although not an eponym, the origin of *tulip* is also interesting. You might think the word originally meant how it sounds—"two lips"; however, it was actually borrowed from a Turkish word for muslin or gauze, *tulbent*. *Turban* has its beginnings in the same word. In fact, the tulip was given its name because the fully opened flower was thought to resemble a turban.

**SORT 13.** Open and Closed Syllables with VCV, VCCV (Doublet or Different), and VV

### Sorting by Pattern

| Open | Closed | | Open |
|------|--------|--|------|
| VCV | VCCV Doublet | VCCV Different | VV |
| **famous** | **slipper** | **pencil** | **poet** |
| clover | happen | chapter | create |
| cocoa | million | expert | cruel |
| humid | muffin | member | dial |
| pupil | sudden | publish | giant |
| | | sentence | lion |
| | | until | quiet |

*Considerations:* This sort introduces students to a new across-syllable pattern: VV. Discuss any unfamiliar words and expand students' understanding of the double meanings of words such as *sentence* (a "grammatical unit" and a "term of punishment") and *pupil* (a "student" and the "opening in the center of an eye"). Begin by asking students to sort the words into two groups by sound: open syllables and closed syllables (long vowels and short vowels). Then they can subdivide each list by pattern. The end results are shown in Sort 13. Once the categories are complete, discuss the results. Although there are few two-syllable words with the VV pattern, it appears much more often in three- and four-syllable words, so it is an important pattern for students to be aware of. Caution them when sorting words with two vowels to pay heed to their sound. The vowels sometimes cross syllable boundaries, as in this sort, so that the sound of each is heard; but at other times, the vowels work as a team, as in *reason*. Because this sort can be completed just by looking at the patterns you may want to provide students with opportunities to sort the words blindly, so that they also attend to sound.

### Talking Points

• Two vowels together are not always a team; sometimes the vowels are situated across syllable boundaries, creating a VV pattern but with the syllable division between them, as in *poet*.

*Integrating Idioms:* "Hey, what are you thinking about? **You're a million miles away.**" (Distracted or daydreaming. If you were literally a million miles away you would have no idea of what other people were doing.)

*Did You Know?* **Pupil** provides an opportunity for students to discover that certain words are entered in the dictionary more than once. Looking up *pupil* will reveal two separate entries, designated with a superscript 1 or 2: pu•pil[1] and pu•pil[2]. Students may wonder why all of the meanings are not listed under one entry. Ask them to speculate before explaining that different entries for a word mean that each meaning has its own story. For example, *pupil*, meaning "student," stems from a word that means "boy," whereas the *pupil* of an eye was borrowed from a word meaning "little doll" because of the miniature image reflected in a pupil. Students might search in the dictionary for other common words with multiple meanings and multiple histories.

　　Just how tall does someone have to be to be considered a *giant*? To a toddler, most parents are giants. According to a Wikipedia entry, 7 feet 5 inches tall has been used as a benchmark for giant size. You might invite students to brainstorm a list of well-known giants from literature (such as Roald Dahl's BFG—Big Friendly Giant; Hagrid from the *Harry Potter* series; Rumblebuffin from C. S. Lewis's *The Lion, the Witch, and the Wardrobe*; the giant of *Jack and the Beanstalk* fame; Paul Bunyan; Polyphemus, the Cyclops in Homer's *The Odyssey*; and the Bible's Goliath).

---

## SORT 14. Open and Closed Syllables with VCV, VCCV (Doublet or Different)

### Sorting by Sound and Pattern

| Open | Closed | | Oddballs |
|------|--------|--|----------|
| VCV | VCCV Doublet | VCCV Different | Consonant and vowel teams |
| **lazy** | **classic** | **basket** | **?** |
| humor | comma | absent | apple |
| recent | gallon | distant | athlete |
| silent | inning | napkin | constant |
| | ladder | picnic | control |
| | mammal | | hundred |
| | tennis | | program |
| | | | reason |

*Considerations:* Up to this point, the V or C elements in VCCV and VCV structures have represented single letters. However, as discussed in the introduction to this section, consonant blends and digraphs and vowel digraphs sometimes occur at the syllable juncture. If individual letters are used to examine across-syllable patterns, students will need to think about an increasing number of patterns. To help them keep in mind the basic patterns that occur across syllables and to limit the number of patterns they must consider, words with digraphs and blends at the juncture of syllables are highlighted as oddballs in this sort. In subsequent sorts, words of this type are categorized as VCV, as VCCV doublet or different, or as VV, with the vowel or consonant team regarded as a unit, V or C.

Begin by going over any unfamiliar words. Explain to students that the sort includes several oddballs for which they should be watchful. Provide the headers; then ask them to sort their words according to the categories they have studied—VCV and VCCV doublet and different—and to place words under the "?" category that do not seem to fit. Their ultimate aim should be to discover characteristics that result in words being classified as oddballs. Suggest that students work in dyads or triads and ask that they share their results with another team when finished. Once everyone is finished, discuss the results. Then ask students to identify any consonant or vowel teams and try to determine which syllable structure is the best match for each oddball. The following chart illustrates the thinking that may result (VCCV doublet and VCCV different have been combined into one column):

| | **V** | **C** | **V** | | **V** | **C** | **C** | **V** | |
|---|---|---|---|---|---|---|---|---|---|
| pr | O | GR | A | m | A | P | P | LE | |
| r | EA | S | O | n | A | TH | L | E | te |

| V | C | V |
|---|---|---|

| V | C | C | V |
|---|---|---|---|
| h | U | N | DR | E | d |
| c | O | N | TR | O | l |
| c | O | N | ST | A | nt |

During the discussion, clarify the pattern in *apple*, which is considered VCCV doublet. Although students may have thought of *pl* as a consonant team, sound does not support this; instead, *l* and *e* together make the vowel sound, /əl/, as they do in many words, for example, *buckle*, *people*, *candle*, and *title*. The first syllable in *apple* consists of *ap*, and the final syllable is *ple* or C*le*. Remind students that awareness of vowel and consonant teams can help with reading unfamiliar words. It is important for students to learn to approach words flexibly. If applying one pattern does not lead to a correct pronunciation during reading, try another. For example, *h-u-m-o-r* is a VCV pattern with an open syllable, but if *t-o-p-i-c* were approached in the same manner, the pronunciation would be tō•pĭc, instead of the actual pronunciation of *topic*, which has a VCV pattern but with a closed syllable. This pattern is discussed in the next sort.

Suggest that students be alert for other words with blends and digraphs at the syllable juncture and explain that in the future, words of this type will be included in one of the basic categories: VCV, VCCV doublet or different, or VV. Ask students who are up to an extra challenge or even a super-duper challenge to try to determine the syllable pattern for one or both of the following words (be sure they understand what the words mean as well; you will almost certainly have to explain the meaning and perhaps the pronunciation for the super-duper challenge):

Challenge: *gypsy* (V = *y*, C = *p*, C = *s*, V = *y*) closed syllable

Super-Duper Challenge: *queuing* [pronounced /Q + ing/] (VV) open syllable

A *queue* means "a long line of waiting people or cars"; it also refers to a long braid. We might say *People are queuing up for the movie*. No letter divisions are listed for *queuing* because just which letters should be considered part of the vowel pattern (V) is debatable; ask students to provide a rationale for their decisions.

### Talking Points

- Sometimes consonants that occur at the juncture of syllables form a team; careful consideration is needed to decide where to divide the syllables, as in *program*, *control*, and *athlete*. Teams can also consist of vowels, as in *rea/son*, not *re/ason*.
- When dividing words with three or more consonants at the juncture, look for consonant blends and digraphs that often work together in words, such as *th* and *dr*.

*Integrating Idioms:* "The teacher said our group's work on the project seems to be **without any rhyme or reason**. She asked if we would get it done on time." (No real purpose or direction. A *rhyme* typically has a pattern or other organization, and *reason* is a motive for acting; without these two, it's unlikely much is being accomplished.)

*Did You Know?* What do *mop*, *map*, and **napkin** have in common? *Mop* was borrowed from the Latin word *mappa*, meaning cloth. In 1496 a similar word, *mappe*, designated a bundle of yarn or cloth used to clean or spread pitch on a ship's planking to keep water out. *Map* has a similar background because early *mappa mundi*, "maps of the world," were made of cloth to last for long sea journeys. *Napkin* comes from the same word with a later adding of *-kin* to mean "little cloth." These "little cloths," even when paper, sometimes serve varied purposes: Popular author J. K. Rowling began the *Harry Potter* series in a café, writing on a paper napkin.

### Literature Links

Truss, L. (2006). *Eats, shoots and leaves: Why commas really do make a difference.* New York: G. P. Putnam's Sons. This picture book, with its cartoon drawings, highlights what happens to meaning when commas are misplaced or omitted. Entertaining for all ages.

---

## SORT 15. Open and Closed Syllables with VCV (Long or Short) and VCCV (Doublet or Different)

| | Sorting by Sound and Pattern | | |
|---|---|---|---|
| Open | Closed | | |
| VCV Long | VCCV Doublet | VCCV Different | VCV Short |
| **moment** | **attic** | **enjoy** | **planet** |
| climate | rabbit | elbow | clever |
| freedom | tunnel | enter | comet |
| local | village | garden | rapid |
| sequel | | mustard | second |
| | | picture | solid |
| | | orbit | travel |
| | | | value |

*Considerations:* After discussing any unfamiliar words, introduce the sort by asking students to categorize the words according to open and closed syllables. This will result in one very long list (closed) and a short list (open). Next, discuss pattern differences in the closed syllable column and, as a group, subdivide the list into the VCCV doublet, VCCV different, and VCV short categories. As the categories are formed, add the corresponding header. *Freedom* is considered a VCV long pattern here, with a vowel team (*ee*) for the first vowel. In *sequel*, the *u* works with the *q* as a team, creating a VCV long pattern. Discuss the results and ask students to tell what they learned. They will likely mention something about the confusing nature of the VCV pattern: It can lead to either a long or a short vowel sound. Caution students when they are reading and writing such words. Remind them that if the syllable ends in a long vowel sound, the consonant that follows will not be doubled when they write the word. However, if the syllable is closed and the vowel sound short, there may or may not be doubled consonants at the juncture—for example, *rabbit/habit, buddy/study,* and *bobbin/robin*. Words with closed syllables require caution in spelling. In reading words with a VCV pattern, it is best to consider the syllable open and the vowel sound long and then try identifying it. If that approach does not produce a recognizable word, the syllable should be considered closed, and a short vowel sound applied. Explain that it is not as difficult as it may seem, just something that wise spellers and readers keep a lookout for.

*Talking Points*

- Although VCV usually signals an open syllable, sometimes this is the pattern of a closed syllable, as the difference between *moment* and *comet*.
- Read words with a VCV pattern as an open syllable first; if this does not produce a known word, try closing the syllable and reading again.
- When writing, if you hear a long vowel, make sure you don't have a double consonant following it, as in *local*, not *loccal*.

*Integrating Idioms:* "Sorry I wasn't home for your call; I went shopping **on the spur of the moment**." (All of a sudden. We typically think of spurs as short little spikes attached to the heel of a rider's boot and used to goad or urge a horse to move more quickly. In this expression, a particular moment is serving as a spur and causing the speaker to suddenly, and without prior planning, decide to go to the mall.)

*Did You Know?* The ancients observed several heavenly bodies that changed their positions relative to each other and to stars that seemed fixed in their positions (the sun and moon; and Mercury, Venus, Mars, Jupiter, and Saturn, thought to revolve about the Earth). The Greeks referred to these bodies as *planetai*, or "wanderers." The word was borrowed by the Romans, the French, and later the English and eventually became **planets**.

**Garden** stems from a Latin word for "fenced or walled area." Then, as now, intruders, whether four-legged or two-legged, were cause for concern to anyone trying to grow plants, so enclosures provided a deterrent. The words *guard* and *kindergarten* are related to *garden*. The latter word is made up of *kinder*, the German word for "children," and *garten*, which means "garden." The word dates back to 1840, 3 years after Friedrich Fröbel started the first kindergarten as a place in which children could be cultivated and bloom.

# SORT 11 Open and Closed Syllables with VCV and VCCV (Doublet)

| Open | Closed | VCV | VCCV Doublet |
|------|--------|-----|--------------|
| diner | dinner | unit | |
| paper | summer | soccer | |
| student | letter | crater | |
| matter | study | better | |
| duty | ribbon | meter | |
| penny | ruler | even | |
| music | bottom | crazy | |
| super | supper | ? | |

# SORT 12   Open and Closed Syllables with VCV and VCCV
(Doublet or Different)

| VCV | VCCV<br>Doublet | VCCV<br>Different |
|---|---|---|
| open | funny | contest |
| limit | history | dizzy |
| follow | bacon | pattern |
| human | sandwich | pretty |
| number | winter | focus |
| rotate | spelling | problem |
| sister | tulip | yellow |
| traffic | insect | ? |

# SORT 13 Open and Closed Syllables with VCV, VCCV (Doublet or Different), and VV

| VCV | VCCV Doublet | VCCV Different | VV |
|---|---|---|---|
| famous | slipper | | pencil |
| poet | quiet | | million |
| dial | sentence | | publish |
| expert | clover | | happen |
| humid | sudden | | until |
| giant | lion | | cocoa |
| member | cruel | | chapter |
| muffin | pupil | | create |

# SORT 14
Open and Closed Syllables with VCV, VCCV (Doublet or Different)

| VCV | VCCV Doublet | VCCV Different |
|---|---|---|
| lazy | classic | basket |
| picnic | control | napkin |
| apple | inning | tennis |
| recent | absent | constant |
| program | mammal | athlete |
| comma | hundred | humor |
| reason | gallon | ladder |
| silent | distant | ? |

Open and Closed Syllables with VCV (Long or Short) and VCCV
(Doublet or Different)

| VCV Long | VCCV Doublet | VCCV Different | VCV Short |
|----------|--------------|----------------|-----------|
| moment | attic | | enjoy |
| planet | second | | tunnel |
| mustard | value | | climate |
| local | elbow | | travel |
| garden | rapid | | freedom |
| clever | rabbit | | picture |
| village | solid | | sequel |
| orbit | enter | | comet |

# Vowel Patterns in Stressed Syllables

## Long Vowel Patterns in Stressed Syllables (DSA Feature M)

This section is the first of several to focus on vowel patterns in stressed syllables. Here long vowels are targeted with short vowels used as a contrasting sound. Later sections deal with *r*-controlled and abstract vowels. Identifying which syllable is stressed or accented can be difficult for students, so you might be wondering, Why study them? Typically, vowel patterns in stressed syllables are easier to spell than those in unstressed syllables because sound provides a clue to the pattern. By identifying the vowel sound, students are able to apply much of their pattern knowledge from previous stages to spell longer words. In contrast, the schwa vowel sound /ə/ of unstressed syllables, which will be studied later at this stage, is less predictable: All five vowels and several vowel combinations can produce the sound. Recognizing stressed and unstressed syllables and realizing which part of a word is the more difficult can alert students to focus their mental energy on the tricky part as they learn to spell the word. Work with stressed syllables can also encourage students to approach unfamiliar words in their reading with flexibility. If pronouncing a word one way does not lead to a known word, shifting the stress to another syllable and trying an alternative pronunciation may. Finally, work with stressed syllables provides an opportunity to help students learn to navigate unfamiliar aspects of the dictionary.

Introduce students to the concept of syllable stress by taking a step back. In advance of the lesson, on the board or a transparency, record the following words and their dictionary entries, which also show syllable division and pronunciation. Cover up the entry word and pronunciation so that these aspects of the words can be revealed one word at a time. Then ask students to clap and count the number of syllables in the words, as *pencil* (2), *principal* (3), *computer* (3), *gym* (1), and *dictionary* (4).

| | | |
|---|---|---|
| *pencil* | **pen•cil** | (pĕn´səl) |
| *principal* | **prin•ci•pal** | (prĭn´sə-pəl) |
| *computer* | **com•put•er** | (kəm-pyo͞o´tər) |
| *gym* | **gym** | (jĭm) |
| *dictionary* | **dic•tion•ar•y** | (dĭk´shə-nĕr´ē) |

Next say something such as:

TEACHER:  When words have more than one syllable, one of the syllables is usually stressed or said with a little more emphasis, as in *pencil. (Points to the word.)* A dictionary often identifies the stressed syllable by placing an apostrophe-like mark called an *accent* after the stressed syllable in the word's pronunciation, as we see here. *(Uncovers the entry word and pronunciation for* pencil *to demonstrate.)* The bolded word is the *entry word*; entry words are usually bolded so you can easily find the word you're searching for; the pronunciation is the part in parentheses. From what you see, which syllable of *pencil* is stressed?

STUDENT:  It's the first syllable, the *pen* part; see, here is the accent mark. *(Points.)*

TEACHER:  That's right. Here the syllable that is stressed is the first syllable. *(Points to bolded word and underlines the first syllable.)* Notice that the entry word separates the syllables with a little dot, but it doesn't show us which of the syllables is stressed, and it doesn't show us how to pronounce the word, either. We might think that the first syllable is pronounced like the writing tool, since it's spelled the same, but look at the second syllable in the entry word. (*Points to* cil.) If you came upon *c-i-l* as a new word in your reading, you would probably pronounce it like the last syllable in *windowsill*, with a short *i* sound. But do we pronounce the letters in *p-e-n-c-i-l* as *pensill*?

STUDENT: No way! That sounds silly.

TEACHER: That's right. It sounds funny to our ears because when we say *pencil*, the second syllable isn't stressed at all; in fact, we say that it is *unstressed*. When a syllable is unstressed, the vowel changes from its usual long or short sound to the schwa sound of "uh." You can always tell when a syllable has this sound, because a dictionary represents it with this special upside-down, backward *e* that we see in the second syllable of *pencil*. (*Points.*) The schwa tells us to pronounce the word as "pensull," not "pensill." We're going to begin our study of syllable stress by exploring vowel patterns and sounds in the stressed syllables of words, but eventually we'll come back to the schwa, because it can be tricky to spell and is the cause of many spelling errors. [Students may notice other schwa vowels during the lesson. You may wish to comment on these, but maintain focus on the stressed syllables at this time.] OK, let's think about the other words we used for counting syllables and see if we can pick out the stressed syllable. What about *principal*; which syllable do you think is stressed?

STUDENT: It's the first one again, just like *pencil*.

TEACHER: (*Uncovers the entry word and pronunciation.*) That's right; when we say *principal*, we stress the first syllable—*prin*. (*Underlines this portion of the word.*)

STUDENT: Is it always the first syllable?

TEACHER: What do you think?

STUDENT: No, because look at *computer*. Who says, "Can I work on the **com**puter?"

TEACHER: Good thinking. So which syllable do we stress in *computer*?

STUDENTS: (*Repeat the word to themselves.*) The second part.

TEACHER: Yes, we stress the second syllable in *computer*. (*Uncovers the information for computer, then models by saying the word and slightly emphasizing the second syllable*—com**pu**ter; *underlines this part of the word.*) [Note: Dictionary entry words divide words into syllables according to meaning units, whereas the pronunciation of the word is divided according to sound. Thus the *t* in the entry word *computer* is included with the second syllable of the entry word, because it is part of a meaning unit, the word root—*put*. It is not included in the second syllable of the pronunciation, because this is not how we say the word. There is no need to call students' attention to this distinction unless they notice the difference.]

TEACHER: All right, what about *gym*?

STUDENTS: You're trying to trick us. That word has just one syllable; you said at the beginning that stress has to do with words that have *more* than one syllable.

TEACHER: (*Uncovers the information for* gym.) Excellent thinking and remembering! That's right. When a word has just one syllable, we don't have to consider stress at all. OK, let's think about the last word, *dictionary*; then we'll check to see what the stress or accent mark for this word looks like in the dictionary. Let's clap and say *dictionary* again: *dic-tion-ar-y*. This is a long word; who will give it a try?

STUDENT 1: I think it's the first syllable.

STUDENT 2: I think it's the third one.

TEACHER: Good job, both of you! Sometimes words with several syllables, like this one, can have more than one stressed syllable. Although a word like *dictionary* may have more than one stressed syllable, one of the stressed syllables is said with greater emphasis than the other. It is the *primary stress*, and the other syllable is the *secondary stress*. [Younger or less capable students may be confused by the additional terms. If so, disregard this portion of the discussion.] Which syllable in *dictionary* is given the main or primary stress?

STUDENT 2: (*Repeats the word.*) It's the first syllable, but the third one gets the other stress.

TEACHER: (*Uncovers the entry word and pronunciation for* dictionary.) That's right; very good observation! Notice that the accent for the syllable that is said with the most emphasis is shown with a heavier line than the less stressed syllable. In some dictionaries, the accented syllable is bolded rather than indicated by the special mark.

At this point, students may be guided to find some of the lesson words, or other polysyllabic words, in the dictionary. Keep the activity engaging by making it a game: Invite each student to suggest one or more polysyllabic words to classmates to guess the stress and then check the accuracy of their responses with a dictionary. Note that dictionaries sometimes vary slightly in how they record a word's pronunciation. The pronunciations provided in this section are from *The American Heritage College Dictionary* (4th ed., 2004). Also, bear in mind that dialect may cause a student to pronounce a word differently from what is shown in a dictionary entry.

Depending on the needs and interests of the group, you might engage students in the States Stress Break included in Sort 63 in Part 2 before moving on to the sorts that follow. Initially, use the States Stress Break word cards just to reinforce students' ability to identify the stressed syllable in the words. At the end of the syllable juncture stage, after students have studied the various vowel patterns, students may revisit the words with the expectation of learning to spell the names of the states. (For further information on working with syllable stress at the syllable juncture stage, see *Word Journeys: Assessment-Guided Phonics, Spelling, and Vocabulary Instruction*, Ganske, 2000.)

The following series of seven sorts focuses on long vowel patterns in stressed syllables. First students identify the syllable that is stressed (first or second), and then they compare and contrast long and short vowel patterns in the stressed syllable. Some students may have a difficult time considering both long and short vowel words. If so, eliminate the short vowel words, or tell students to focus only on long vowel stressed syllables and to categorize all other words as oddballs.

*What Is Known:* (Sorts 16–22). Students should be confident in their use of long and short vowel patterns in single-syllable words; a few specific patterns may be new to them. They should also be familiar with stress and syllables. Though likely not confident in identifying the stressed syllable in a word, they should know that it can occur in different syllables.

*What Is New:* (Sorts 16–22). Examining vowel patterns in stressed syllables will be new; also, because students were just introduced to the open syllable long vowel pattern earlier in this book, it is still relatively new to them; a few other patterns may also be new. For example, the long *e* pattern *eCe* (*compete*) and *y* as a short vowel pattern (*symbol*).

## SORT 16. Long and Short *a* in Stressed Syllables

### Sorting by Syllable Stress

| 1st Syllable Stress | 2nd Syllable Stress | Oddball |
|---|---|---|
| **bracelet** | **afraid** | **?** |
| April | amaze | [none] |
| basement | complain | |
| basic | contain | |
| chocolate | erase | |
| crayon | escape | |
| daily | explain | |
| fable | obey | |
| later | perhaps | |
| nation | remain | |
| raisin | | |
| rather | | |
| Saturday | | |
| shadow | | |

*Considerations:* Introduce the sort in a manner similar to the following:

1. Read through the template of words and discuss any that might be unfamiliar, perhaps *fable* and *nation*.

2. Ask students if they noticed anything about the words. They should have detected that nearly all of the words have a long *a* sound. If they do not mention that a few of the words have the short *a* sound, bring this to their attention.

3. Put out the headers *1st Stress* and *2nd Stress* with their respective key words (*bracelet* and *afraid*) and the card used for oddballs ("*?*"), though the words can be sorted without it.

4. Say "bracelet" and slightly emphasize the first syllable, **bracelet**. Explain that *bracelet* has been placed in the first category because the first syllable is stressed. Follow a similar process with *afraid* to highlight its placement in the 2nd stress category.

5. Explain to students that with their help you will be sorting the remaining words under the appropriate 1st Stress or 2nd Stress category. Choose a short vowel word to model another example. Invite students to attempt the next word. (Sometimes it can be helpful to read the words aloud without showing them to students. This takes away any visual distraction and allows full concentration to be on the sound. Be sure to pronounce the words with natural emphasis.)

6. When all of the words have been sorted, read down the column of 1st Stress words; slightly accentuate the stressed syllable. Ask students if they can hear the accent or stress on the first syllable. If anyone has difficulty, ask the group to reread the column with you. Identify the vowel sound in the stressed first syllable of each word and discuss. Point out that because long vowels often occur in stressed syllables, hearing a long vowel sound can help to identify which syllable is stressed.

7. Repeat the process with the other column. Discuss the results, drawing students' attention to the difference in stress from the first category. Identify the vowel sound in each stressed syllable. Point out that with the exception of *chocolate* all of the words have either a long or a short *a* vowel sound in the stressed syllable.

8. *Saturday*, with its long and short *a* sounds, may give rise to special debate; although the third syllable, *day*, receives some stress, the primary stress is on the first syllable. Because dialect may influence the pronunciation of this and other words, avoid being overly concerned about correctness; instead, allow for individual differences by suggesting the oddball category as a way to resolve such questions.

9. Explain to students that vowel patterns in stressed syllables tend to be easier to spell because the sound provides a clue, as, for example, the *aCe* pattern in *basement*, which is stressed, compared with the same pattern in *chocolate*, which is not.

## Sorting by Sound and Pattern

| Short *a* | aCe | ai | Open *a* | Oddball |
|---|---|---|---|---|
| **shadow** | **bracelet** | **afraid** | **fable** | **?** |
| perhaps | amaze | complain | April | chocolate |
| rather | basement | contain | basic | daily |
| Saturday | erase | (daily) | crayon | obey |
| | escape | explain | (daily) | |
| | | raisin | later | |
| | | remain | nation | |

After completing the sound sort with stressed syllables for Sort 16, or at a later time, ask students to suggest other ways to categorize the words. Likely someone will suggest sorting by pattern. The results would be the same as shown in the sound and pattern sort above except that the short *a* and open *a* categories would be combined. If no one mentions it, suggest that students try sorting by pattern and vowel sound, as shown. The group session would go something like this (a similar process can be used for Sorts 17–22):

1. Put out *shadow*, *bracelet*, *afraid*, and *fable* as key words; add the question mark for oddballs. Highlight or underline the vowel pattern in each stressed syllable. If someone suggests that the two categories represented by *shadow* and *fable* should be combined, since they both have the *a* pattern, say something such as:

"That is one way the words could be looked at, because both *shadow* and *fable* do have *a*'s, but because we want to think about sound as well as pattern, we're going to keep them separate. Listen: The *a* makes a short sound in *shadow* and a long sound in *fable*. Because the vowel sound ends the syllable in *fable*, it makes a long sound; it's like the other open-syllable words we studied earlier. It is kind of confusing, because the vowel is tucked between two consonants just as it is in *shadow*. Patterns like these that look alike on the surface can cause problems during reading, too. Obviously, we'll need to be careful about our placement of words with the *a* pattern."

2. Ask students to help you sort the words into their appropriate categories.

3. *Chocolate* is an oddball; although it has the *aCe* pattern, the pattern does not make a long *a* sound. *Obey* is also an oddball; it has a long *a* sound but there is no *ey* category. *Daily* is an oddball because it has both open *a* and *ai* patterns. Allow students to place the word in any of the three pattern categories.

4. Review the categories for the appropriate sound and pattern; discuss the results and add the category headers. As part of the discussion, you might temporarily move an open *a* word or two to the short *a* category and ask students how the word(s) would be pronounced. You might also ask them how *s-h-a-d-o-w* would be pronounced if it had an open *a*. Invite students to brainstorm other long *a* patterns in stressed syllables, as, for example, *ay* in *decay* or *mayor*. Explain that in the future they will be examining other vowel patterns in stressed syllables.

## Talking Points

- Vowel patterns in the stressed syllable tend to be easier to spell.
- A particular vowel pattern may be stressed in the first syllable of one word (*bracelet*), in the second syllable of another (*escape*), and not at all in some other word (*chocolate*).
- Three common long *a* patterns found in stressed syllables are *aCe*, *ai*, and *open a*, as in *amaze*, *contain*, and *later*.

**Integrating Idioms:** "Are you sure, **beyond a shadow of a doubt**, that he took your paper?" (Completely. If the only doubt you had could be compared to a shadow, there would be little substance to it; taking the matter a step further and saying "*beyond* a shadow of a doubt" suggests no possibility of a doubt.)

**Did You Know? Saturday,** like the other days of the week, gets its name from a celestial body—the sun, moon, or planets. *Saturday* was originally called *Saturn's Day* (the Latin expression would have been *Dies Saturni*) and was named after the Roman god of agriculture. In ancient times, each year a 7-day period of high-spirited and carefree celebration called *Saturnalia* was held in his honor. The way that many people still like to enjoy themselves on a Saturday evening is a good reminder of Saturn's connection to this day.

The rest of the days, in order, translated from the Latin as *Sun's Day, Moon's Day, Mars's Day, Mercury's Day, Jupiter's* or *Jove's Day,* and *Venus's Day.* The relationship of the sun and moon to the names of our days of the week is obvious, but what about the other days that were named after planets? How did *Tuesday* evolve from *Mars's Day,* and so on? The days named after planets were names of gods, as *Saturday* for Saturn. However, because Old English (the ancestor of modern-day English) was a Germanic language, when the names of the days of the week were borrowed into early English, writers not only translated the Latin words but also substituted similar German or Norse gods for the names of four of the Roman gods. So instead of *Mars's Day* it was *Tiu's Day* ("Tuesday"). Tiu, like Mars, was a god of war. *Mercury's Day* became *Woden's Day* ("Wednesday"). Mercury was quick, well-spoken, and known for his general skill, and Woden as the supreme god would have been recognized for similar traits. *Jupiter's Day* became *Thurin's* or *Thor's Day* ("Thursday"). Jupiter was the supreme Roman god, and Thor, a son of Woden's, was the most popular god. He was known as the "thunder god" because whenever he traveled across the sky in his chariot, the sound of the wheels made thunder. *Venus's Day* became *Frigga's Day* ("Friday"). Both Venus and Frigga, the wife of Woden, were goddesses of love and beauty. So why was *Saturn's Day* not replaced? Apparently the Germanic people had no similar god to substitute, so they just translated the Roman god's name. A table comparing current English spelling to that of the ancient Latin and Old English follows. Contemporary French and Spanish spellings are also included. These were also derived from the Latin but without the substitution of different gods, so the names of the Roman gods are more discernable in their spellings. The weekend days, with their religious significance, were altered in the French and Spanish forms to words related to *Sabbath* and to a phrase meaning "Lord's Day."

| English | Latin | Old English | French | Spanish |
|---------|-------|-------------|--------|---------|
| Sunday | *Dies Solis* | *Sunnandaeg* | *dimanche* | *domingo* |
| Monday | *Dies Lunae* | *Monandaeg* | *lundi* | *lunes* |
| Tuesday | *Dies Martis* | *Tiwesdaeg* | *mardi* | *martes* |
| Wednesday | *Dies Mercurii* | *Wodnesdaeg* | *mercredi* | *miércoles* |
| Thursday | *Dies Jovis* | *Thunresdaaeg* | *jeudi* | *jueves* |
| Friday | *Dies Veneris* | *Frigedaeg* | *vendredi* | *viernes* |
| Saturday | *Dies Saturni* | *Saeternesdaeg* | *samedi* | *sábado* |

(*Note*: The word *Saturday* is included in this sort; for the other days of the week see: *Sunday*, Sort 54; *Monday*, *Tuesday*, and *Thursday*, Sort 22; *Wednesday*, Sort 17; and *Friday*, Sort 19.)

## Literature Link

D'Aulaire, I., & D'Aulaire, E. P. (1967). *D'Aulaires' book of Norse myths.* New York: Doubleday.

D'Aulaire, I., & D'Aulaire, E. P. (1992). *D'Aulaires' book of Greek myths.* New York: Delacorte Books for Young Readers.

Vinge, J. P. (1999). *The Random House book of Greek myths.* New York: Random House for Young Readers.

## SORT 17. Long and Short e in Stressed Syllables

### Sorting by Syllable Stress

| 1st Stress | 2nd Stress | Oddball |
|------------|------------|---------|
| **fever** | **delete** | **?** |
| deeply | asleep | [none] |
| effort | between | |
| either | complete | |
| evening | degrees | |
| female | expect | |
| ketchup | extreme | |
| legal | idea | |
| never | indeed | |
| people | succeed | |
| secret | supreme | |
| Wednesday | trapeze | |

## Sorting by Sound and Pattern

| Short e | ee | eCe | Open e | Oddball |
|---------|-----|-----|--------|---------|
| **effort** | **asleep** | **delete** | **fever** | **?** |
| expect | between | complete | female | either |
| ketchup | deeply | evening | idea | people |
| never | degrees | extreme | legal | |
| Wednesday | indeed | supreme | secret | |
| | succeed | trapeze | | |

*Considerations:* VCe is a new pattern for *e*, as the pattern seldom occurs in one-syllable words. Also, as a point of information, although *Wednesday* looks as though it has three syllables due to its three separate vowels, it has only two. Discuss meanings as needed, but check for understanding of *trapeze* and the multiple meanings of *degrees* (university-related, temperature, and others). The same basic process described for introducing Sort 16 may be used here. When discussing the results, there is no oddball for the syllable stress sort, unless students pronounce *either* with a long *i*. *People* and *either* are oddballs in the sound and pattern sort. Although each has a long *e* sound in the stressed syllable, their long *e* patterns are not included in the sort. Students may be able think of other long *e* patterns. Also, some students may suggest that *delete* has an open syllable as well as eCe. Remind them that the vowel pattern needs to be in the stressed syllable. Say the word with them, slightly emphasizing the second syllable. If they continue to pronounce it with a long *e* sound in each syllable, suggest that they place the word as an oddball.

### Talking Points

- Three long *e* vowel patterns often found in stressed syllables are *ee*, eCe, and open *e*, as in *between*, *delete*, and *fever*.
- Although very few one-syllable words have eCe, this pattern is found in the second syllable of numerous polysyllabic words.
- Because various patterns can represent the same sound in a stressed syllable, when trying to spell one if you're not sure which is the right one, check a dictionary or ask an expert.

### Integrating Idioms:
"I'd like to create a model of the White House for my project, but I know **it'll never fly** with Ms. Papier, because she said it had to be a report." (It will never be approved. The project won't get the go-ahead from Ms. Papier, just as airplanes sometimes don't get clearance to take off.)

### Did You Know?
**Ketchup** is also called *catchup* and *catsup*. Although all three variations are in use today, *ketchup* has been around the longest; it came into use in 1711. The word is thought to have been borrowed from a Malay word (*kechap*) for a sauce that contained fish brine and sauces, but no tomatoes. During the 1700s and 1800s *ketchup* referred to any sauce that had vinegar as a base. The other ingredients were anything that was available—walnuts, mushrooms, and so forth. What might you add to the vinegar if you were going to make this type of ketchup?

    **Fever** derives from the Latin word *febris*, a connection still apparent in several "$100 words," including *febrile*, which means "feverish," *febrifuge*, a medication used to reduce a fever, and *febrifacient*, which means "fever-producing." With 98.6°F considered normal body temperature, just what temperature is considered a *fever*, "an abnormally high body temperature"? A temperature greater than 100°F is indicative of a fever, and if greater than 104°F should receive immediate medical attention. Two well-known diseases characterized by high fevers are *scarlet fever*, caused by bacteria, and *yellow fever*, a tropical disease caused by a mosquito-transmitted virus.

---

## SORT 18. More Long and Short *e* in Stressed Syllables

### Sorting by Syllable Stress

| 1st Stress | 2nd Stress | Oddball |
|---|---|---|
| **season** | **believe** | **?** |
| breakfast | achieve | [none] |
| diet | agreed | |
| eastern | beneath | |
| healthy | instead | |
| heavy | proceed | |
| jealous | relief | |
| meaning | repeat | |
| needle | retrieve | |
| ready | | |
| science | | |
| seedling | | |
| sweater | | |
| weather | | |
| western | | |

### Sorting by Sound and Pattern

| Short *ea* | *ee* | Long *ea* | *ie* | Oddball |
|---|---|---|---|---|
| **ready** | **agreed** | **season** | **believe** | **?** |
| breakfast | needle | beneath | achieve | diet |
| healthy | proceed | eastern | relief | science |
| heavy | seedling | meaning | retrieve | western |
| instead | | repeat | | |
| jealous | | | | |
| sweater | | | | |
| weather | | | | |

*Considerations:* This sort expands on Sort 17 in two ways. It reviews two additional long *e* patterns—*ea* and *ie*—and it includes numerous short *e* words spelled with *ea*. Before introducing the sort, discuss any unfamiliar words, perhaps *relieve* and *seedling*. This is also a good time to make students aware of meaning connections that may help them to spell some short *e* words: *breakfast* = *break* + *fast*, *healthy* = *heal*, *heavy* is related to *heave*. You might call students' attention to the final *-e* in *believe*, *achieve*, and *retrieve* and explain that it is not part of the long vowel pattern but instead closes off the *v*, which does not end English words. Prompt students to be on the alert for words that may be tricky. Introduce the sound and pattern sort in a manner similar to that described for Sort 16. Discuss the results when complete, being sure to talk about the oddballs *diet*, *science*, and *west-*

*ern.* The first two sound incorrect due to the syllable division occurring between the *i* and *e* (VV structure), and the third has a short *e* pattern that does not fit the categories.

### Talking Points

- Two more ways to spell long *e* in a stressed syllable are *ea* and *ie* as in *repeat* and *relief.*
- In a stressed syllable, the *ea* pattern can produce either a long or a short *e* sound, as in *season* and *ready.*
- Sometimes *ie* works as a team, as in *relief,* and sometimes the letters are in separate syllables, as in *diet.*
- A related word can sometimes help to determine a vowel spelling, as in *heal* for *healthy.*
- The sound of /v/ at the end of a word is spelled *ve,* as in *achieve.*

**Integrating Idioms:** "She's **under the weather** today, so we're supposed to go on to school without her." (Slightly ill. If you were out walking in stormy weather and it was sleeting, snowing, or hailing, you would not be feeling well and would want to get out of it. The same is true of airlines; to avoid being under weather and in turbulence, they fly *above* the weather, so you can have a positive experience.)

**Did You Know?** Achievers are sometimes those who have made their way to the head of the class or of an organization. **Achieve** comes from an Old French phrase, *à chef,* meaning "at an end," or from the Latin word for "to bring to a head," *accapare* (for a discussion of related words see Part 3, Sort 40). Those who achieve typically have the help of other fine "heads" or "chiefs"—teachers, parents or guardians, and other mentors.

On a chilly or cold day we put on a **sweater** to keep warm, so why call the garment a *sweater?* In the early 1800s heavy blankets were put around the bodies of racehorses to make them perspire heavily during training. Not surprisingly, the blankets were called *sweaters.* By late 1850 the word referred to flannel underclothing that athletes wore to work off weight. A generation later the word took on a new meaning in the realm of sports: It referred to woolen vests and pullovers worn by rowers and other athletes. This connection led to the word's current meaning. Will this meaning last? If not, what might be the next reference for *sweater?*

## SORT 19. Long and Short *i* in Stressed Syllables

### Sorting by Syllable Stress

| 1st Stress | 2nd Stress | Oddball |
|------------|------------|---------|
| **minus** | **excite** | **?** |
| building | behind | [none] |
| crisis | beside | |
| differ | decide | |
| figure | describe | |
| Friday | despite | |
| frighten | extinct | |
| highway | polite | |
| justice | tonight | |
| kitchen | | |
| library | | |
| lightning | | |
| pilot | | |
| spider | | |
| window | | |

### Sorting by Sound and Pattern

| Short *i* | *iCe* | *igh* | Open *i* | Oddball |
|-----------|-------|-------|----------|---------|
| **figure** | **excite** | **lightning** | **minus** | **?** |
| differ | beside | frighten | crisis | behind |
| extinct | decide | highway | Friday | building |
| kitchen | describe | tonight | library | justice |
| window | despite | | pilot | |
| | polite | | spider | |

*Considerations:* Discuss word meanings as needed; then introduce the sort in a manner similar to Sort 16. After each activity, discuss the category characteristics. Ask students why *justice, behind,* and *building* are oddballs in the second sort. (In *justice* the stressed syllable has a short *u*, and the *iCe* pattern does not make a long sound. *Behind* has a long *i* sound, but there is no category for its *iCC* pattern. The short *i* pattern in *building* is *ui*.) In case students wonder about the peculiar short *i* spelling in *building,* which also occurs in the related words *built, builder, and build,* how we came to have this unusual spelling is unknown. One hypothesis is that it is a combination of two earlier spellings—*bilden* and *bolden.* Before the session ends, remind students that, when reading words with an *iCV* pattern as in *minus* and *figure,* it is important to pay careful attention to the context and to read flexibly, because the vowel sound can be either long (open) or short (closed). Again, if applying one sound to the pattern does not produce a known word, try another.

### Talking Points

- Three common ways to spell long *i* in polysyllabic words are *iCe, igh,* and open *i,* as in *decide, frighten,* and *minus.*
- As with *aCe,* as in *chocolate, iCe* does not always make a long sound; the sound depends on whether or not the syllable is stressed—*excite* versus *justice.*

*Integrating Idioms:* "Mr. M. just gave us that hard quiz yesterday. Hopefully he won't give us another today, because I didn't read the new chapter last night. I know they say that **lightning never strikes twice in the same place**, but I'm not sure that includes Mr. M." (It is really unlikely that the same problem will happen again. Just as lightning doesn't follow the same path twice, so, too, it is extremely unlikely that Mr. M. will provide his class with another sudden quiz.)

*Did You Know?* Although we think of a **window** as transparent, hidden in the origins of this word is a wonderful metaphor. Scandinavians who invaded and settled in England sometime during the early Middle Ages (before 1200) are the source of this word. There is no record of the exact word they gave us, but it was related to *vindauga*, an Old Icelandic word for "window," a compound of *vindr* (wind) and *auga* (eye). Besides being poetic, the metaphor of "wind eye" for *window* suggests an openness that would have characterized windows of the time, as there would have been no glass. Scandinavians (Norse) and Old English poets loved to use this type of figurative language, known as *kenning*, where they replaced a single noun with a compound. Other examples are "whale road" for *sea* and "storm of swords" for *battle*. Can you think of other examples of kenning, or perhaps create one yourself? (For a discussion of *library* and its origins, see Sort 1.)

## SORT 20. More Long and Short *i* in Stressed Syllables

### Sorting by Syllable Stress

| 1st Stress | 2nd Stress | Oddball |
| --- | --- | --- |
| **finish** | **advice** | **?** |
| crystal | apply | [no words] |
| hyphen | arrive | |
| island | divide | |
| listen | good-bye | |
| mystery | July | |
| ninety | provide | |
| rhythm | reply | |
| river | supply | |
| symbol | surprise | |
| symptom | survive | |
| system | | |
| visit | | |

### Sorting by Sound and Pattern

| Short *i* | Short *y* | *iCe* | Long *y* | Oddball |
| --- | --- | --- | --- | --- |
| **finish** | **symbol** | **advice** | **July** | **?** |
| listen | crystal | arrive | apply | island |
| river | mystery | divide | hyphen | good-bye |
| visit | rhythm | ninety | reply | |
| | symptom | provide | supply | |
| | system | surprise | | |
| | | survive | | |

***Considerations:*** Discuss words that may be somewhat unfamiliar—perhaps *symptom, system,* and *hyphen*. You might also point out that there are several acceptable ways to spell *good-bye,* including *goodbye* and *good-by. Y* as a short vowel is a new feature, although students may be familiar with its use in words such as *gym* and *myth*. They may wonder how it is that *rhythm* has more than one syllable but just one vowel. Invite their speculations. The inclusion of words with both short and long vowel sounds for the y spelling adds additional challenge to this sort. Introduce the words with as much support as necessary; discuss the results. The first sort has no oddballs unless the dialect of students leads to some. In the sound and pattern sort there are two oddballs to discuss. *Island* has a long vowel sound in the stressed syllable, but its VCCV pattern suggests a short *i* sound. *Good-bye* has a long *i* sound in the stressed syllable, but the pattern is *ye* (as also in *dye*). You might close the group session by asking students to suggest tricky aspects of some of the words that will require careful attention when spelling. Although responses will vary, suggestions may include the silent letters in *listen* and *island*; the unstressed *o* or *e* in *symbol, symptom,* and *system*; and the silent *e* in *ninety*.

### Talking Points

- Y sometimes acts as a vowel; its sound can be long or short, as in *system* and *hyphen*; when y occurs at the end of a syllable it creates an open syllable and has a long vowel sound, as in *supply*.
- As with *ea*, caution is needed when reading words with y; in addition to its consonant sound and long and short *i* possibilities, it can also make a long *e* sound, as in *city*. Context clues and flexibility will help to ensure a correct word identification.

***Integrating Idioms:*** "I know the movie was good, but you saw it three times last week. Didn't you **get it out of your system** yet?" (Have enough of it. Sometimes systems, like engines, get matter in them that prevents them from working normally. The person in the sentence example seems to be obsessing on a movie, doesn't want to move ahead to something new, and may not be attending to other tasks that need to be completed.)

***Did You Know?*** **Good-bye** (or whichever spelling you prefer) is a contraction of the phrase "God be with ye (you)." Just as there are several ways to spell the word today, there are numerous earlier forms of the expression, including *God be wy you, god b'w'y, godbwye, god buy' ye,* and *good-b'wy*. Over time the word *God* was replaced with *good,* as it was in the phrase *good day*. The change may have come about because people lost sight of the original meaning of the phrase or because of confusion between *god* meaning "good" and God.

    **July** takes its name from *Gaius Julius Caesar,* a famous Roman general and statesman who was born during this month. Just how it is that *Julius* has a first syllable stress and *July* a second is unknown. The first syllable of July was commonly stressed into mid-1700 and continues to be heard today in much of the southern part of the United States.

## SORT 21. Long and Short *o* in Stressed Syllables

### Sorting by Syllable Stress

| 1st Stress | 2nd Stress | Oddball |
|---|---|---|
| **ocean** | **compose** | **?** |
| bony | alone | [none] |
| bowling | approach | |
| clothing | below | |
| common | forgot | |
| honest | improve | |
| lonely | remote | |
| modern | suppose | |
| movement | unknown | |
| notebook | | |
| notice | | |
| owner | | |
| product | | |
| robot | | |
| total | | |

### Sorting by Sound and Pattern

| Short *o* | *oCe* | *ow* | Open *o* | Oddball |
|---|---|---|---|---|
| **honest** | **compose** | **below** | **ocean** | **?** |
| common | alone | bowling | bony | approach |
| forgot | lonely | owner | clothing | improve |
| modern | notebook | unknown | notice | movement |
| product | remote | | robot | |
| | suppose | | total | |

***Considerations:*** Discuss any unfamiliar words. If *remote* is discussed, ask students to consider a common meaning connection among the following uses of the word: *dinosaurs as creatures of the remote past, a remote-controlled car,* and *a remote chance of going to a movie.* They should come up with something like "distant" or "far removed in time, space, possibility." Begin the sort in a way similar to that described for Sort 16. Discuss the results. How are categories alike or different? *Improve* and *movement* are oddballs in the sound and pattern sort. Despite their VC*e* pattern in the stressed syllable, they have no long *o* pattern. By contrast, *approach* has a long *o* with a second-syllable stress, but *oa* is not a targeted feature. You might ask students if they can think of any other pattern from their studies of patterns in single-syllable words that can make the long *o* sound. Numerous words have *oCC*, as in *almost, enroll, hostess, molten,* and *soldier.*

### Talking Points

- Common long *o* patterns in accented syllables include *oCe, ow,* and open *o* as in *alone, below, robot. Oa* and *oCC* are two more long *o* patterns.
- Flexibility is needed when reading words with long *o* patterns; what looks like long *o* may not be, as in *remote* versus *improve,* and *robot* versus *modern.* Similarly, what looks like short *o* may actually be long *o,* as in *adopt* versus *almost.*

*Integrating Idioms:* "I've saved up fifty dollars, but that's just a **drop in the ocean** of what I'll need to buy the bike." (A very small amount. Imagine how many drops there must be in the ocean, or in a bucket of water for that matter, as the idiom sometimes is worded *drop in the bucket*, and you'll have an idea of how incredibly much farther this person has to go to save enough for the bike.)

*Did You Know?* Many words in our language have been borrowed from other languages, for example, the days of the week; others, such as *sandwich*, get their name from a person or place; and still others come about because someone created a word that became popular and was accepted as part of our language. That was the case with **robot**. In 1921 a new play was performed that featured mechanical men who revolt and threaten to take over the world. The robots eventually become human and save the world. This was the first time the word had been used to describe mechanical men. The word caught on quickly, and its meaning was extended to include people who seem to have no feelings and who respond in a mechanical way. There has long been a synonym for robot— *automaton* (ô•tŏm•ə•tən). This word has been part of our language since the early 1600s and came from a phrase that meant "self-acting." Estimates are that there are now tens of thousands of robots in use in the United States. Though they may look nothing like a human, they are machines that are programmed to move parts, materials, tools, and so forth to complete tasks. When a person creates a word that catches on, as when the playwright wrote about robots, we say he *coined* the word. You might invite students to read or hear the delightful fiction story *Frindle* by Andrew Clements. The story tells how a fifth grader went about coining a new word for "pen." Students may also enjoy brainstorming or writing about new words they would like to coin.

## SORT 22. Long and Short *u* in Stressed Syllables

### Sorting by Syllable Stress

| 1st Stress | 2nd Stress | Oddball |
|---|---|---|
| **tuna** | **perfume** | **?** |
| beauty | amuse | Thursday |
| future | balloon | |
| hungry | cartoon | |
| Monday | cocoon | |
| pumpkin | computer | |
| punish | erupt | |
| toothache | excuse | |
| truly | include | |
| Tuesday | pollute | |
| uncle | reduce | |
| | shampoo | |

### Sorting by Sound and Pattern

| Short *u* | *u*Ce | *oo* | Open *u* | Oddball |
|---|---|---|---|---|
| **pumpkin** | **perfume** | **cartoon** | **tuna** | **?** |
| erupt | amuse | balloon | computer | beauty |
| hungry | excuse | cocoon | future | Monday |
| punish | include | shampoo | truly | Thursday |
| uncle | pollute | toothache | | Tuesday |
| | reduce | | | |

*Considerations:* Discuss any unfamiliar words. For *uncle*, check to see that students understand that this is the brother of their father or mother, and for *excuse* ask students for two ways to pronounce the word and to explain what each word means: final consonant sound of /z/ when the word is a verb and /s/ when it is a noun. (See Additional Sorts for a homograph activity with words that have multiple pronunciations.) Because vowels other than *u* can produce the long *u* sound, you might introduce this sort by reading the words aloud to see what students notice about the vowel sounds. Then engage them in the syllable stress and sound and pattern sort as described in Sort 16. Discuss the results; in both sorts *Thursday* is an oddball, because its vowel is neither long nor short. The other three oddballs in the sound and pattern sort all have appropriate sounds, short *u* in *Monday* and long *u* in *beauty* and *Tuesday*, but have patterns with no categories. The multiple ways of representing long *u* present a spelling challenge. Ask students if they notice anything about the words that might provide a clue to their spelling. Accept any reasonable and justified response. (For a discussion of the origin of *Thursday*, see Sort 16.)

## Talking Points

- Three patterns that produce the long *u* sound are *uCe*, *oo*, and open *u*, as in *amuse*, *cartoon*, and *future*.
- As with the other long vowel patterns studied, care and flexibility are needed when reading words with a VCV pattern with *u*, because it can be long or short, as in *tuna* or *punish*.

*Integrating Idioms:* "We tried asking for an extension on our project, but that idea went over **like a lead balloon**." (Failed. Balloons are usually filled with helium or air, so they are very lightweight and easily float up in the air. A lead balloon would go nowhere.)

*Did You Know?* **Pumpkin** comes to us from a Greek word *pepon*, meaning "cooked by the sun." Unlike some vegetables in the garden that could be eaten "green," this squash was inedible until it had been "baked" on the vine out in the sun for a long enough time. Pumpkins originated in the Americas and were a mainstay of the Pilgrims.

**Uncle** derives from *avunculus*, a Latin word for "mother's brother." Although today we regard an uncle as the brother of either parent, there is one uncle that is shared by every American—*Uncle Sam*. The United States is often personified as a tall, thin man with a flowing white beard, wearing red-and-white-striped trousers, a blue coat with tails, and a tall hat banded with stars. This well-known image of Uncle Sam was created at the time of the American Civil War by a British cartoonist named Sir John Tenniel, famous for his illustrations of *Alice in Wonderland* and *Through the Looking Glass*. Tenniel portrayed the United States as an awkward, unsophisticated person—striped pants, big heavy shoes, and a straw hat—and modeled the figure after Abraham Lincoln, who was president at the time. Despite the figure's unattractiveness, it caught on with Americans and was soon refined by an American cartoonist into the image we know today. Origin of the name *Uncle Sam* is less certain. The most likely story seems to be that *Uncle Sam* stems from a humorous interpretation of the letters "U.S." printed on casks of meat provided to army men during the War of 1812. The supplier was Samuel Wilson, who was locally known as "Uncle Sam," because meat labeled *U.S.* was said to have come from "**Uncle Sam.**" In 1961 Congress made Sam Wilson the official namesake of Uncle Sam.

# SORT 16 Long and Short *a* in Stressed Syllables

| Short a | aCe | ai | Open a |
|---------|-----|-----|--------|
| **1st Stress** | **2nd Stress** | | **?** |
| shadow | bracelet | | afraid |
| fable | complain | | escape |
| contain | obey | | crayon |
| basement | Saturday | | daily |
| raisin | erase | | amaze |
| chocolate | nation | | explain |
| remain | April | | later |
| basic | rather | | perhaps |

# SORT 17   Long and Short *e* in Stressed Syllables

| Short e | ee | eCe | Open e |
|---------|-----|-----|--------|
| **1st Stress** | **2nd Stress** | | **?** |
| effort | asleep | | delete |
| fever | idea | | supreme |
| indeed | secret | | people |
| either | deeply | | evening |
| extreme | female | | legal |
| complete | succeed | | trapeze |
| degrees | between | | Wednesday |
| ketchup | never | | expect |

# SORT 18 More Long and Short *e* in Stressed Syllables

| Short ea | ee | Long ea | ie |
|----------|-----|---------|-----|
| **1st Stress** | **2nd Stress** | | **?** |
| ready | agreed | | season |
| believe | sweater | | diet |
| meaning | seedling | | heavy |
| instead | beneath | | science |
| weather | relief | | breakfast |
| repeat | jealous | | eastern |
| needle | achieve | | retrieve |
| western | healthy | | proceed |

# SORT 19  Long and Short *i* in Stressed Syllables

| Short i | iCe | igh | Open i |
|---------|-----|-----|--------|
| **1st Stress** | **2nd Stress** | | **?** |
| figure | excite | | lightning |
| minus | polite | | justice |
| describe | decide | | pilot |
| behind | frighten | | crisis |
| tonight | library | | highway |
| spider | beside | | building |
| despite | Friday | | differ |
| kitchen | window | | extinct |

# SORT 20 More Long and Short *i* in Stressed Syllables

| Short i | Short y | iCe | Long y |
|---------|---------|-----|--------|
| **1st Stress** | **2nd Stress** | | **?** |
| finish | symbol | advice |
| July | survive | mystery |
| hyphen | system | arrive |
| ninety | surprise | supply |
| island | good-bye | provide |
| reply | apply | symptom |
| crystal | divide | rhythm |
| visit | listen | river |

# SORT 21 Long and Short *o* in Stressed Syllables

| Short o | oCe | ow | Open o |
|---------|-----|-----|--------|
| **1st Stress** | **2nd Stress** | | **?** |
| honest | compose | | below |
| ocean | approach | | clothing |
| notebook | remote | | unknown |
| robot | lonely | | notice |
| bowling | total | | movement |
| suppose | alone | | bony |
| improve | owner | | product |
| modern | common | | forgot |

# SORT 22 Long and Short *u* in Stressed Syllables

| Short u | uCe | oo | Open u |
|---------|-----|-----|--------|
| **1st Stress** | **2nd Stress** | | **?** |
| pumpkin | perfume | | cartoon |
| tuna | toothache | | Monday |
| excuse | Thursday | | pollute |
| cocoon | amuse | | computer |
| include | future | | shampoo |
| Tuesday | beauty | | reduce |
| truly | balloon | | hungry |
| uncle | punish | | erupt |

## R-Controlled Vowel Patterns in Stressed Syllables  (DSA Feature N)

The following five sorts review the sounds and patterns of r-controlled vowels, but in the context of stressed syllables in polysyllabic words. There are still multiple patterns that produce the same sound, making r-controlled vowels challenging to spell, though perhaps less so than they are when the patterns occur in unstressed syllables. To introduce each of the sorts in this section, ask students to work with a partner to determine categories for the words, making sure the categories are mutually exclusive (namely, defined in ways that prevent words from being classified in more than one category, unless they are ultimately placed as oddballs). After discussing their results, if sound and pattern were not used as the bases for their sorting, ask students to re-sort their words by sound and pattern, using the indicated key words as guides to the categories. Discuss the results, add the header cards, and encourage students to share insights for spelling words with r-controlled vowels. Extend their thinking through a discussion of the talking points.

*What Is Known:* Students are familiar with most of the r-controlled patterns from studies of one-syllable words at the within word pattern stage. They are aware that several patterns can represent a particular r-controlled sound. They also know what stressed syllables are and can identify the accented syllable in longer words.

*What Is New:* Examining r-controlled patterns in the stressed syllables of polysyllabic words is new. Also, students likely lack experience with several of the patterns, including *ere, orr,* and *arr.*

---

## SORT 23. *R*-Controlled Vowels with V*re* Patterns in Stressed Syllables

### Sorting by Sound and Pattern

| *are* | *ere* | *ire* | *ore* | *ure* | Oddball |
|---|---|---|---|---|---|
| **barely** | **sincere** | **admire** | **before** | **surely** | **?** |
| aware | adhere | desire | boredom | endure | failure |
| beware | merely | entire | explore | secure | terrible |
| compare | severe | fireman | | | therefore |
| | | inspire | | | |
| | | retire | | | |

*Considerations:* Discuss words with meanings that may be unfamiliar, such as *adhere, merely, endure,* and *secure.* Except for the two oddballs, the words in this sort can easily be classified by either sound or pattern, because multiple patterns for the same sound have not been included as separate categories. This aspect of the sort should make this set of words easier to spell. The oddballs *terrible* and *therefore* provide a glimpse of the multiple patterns that can produce the same sound. *Failure* is an oddball because the first syllable is stressed, not *ure.*

### Talking Points

- Words with the V*re* pattern have a long vowel pattern with an *r*-influenced or controlled vowel, as in *explore* compared with *explode.*
- There are often multiple ways to spell a particular r-controlled vowel, as in *barely, terrible,* and *therefore.*

*Integrating Idioms:* "We nearly **died of boredom** before the movie was over." (Suffered from lack of stimulation. Though it is unlikely anyone ever died from being bored, boredom can be excruciating.)

*Did You Know?* If someone has ever **inspired** you, you likely felt energized and invigorated; it's no wonder, as the word literally means "to blow or breathe into," although it was likely thoughts or feelings that were inhaled rather than air. Other related words include *aspire, conspire, perspire,* and *transpire.* Word families, such as the *spir* family, are a primary focus of the next part of this book.

When we think of *sincere* we think of someone or something that is "genuine," "true," or "pure." Although most experts believe that *sincere* stems from the Latin word for "clean" or "pure," there is an old story that lends a bit more color to the word's roots. According to it, the word's origin goes back to the days of the famous Italian sculptor, painter, architect, and poet Michelangelo, who lived from 1475 to 1564. Sculptors of his time often used marble blocks to carve out their sculptures. The marble sometimes had imperfections. Roman quarrymen would often rub wax on the marble to hide such flaws from the eyes of prospective purchasers. To stop the deceptive practice, the Roman government dictated that all marble had to be *sine cera,* which means "without wax." In time, the phrase was applied more generally to mean "without deception."

---

## SORT 24. *R*-Controlled *o* in Stressed Syllables

### Sorting by Sound and Pattern

| *or* | *ore* | *orr* | Oddball |
|------|-------|-------|---------|
| **order** | **ignore** | **sorry** | **?** |
| afford | adore | borrow | resource |
| corner | ashore | horror | worry |
| forty | foreman | sorrow | worthless |
| forward | restore | tomorrow | |
| inform | | torrent | |
| northern | | | |
| report | | | |
| stories | | | |

*Considerations:* Discuss the meanings of any unfamiliar words. Possibilities include *afford, forward* (compare with *foreword*), *foreman, restore,* and *torrent.* Except for two of the oddball words, whose vowel patterns are influenced by *w,* there is no sound contrast in this sort. The importance here is for students to bear in mind that there may be several different ways to spell a particular *r*-controlled sound and to develop spelling awareness so that, if they are not sure of a spelling, they will know that they need to take action and look it up in a dictionary or check with an expert.

### Talking Points

- *R*-controlled vowels with long and short *o* patterns produce the same sound, /ôr/, as do the *or*, *ore*, *orr*, and *our* patterns of this sort, as in *order, ignore, sorry,* and *resource.*
- *W* nearly always influences the sound of *or*, as in *worry* and *worthless.*

*Integrating Idioms:* "To **make a long story short**, my homework was thrown out with the trash this morning." (Summarize the main points or get to the main idea of a happening. Writers often delete extraneous matter when they revise a story, thereby shortening it up to the essentials.)

*Did You Know?* As bothersome as it can be to ***worry*** about something, the word has a far more gentle meaning now than it once had when it meant "to kill by violence." Over the centuries, the word evolved from its harsh Old English meaning to the softened meaning of "to harass or distress" to the commonly used meaning of today, "to feel troubled or uneasy."

## SORT 25. *R*-Controlled *a* in Stressed Syllables

### Sorting by Sound and Pattern

| *ar* | *are* | *air* | *arr* | Oddball |
|------|-------|-------|-------|---------|
| **party** | **declare** | **repair** | **carry** | **?** |
| barber | barefoot | dairy | arrow | parents |
| farther | prepare | despair | carrots | toward |
| harvest | rarely | fairly | narrow | |
| market | | prairie | sparrow | |
| partner | | | | |
| scarlet | | | | |

*Considerations:* Discuss any words that may be unfamiliar to some students, such as *harvest*, *scarlet*, *declare*, *dairy*, *despair*, and *prairie*. (The last is discussed in the "Did You Know?" section for this sort.) Clarification should also be given for the meaning of *farther*. *Farther*, in this sort, and *further*, in the next, have often been used interchangeably. However, according to a recent rule noted in the third edition of the *American Heritage Dictionary of the English Language*, the use of *farther* should be limited to "physical distance" and *further* used for "advancement along a nonphysical dimension." This sort explores the long and short sounds of *r*-controlled vowels with *a*. Although *ar* usually has the sound heard in *art*, it can also sound like a long influenced pattern, as in the oddball word *parents*. There are several ways to spell the long *a* sound influenced by *r*, including *are*, *air*, and *arr* (categories in this sort), and *er* and *err* (*merit* and *cherry*). Students may notice the influence of the *w* in *toward* on the *ar* vowel pattern. If they do not, call their attention to this, and encourage them to brainstorm other words with a *war* spelling (for example, *award*, *awkward*, *warning*, and *warrant*).

### Talking Points

- The /är/ sound is usually spelled *ar*, as in *party*, and similarly, the *ar* pattern in a word is usually pronounced as in *art*.
- There are several ways to spell the /âr/ sound; some common spellings include *are*, *air*, and *arr*, as in *prepare*, *fairly*, and *carry*.
- A preceding *w* usually causes *ar* to sound like /ôr/ as in *award* or /ər/ as in *awkward*.

*Integrating Idioms:* "Mom said that my brother and I have to **carry our own weight** now that Dad's in the hospital." (Do our share. If you literally carried your own weight, you would be no worry or trouble for anyone else.)

*Did You Know?*  Much of the Midwest (this usually includes Illinois, Indiana, Iowa, Kansas, Michigan, Minnesota, Missouri, Nebraska, Ohio, and Wisconsin) was once covered by tall grasses. The French were the first to come to the lands that we now know as Iowa, Illinois, and Indiana and some of the adjoining areas. What they saw were vast expanses of grasses, growing 5 to 9 feet tall and crowded with insects, creatures of various sorts, and flowers, but not a tree in sight, so they called it **prairie**, the French word for "meadow." In time some of the plants and animals took on the "prairie" descriptor, as in *prairie dog, prairie chicken* (grouse), *prairie beans*, and so forth. In the 1700s, when settlers headed west across the prairies, they traveled in covered wagons, known as *prairie schooners*, because of their resemblance to ships sailing through the grasses. Today both Illinois and North Dakota bear the nickname *Prairie State*, but only tiny remnants of the tall grass prairie remain; the rest has been converted into farmland by burning and draining.

## SORT 26. *R*-Controlled /ûr/ in Stressed Syllables

### Sorting by Sound and Pattern

| *er* | *ir* | *ur* | Oddball |
|------|------|------|---------|
| **person** | **dirty** | **during** | **?** |
| determine | birdhouse | disturb | hurry |
| nervous | chirping | furnish | series |
| perfect | thirsty | further | spirit |
| prefer | thirty | jury | |
| thermos | | purple | |
| verdict | | purpose | |
| | | sturdy | |

*Considerations:* Discuss any words that may be unfamiliar, such as *thermos, verdict, sturdy,* and *series*. Also, use of the word *further* should be reviewed (see Sort 25). As in Sort 24, this sort includes no sound contrast except for two of the oddball words (*series* and *spirit*). All of the other words include the /ûr/ sound but with various spellings—*er, ir,* and *ur* (and *urr* in the oddball word *hurry*). Just as with one-syllable words, words with /ûr/ in the stressed syllable are difficult to spell. Sound provides no help in determining the correct pattern. Students need to realize this and exert caution when spelling such words if they are uncertain of the pattern.

### Talking Points

- In stressed syllables the /ûr/ sound is usually spelled with *er, ir,* or *ur*; similarly, *er, ir,* and *ur* are typically pronounced as /ûr/ in unfamiliar words, as in *person, dirty,* and *further*.
- Because of the spelling variations, when in doubt about how to spell the /ûr/ sound, consult a dictionary or an expert.

*Integrating Idioms:*  "She **gave me a dirty look** when I asked for a pencil." (Frowned or looked angry. Something dirty is usually unpleasant, as a dirty look would be.)

*Did You Know?*  The word **person** comes from the Latin *persona*, a word that originally meant "mask," as in an actor's mask. Over time the word came to be associated with the real character or role of the character and eventually with the actual person, an individual. Although we sometimes use the word *persons* as the plural of *person*, when a group of persons is the reference, the more commonly used word is *people*, as in *Today more than 6,500,000,000 people live on earth, of which over 300,000,000 live in the United States.* (For a minute-by-minute counting of the persons of either the world or the United States, go to the U.S. Census Bureau's Population Clocks website at *www.census.gov/main/www/popclock.html.*)

## SORT 27. *R*-Controlled *e* in Stressed Syllables

| Sorting by Sound and Pattern | | | |
|---|---|---|---|
| *er* (Short) | *ear* (Short) | *ear* (Long) | Oddball |
| **sternly** | **early** | **nearby** | **?** |
| alert | earning | appear | career |
| hermit | earthquake | clearing | pioneer |
| merchant | learner | dreary | |
| observe | rehearse | spearmint | |
| reserve | | teardrop | |
| sermon | | weary | |
| service | | yearbook | |

*Considerations:* Discuss any words that may be unfamiliar, such as *hermit, merchant, dreary,* and *pioneer* (the last is discussed in the "Did You Know?" section). This sort introduces *ear* as an /ûr/ pattern for review and contrasts it both with the same sound (spelled *er*) and with the same pattern, *ear* but with the sound heard in *dreary.* When trying to read unknown words with an *ear* spelling, the sound is more likely to be the long *r*-controlled sound (*dreary*); however, if applying that sound does not lead to a known word, the alternative sound of /ûr/ should be used. A mnemonic might be of help in remembering the spelling of *rehearse:* When actors re*hear*se, they *hear* lines said again and again. Ask students to brainstorm known spellings pronounced as /îr/ (for example, *ere,* previously introduced, and *ear* and *eer* from this sort).

### Talking Points

- The *ear* pattern can be pronounced with a short as well as a long *r*-influenced vowel sound, as in *earning* versus *clearing.*
- There are different ways to spell /îr/, including the common *ear, ere,* and *eer.*

*Integrating Idioms:* "I'm turning in my paper on Friday, even though it's not due until Tuesday. You know . . . **the early bird catches the worm.**" (Being ahead of schedule can benefit you. In the heat of the sun worms are typically underground, but early morning will often find them on the surface, making it easy for an early-rising bird to enjoy a good meal.)

*Did You Know?* The notion of **pioneers** as settlers of the wilderness is very different from the original meaning of the word, which related to the military. These pioneers prepared the way for the armies that followed by clearing paths and building roads. In the early 1800s, when a writer applied the term to describe those who were venturing into new territory, settling there, and paving the way for others, the word became popular. *Pioneer* now often refers to someone who is the first to discover or explore, as in *space pioneers* or *pioneers of medicine.*

# SORT 23 — R-Controlled Vowels with V*re* Patterns in Stressed Syllables

| are | ere | ire | ore | ure |
|-----|-----|-----|-----|-----|

| | | |
|---|---|---|
| barely | sincere | admire |
| before | surely | explore |
| severe | retire | beware |
| failure | therefore | fireman |
| inspire | aware | secure |
| merely | endure | terrible |
| entire | desire | boredom |
| compare | adhere | ? |

# SORT 24 _R-Controlled o in Stressed Syllables_

| or | ore | orr |
|---|---|---|
| order | ignore | sorry |
| horror | restore | sorrow |
| resource | worry | torrent |
| borrow | ashore | inform |
| report | northern | foreman |
| forty | worthless | corner |
| tomorrow | forward | adore |
| afford | stories | ? |

# SORT 25 *R-Controlled a in Stressed Syllables*

| ar | are | air | arr |
|----|-----|-----|-----|
| party | declare | repair | |
| carry | fairly | toward | |
| sparrow | rarely | farther | |
| market | carrots | barefoot | |
| prairie | barber | dairy | |
| prepare | narrow | partner | |
| harvest | parents | arrow | |
| despair | scarlet | ? | |

# SORT 26 *R*-Controlled /ûr/ in Stressed Syllables

| er | ir | ur |
|---|---|---|
| person | dirty | during |
| further | purple | thirty |
| perfect | chirping | nervous |
| jury | series | disturb |
| determine | birdhouse | hurry |
| purpose | spirit | prefer |
| thermos | furnish | thirsty |
| sturdy | verdict | ? |

# SORT 27  R-Controlled *e* in Stressed Syllables

| er | ear (Short) | ear (Long) |
|---|---|---|
| sternly | early | nearby |
| yearbook | appear | observe |
| sermon | pioneer | earthquake |
| earning | spearmint | reserve |
| weary | hermit | clearing |
| rehearse | teardrop | service |
| alert | dreary | learner |
| career | merchant | ? |

## *Abstract Vowel Patterns in Stressed Syllables*

*Abstract vowels* are neither long nor short nor *r*-controlled. The following two sorts review abstract vowels in the context of longer words. As with *r*-controlled vowels, introduce the sorts by asking students to work with a partner to sort the words into categories. Remind them to examine the characteristics of each category carefully so they can describe them. Students have had much experience with sorting by sound and pattern, so many may arrive at the same categories as those listed. If they do not, after discussing their results, suggest that students re-sort the words by sound and pattern, using the key words as a guide.

**What Is Known:** Students have worked with all of the abstract vowel patterns at the within word pattern stage. They have also examined patterns in stressed syllables.

**What Is New:** Examining abstract vowels in polysyllabic words is new; also, the sound of *ou* as in *trouble* may be new.

---

**SORT 28.** Abstract Vowels with *o* in Stressed Syllables

### Sorting by Sound and Pattern

| *oi* /oi/ | *oy* /oi/ | *ou* /ou/ | *ow* /ou/ | *ou* /?/ |
|-----------|-----------|-----------|-----------|----------|
| **avoid** | **loyal** | **county** | **power** | **trouble** |
| appoint | annoy | announce | allow | country |
| moisture | destroy | counter | brownie | enough |
| poison | employ | doubtful | coward | southern |
| | | thousand | shower | |
| | | without | towel | |

**Considerations:** Discuss any unfamiliar words; *county* and *loyal* may benefit from clarification. This sort reviews the *oi* and *oy* spellings of /oi/ and the *ou* and *ow* spellings of /ou/ and presents another pronunciation for the *ou* spelling. Students previously worked with *ow* as a long *o* spelling (see Sort 21). By now, given the key words and instructions to sort by sound and pattern, students should be able to categorize the words without other preliminary sorting. However, if needed, ask students to begin with a sound or pattern sort. Either will result in a combining of some of the categories shown in Sort 28. Then they can re-sort with attention to aural and visual cues. Discuss the results, including talking points. There are many additional sounds for *ou*, as in *though*, *through*, and *thought*; encourage students to find such oddballs during a word hunt.

### Talking Points

- *Oi* and *oy* are used to spell the /oi/ sound; *oy* is usually used at the end of a syllable, as in *employ* and *loyal*.
- *Ou* and *ow* are used to spell the /ou/ sound; *ow* is usually used at the end of a syllable, as in *power* and *allow*.
- *Ou* and *ow* can be pronounced in multiple ways; when reading words with these spellings, if one sound doesn't lead to a known word, try another.

*Integrating Idioms:* "I might as well **throw in the towel**; I'm never going to finish this by tomorrow." (Give up and admit defeat. This expression stems from boxing, in which a fighter used to concede defeat by throwing the towel with which he wiped his face into the boxing ring. The expression "throw in the sponge" means the same thing.)

*Did You Know?* The **brownie** is all-American, though there is disagreement regarding its origins. According to one story, in a careless moment a cook forgot to add baking powder, a rising agent, to the batter in a chocolate cake recipe. According to another, the brownie was invented in 1892 at a Chicago hotel. Box lunches were being prepared for an exposition, and the brownie seemed like a good way for ladies to be able to enjoy a cake-like dessert and keep their hands clean. Though the brownie originated in America, it is now found in many parts of the world. Which of the origin stories do you agree with? Can you imagine another possibility?

## SORT 29. Abstract Vowels with *a* in Stressed Syllables

### Sorting by Sound and Pattern

| *au* | *aw* | *al* | Oddball |
|------|------|------|---------|
| **author** | **awful** | **almost** | **?** |
| applaud | awesome | already | all right |
| August | awkward | also | laughter |
| daughter | drawback | although | |
| exhausted | flawless | altogether | |
| faucet | lawyer | always | |
| laundry | | | |
| naughty | | | |
| sausage | | | |

*Considerations:* Discuss any unfamiliar words, such as *drawback* and, for some students, *sausage*. All three patterns in this sort produce a similar sound. Spelling can be aided by realizing that *aw* is usually used at the end of a syllable (*flawless*) and that when /l/ immediately follows the /ô/ sound the spelling is likely *al* (*always*). Although *all right* sounds as though it is one word, standard English dictates that it be spelled as separate words.

### Talking Points

- There are multiple ways of spelling the /ô/ sound, including *au*, *aw*, and *al*, as in *laundry*, *awful*, and *also*. *Aw* is usually used at the end of a syllable.

*Integrating Idioms:* "I thought I'd **split my sides with laughter** when I first heard Jon Sciezska's *The Stinky Cheese Man* read." (Laugh so hard that your skin would burst. Other, similar expressions with *laughter*, according to Webster's Online Dictionary [*www.websters-online-dictionary.org/definition/laughter*], include *convulse with laughter, die with laughter, explode with laughter, howl with laughter, roar with laughter, scream with laughter, shake with laughter, shout with laughter, shriek with laughter,* and *yell with laughter.* Invite students to brainstorm or create some other expressions with *laughter* and to consider the meanings of the following two quotes cited at the same website: "Laughter translates into any language" [graffiti] and "Laughter is the shortest distance between two people" [Victor Borge, a witty pianist, 1909–2000].)

*Did You Know?*  The meaning of **naughty**, like *worry* (see Sort 24), has softened over time. In the 1400s it was used to describe a very bad or wicked person. A century or so later it had the sense of "inferior quality," as in *naughty olives* that would likely have to be thrown away. Today the word is most often applied to children and their minor mischievous offenses.

# SORT 28 Abstract Vowels with *o* in Stressed Syllables

| oi /oi/ | oy /oi/ | ou /ou/ | ow /ou/ | ou /ŭ/ |
|---------|---------|---------|---------|--------|
| avoid | | loyal | | county |
| power | | trouble | | thousand |
| employ | | southern | | doubtful |
| appoint | | allow | | annoy |
| enough | | counter | | coward |
| destroy | | towel | | moisture |
| brownie | | announce | | country |
| poison | | without | | shower |

# SORT 29 Abstract Vowels with *a* in Stressed Syllables

| au | aw | al |
|---|---|---|
| author | awful | almost |
| flawless | sausage | laundry |
| applaud | already | all right |
| although | August | awkward |
| naughty | drawback | always |
| also | altogether | exhausted |
| daughter | laughter | awesome |
| lawyer | faucet | ? |

# Unstressed Syllables
(DSA Feature O)

Sorts in the previous three sections have dealt with vowel patterns in stressed syllables. In this part (Sorts 35–41) we explore unstressed syllables and the schwa vowel sound /ə/. In all but the last sort, the unstressed syllable is the final syllable. The schwa vowel sound of an unstressed syllable (pronounced as "uh") is difficult to spell because so many different patterns can represent it, and sound is of no help, as the bolded letters in the following examples show: *ag**ai**n, fast**e**n, foss**i**l, butt**o**n, foc**us**, mount**ai**n, curi**ou**s*. Sometimes meaning can provide a clue to the correct spelling; for example, comparative adjectives end in *-er* (*high**er**, dimm**er***) rather than *-ar* or *-or*. Sometimes the letters surrounding the schwa sound can be of help; for instance, if the final syllable of *cancel* was spelled with an *-le*, the second *c* would lose its soft sound /s/. As students explore the patterns in this section and search for more examples of the patterns through word hunts, they also will learn the helpful strategy of *Best Guess*; some patterns, such as *-le* for final /əl/, are far more common than others, and knowing which ones are makes it possible to guess at the spelling when there are no other options. Nonetheless, it is particularly important for students to realize that when they are learning to spell words with the schwa, that portion of the word is likely to require careful attention so the pattern can be memorized. When confronted with writing the schwa of an unfamiliar word, wise spellers check in a dictionary or ask an expert to confirm the correct spelling. For further tips on teaching and learning with unstressed syllables, see *Word Journeys* (Ganske, 2000), Chapter 6.

***What Is Known:*** Students are familiar with identifying the accented syllable in words. Several of the patterns in this section, especially those in Sorts 30–33, were examined as long or short vowel patterns at the within word pattern stage.

***What Is New:*** Although students were exposed to the schwa at the beginning of the section on "Long Vowel Patterns in Stressed Syllables," work with unstressed syllables and the schwa is new.

---

## SORT 30. Unstressed Final Syllables with Long *a* Patterns

### Sorting by Sound and Pattern

| *-ace* | *-age* | *-ain* | Oddball |
|--------|--------|--------|---------|
| **surface** | **manage** | **certain** | **?** |
| furnace | bandage | bargain | engage |
| menace | cabbage | curtain | obtain |
| necklace | courage | fountain | practice |
| palace | damage | mountain | |
| | garbage | villain | |
| | luggage | | |
| | message | | |
| | package | | |

***Considerations:*** Before distributing the templates of words to the students, you might introduce the study of unstressed syllables by dictating a short spelling quiz with *obtain, certain, explain, villain, cur-*

*tain, complain, bargain,* and *fountain.* If desired, include or substitute some of the following words, being sure to include words with long vowels, as well as a schwa: *engage, garbage, teenage, bandage, disgrace, furnace, fireplace, palace.* When discussing the results, ask students what made some of the words more difficult to spell than others. If they do not mention that the same spelling pattern can be used to spell different sounds, draw their attention to this. Ask them how this might be explained (the sound in the stressed syllable provides a clue to the spelling pattern, whereas in an unstressed syllable you cannot tell which pattern to use). Place the headers on the table or overhead and distribute the templates of words. Ask students to cut apart the word cards and sort them by the vowel patterns shown on the headers. When they are finished, draw students' attention to the first-syllable stress in each of the key words (*surface, manage,* and *certain*). Remind them of the work they have done with stressed syllables. Then point to the second syllable and explain that now they are ready to turn their attention to the unstressed syllable, which, as they likely discovered from the quiz, is more difficult to spell because of the schwa vowel sound. Tell students that for this sort and for most of the others that they will study related to unstressed syllables, the second syllable will be the one that is unstressed. Ask them to review their categories to find any words that have the appropriate pattern but a different sound. These should be moved to the oddball category. Discuss the results, including the oddballs *engage* and *obtain,* both of which have a stressed final syllable, and *practice,* which does have an unstressed final syllable but a different spelling pattern. Talk about the meanings of any unfamiliar words, perhaps *villain* and *menace.* Before ending the session, remind students to pay attention to how an unstressed syllable is spelled in order to remember it.

## Talking Points

- Vowel patterns in unstressed syllables are difficult to spell, because there are many patterns for the schwa sound.
- When reading an unfamiliar word, if applying a long vowel sound to a known long vowel pattern does not lead to a recognizable word, try shifting the stress to another syllable and reading the pattern with a schwa sound. (*Villain,* for example might be misread as /vĭl•lān/; by shifting the stress to the first syllable, the correct word can be detected, /vĭl•lən/.)

*Integrating Idioms:* "I know I wore your shirt without asking you, but don't **make a mountain out of a molehill**." (Exaggerate a small problem. When moles burrow underground, their tunnels barely raise the ground above; to call the slight upheaval a *mountain* would be a gross exaggeration.)

*Did You Know?* A **palace** is typically associated with royalty and as a residence is impressively large and luxurious. The palaces of fairy tales are often situated on a hill or other prominent place, away from the ordinary people. The word is derived from Palatine Hill in Rome, where people of power and wealth had their homes beginning around 330 B.C., including the emperors Augustus, Tiberius, and Nero. The Latin word for this hill, *Palatium,* eventually evolved into *palace* and came to be associated with any expensive and splendid house.

## SORT 31. Unstressed Final Syllables with /ən/

### Sorting by Meaning (Parts of Speech)

| Verbs | Nouns | Oddball |
|---|---|---|
| **darken** | **dozen** | **?** |
| awaken | button | urban |
| fasten | cabin | |
| loosen | chicken | |
| sharpen | cotton | |
| strengthen | cousin | |
| tighten | dragon | |
| | eleven | |
| | lemon | |
| | margin | |
| | method | |
| | pardon | |
| | robin | |
| | siren | |
| | slogan | |
| | woman | |

### Sorting by Pattern and Meaning

| Verbs | Nouns | | | | (Adjective) |
|---|---|---|---|---|---|
| *-en* | *-an* | *-en* | *-in* | *-on* | Oddball |
| **darken** | **slogan** | **dozen** | **cabin** | **lemon** | **?** |
| awaken | woman | chicken | cousin | button | urban |
| fasten | | eleven | margin | cotton | |
| loosen | | siren | robin | dragon | |
| sharpen | | | | method | |
| strengthen | | | | pardon | |
| tighten | | | | | |

**Considerations:** Discuss any unfamiliar words, such as *pardon, margin, urban,* and *slogan.* Students may need an example of the last word, say, for instance, "sometimes runners and joggers use the following slogan: *Motion is lotion.*" Talk about the meaning of the phrase, and ask students to think of slogans they have heard in advertising or politics. Introduce this set of words as a two-category meaning sort: verbs and nouns. Discuss the results. Many will recognize *urban* as an adjective and therefore an oddball; they will also likely notice that all of the verbs end in *-en.* Then ask students to re-sort the words by meaning and pattern. This type of combined sort will be new to them, so after putting out the key words and headers, model the sorting with a think-aloud, if necessary. Discuss the results. As students collect and examine other words with the same patterns through word hunts, encourage them to be on the lookout for patterns that occur frequently. This will help them to develop a "best guess" strategy for final /ən/.

*Talking Points*

- There are many ways to spell unstressed final syllable /ən/; meaning can be of help, for example, verbs tend to be spelled -en, as in *sharpen* and *darken*.

*Integrating Idioms:* "Whenever I say that I'm going to buy a new skateboard if my essay wins the contest, Mom tells me I shouldn't **count my chickens before they hatch**." (Plan on something until you're certain it will happen. According to *The American Heritage Dictionary of Idioms* [Ammer, 1997], this expression stems from one of Aesop's fables, in which a milkmaid dreams about getting rich from some chickens she hopes to buy with the milk that she is carrying in a pail on her head. She tosses her head as she dreams of wealth, spilling the milk.)

*Did You Know?* Our decimal system shows much consistency with its counting, as in "twenty-one, twenty-two, twenty-three . . . ninety-seven, ninety-eight, ninety-nine." Though we do not say "tenty-three, tenty-four," a similar consistency exists in the tens through application of the "ten"-related suffix *teen*, as in *thirteen, fourteen . . . eighteen, nineteen*. But what about **eleven** and *twelve*? Unlike the teens, these two numbers derived from Old English words that were made up of the roots for "one" (or "two" in the case of *twelve*) and "left over." So *eleven* literally means "one left over" or "one past ten" and *twelve* means "two left over" or "two past ten."

## SORT 32. Unstressed Final Syllables with /ər/

### Sorting by Meaning

| People Nouns | Other Nouns |
|---|---|
| **brother** | **finger** |
| doctor | answer |
| father | collar |
| grocer | cover |
| mayor | dollar |
| mother | drawer |
| neighbor | error |
| sailor | favor |
| soldier | harbor |
| swimmer | honor |
| traitor | litter |
| | mirror |
| | sugar |

### Sorting by Pattern and Meaning

| People Nouns | | Other Nouns | | |
| --- | --- | --- | --- | --- |
| *-er* | *-or* | *-er* | *-or* | *-ar* |
| **brother** | **doctor** | **finger** | **favor** | **sugar** |
| grocer | mayor | answer | error | collar |
| father | neighbor | cover | harbor | dollar |
| mother | sailor | drawer | honor | |
| soldier | traitor | litter | mirror | |
| swimmer | | | | |

*Considerations:* This is the first of two sorts related to the unstressed final syllable /ər/. During their within word pattern studies and earlier work at the syllable juncture stage, students explored the confusing aspects of the r-controlled /ûr/ sound, which can be spelled with *-er* (*her*), *-ir* (*first*), and *-ur* (*fur*). Spellings of the /ər/ sound in unstressed final syllables are equally confusing but involve different patterns: *-er*, *-ar*, and *-or*. Start by discussing any words that may be unfamiliar, such as *traitor*, as well as words with multiple meanings, as in *litter* ("trash," "a cat box," and a "type of framework for carrying a person"). Introduce the sort by asking students to categorize the words by meaning: People Nouns and Other Nouns. Point out to students that although several of the words in this sort can function as verbs, for example, *answer* and *honor*, their use as nouns is the focus here. Students who are ready for greater challenge may be asked to determine categories through open sorting or with only the help of key words. Discuss the results, and then ask students to re-sort the words by meaning and pattern, as shown above. Ask students to speculate on the best-guess pattern or patterns for final /ər/. After they have collected more words through word hunts, check to see whether they need to change their hypothesis. They should conclude that *-er* is most commonly used.

### Talking Points
• Final /ər/ can be spelled several ways; the most common is *-er*, as in *swimmer* and *cover*.

*Integrating Idioms:* "Don't worry about my sister; I can always **twist her around my little finger**." (Easily influence her. A person's pinkie is very small, so it would take very little to wrap something around it.)

*Did You Know?* **Dollar** has its origin in Jachymov, a small town in central Europe. In the 1500s the town was known by its German name—Sankt Joachimsthal—and was the namesake for coins called *joachimstaler* that were minted with silver from a nearby mine. The name of the coin was shortened in German to just *taler* and was borrowed into English as *daler*, a word that referred to various similar coins. Thomas Jefferson proposed that the "dollar" be adopted as the United States unit of currency, and in 1785 this was formalized by the Continental Congress.

## SORT 33. More Unstressed Final Syllables with /ər/

### Sorting by Meaning (Parts of Speech)

| Noun (Person) | Adjective |
|---|---|
| **farmer** | **younger** |
| actor | fewer |
| beggar | hotter |
| burglar | polar |
| editor | regular |
| governor | similar |
| miser | smarter |
| plumber | smoother |
| sculptor | solar |
| settler | stellar |
| shopper | |
| sponsor | |
| visitor | |
| voter | |

### Sorting by Pattern and Meaning

| Noun (People) | | Adjective | | |
|---|---|---|---|---|
| *-er* | *-or* | *-er* | *-ar* | Oddball |
| **farmer** | **actor** | **younger** | **solar** | **?** |
| miser | editor | fewer | polar | beggar |
| plumber | governor | hotter | popular | burglar |
| settler | sculptor | smarter | regular | |
| shopper | sponsor | smoother | similar | |
| voter | visitor | | stellar | |

*Considerations:* Discuss any unfamiliar words, perhaps *miser, sponsor,* and *stellar.* This sort extends work from the previous sort with final /ər/ through the inclusion of adjectives. Ask students to sort the words into meaning categories based on part of speech, as shown. Discuss what the students notice about the two categories. Ask them to re-sort the words by meaning and pattern, then share their results with a partner, being sure to talk about their observations and any helpful generalizations for spelling. Discuss their ideas and clarify and elaborate as needed. If an idea is suggested that seems questionable but is plausible, say something such as, "I can see why you think that. As we gather more words, let's keep a close lookout for words that will support or disprove your idea." Some likely generalizations follow:

### Talking Points

- Nouns related to people usually end in *-er* or *-or* (*farmer* and *governor*).
- Adjectives that compare end in *-er*, as in *hotter* and *smarter*; *-ar* is often used for other adjectives (*polar* and *similar*).

*Integrating Idioms:* "We're holding elections next week at school to see how our **voter** results compare with the rest of the country, and I still can't decide whether to **vote a straight ticket or a split ticket**." (Vote for only candidates of one party or divide the votes between the two parties. The meaning of *ticket* as the "listing of candidates on a ballot" probably stems from mid-1500 when the word referred to a public notice.)

"My friend loaned me this hat to wear for the parade, since I forgot mine. I hate it, but **beggars can't be choosers**." (You can't criticize what you get for free. If you are really in need of a certain item and someone gives it to you, you're in no position to find fault with it.)

*Did You Know?* **Plumber** evolved from *plumbum*, the Latin word for "lead." As far back as Roman times, many pipes used to carry water in a building were made of lead. This lead structure came to be called *plumbing* and the person who dealt with its maintenance and installation a *plumber*. The root of *plumbum* (*plon*) made its way into English as the name for a lead weight attached to a line and dropped to determine a straight vertical line on a flat surface, such as a wall, or in water to determine depth. Use of such a *plumb line* to measure depth or verticality eventually led to the figurative meaning "to examine closely or in depth," as in *The detective stayed up late and plumbed the many available clues, looking for a common link to solve the mystery.*

## SORT 34. Unstressed Final Syllables with /chər/ and /zhər/

### Sorting by Sound and Pattern

| -cher /chər/ | -ture /chər/ | -sure /zhər/ | Oddball |
|---|---|---|---|
| **pitcher** | **nature** | **measure** | **?** |
| catcher | capture | leisure | danger |
| rancher | creature | pleasure | injure |
| stretcher | culture | treasure | |
| teacher | feature | | |
| | furniture | | |
| | gesture | | |
| | mixture | | |
| | pasture | | |
| | posture | | |
| | texture | | |
| | torture | | |

*Considerations:* Discuss the meanings of any words that may be unfamiliar or need clarifying, perhaps *culture, gesture, leisure,* and in some areas *pasture*. Although the words in this sort all have similar-sounding final syllables, there are slight variations that, when coupled with meaning, can provide clues to the different spellings. To illustrate the help that sound and meaning clues can provide, introduce the sort as a teacher-guided blind sort. Explain to students that after you model the placement of a few of the words, you will read the rest of the words aloud while they determine their placement without looking at the spelling. Ask them to think carefully about the sound of the final syllable and any meaning connections that may be of help. Model the placement of one or more words in each category by saying the word carefully but naturally and then placing the word under the appropriate key word (do not stack the cards; students should be able to see the spellings once their placement is decided). Continue to read aloud others of the words; as students begin to catch on, ask them to point to the category they think is correct. Lay the card down and verify whether the word fits or not before reading the next word. Save the oddballs until the latter part of the sort to avoid confusion. If students have difficulty distinguishing between the two /chər/ patterns, think aloud to reveal that *-er* is used with base words that end in /ch/. Talk about the results. Students' observations should raise generalizations similar to those listed next; if not, make them aware of them.

### Talking Points

- In words that end with /zhər/, the final syllable is spelled *-sure*, as in *treasure*.
- Many words end in /chər/; if the word includes a base word that ends in /ch/, the ending is *-er*, as in *rancher* and *catcher*; if not, the ending is *-ture*, as in *creature* and *nature*.

**Integrating Idioms:** "This old computer needs to be **put out to pasture**." (Retired from use. This expression comes from the traditional practice of keeping farm animals that were too old to work, especially horses, in a pasture.)

**Did You Know?** What do **treasure** and a *thesaurus* have in common? Both relate to storing: the one is "stored wealth" in the form of valuables, such as money or jewels, and the other is a "storehouse of synonyms." Both words evolved from the Greek word *thesauros*, meaning "something stored up or laid away." Although it is currently regarded as a book of synonyms, *thesaurus* initially carried the meaning of a "monetary treasury."

## SORT 35. Unstressed Final Syllables with /əl/

### Sorting by Sound and Pattern

| *-le* | *-al* | *-el* | Oddball |
|-------|-------|-------|---------|
| **angle** | **rural** | **angel** | **?** |
| bottle | equal | cancel | canal |
| couple | final | channel | fossil |
| little | normal | level | |
| middle | plural | model | |
| pickle | | nickel | |
| simple | | novel | |
| wrinkle | | vowel | |

**Considerations:** This sort introduces students to final /əl/, which, like other unstressed syllable patterns examined in this section, can be represented in several ways, here as *-le*, *-el*, *-al*, and *-il*. The sort highlights the very common *-le* pattern and reviews the structure of syllables. If students need greater awareness of how confusing it can be to spell unstressed syllables, you might dictate a few of the words to them before distributing the word cards and discuss the results of their spelling. Before introducing the sort, go over any words students do not know, perhaps *rural* and *canal*. Ask if they can think of a recently studied word that is an opposite, or *antonym*, of *rural* (*urban*; see Sort 31).

After discussing unfamiliar vocabulary, ask students to pair up and, with their partners, determine the sort categories (the category headers should be reserved for later). Remind them to carefully define the categories so that a word matches just one category; otherwise, it should be placed as an oddball, or the categories should be redefined. A sound-and-pattern sort, such as depicted in Sort 35, may result; if not, after discussing the students' results, ask them to re-sort the words according to the pattern and sound of the unstressed syllable. Discuss the new results, including the two oddballs and add the category headers. Contrary to the other *-al* words, the *-al* in *canal* is stressed and therefore not a schwa vowel. *Fossil* includes a schwa but has a pattern that is not represented as a category. Ask students to share any generalizations they notice. Use the talking points to expand on their ideas. As an extension during this session or at a later time, review the structure of syllables, being sure to highlight V*le*. As students work with the patterns and word hunt for additional examples, invite them to see whether they can determine which is the most frequently occurring pattern.

The *-le* pattern, which appears in many words, wins the frequency competition for /əl/ and is truly the best guess. So many words include this pattern that it is considered one of the six basic syllable patterns (the others have previously been studied: closed, open, VCe, vowel team, and *r*-controlled). When identifying a syllable with *-le*, as in the word *syllable*, the consonant preceding the *-le* is considered part of the syllable. (See also Sort 14.) In the case of *syllable*, the final syllable is *-ble*, and the *l* is part of the vowel pattern, *le*, rather than part of a *bl* blend. So where do words with final *-le* fit when the structure of the word is being examined? You may remember that there are several across-syllable patterns. These include VCCV, in which the consonants may be either doublets or different, as in *manner* and *basket*; VCV open, as in *paper*; VCV closed, as in *robin*; and VV, as in *create*. From this point on, when syllable structures are examined in this book, the *-le* syllable pattern is designated by a superscript *le* immediately following the V designation. For example, in this sort the structure for the word *little* is VCCV$^{le}$ Doublet. The V$^{le}$ reveals that the second vowel pattern is *-le*. The structure of *simple* is also VCCV$^{le}$ but not a doublet. *Able* has a VCV$^{le}$ open structure. Though not included in this sort, *triple* is an example of a VCV$^{le}$ closed structure. You might ask students to determine the structure of the other *-le* words included in this sort or of those they find when word hunting.

## Talking Points

- The /əl/ in unstressed syllables can be spelled in several ways (*-al, -il, -el, -le*), but the most common or best guess for spelling this sound is *-le*, as in *simple*.
- When examining the structure of syllables with final *-le*, the preceding consonant is part of the syllable, and *-le* acts as a vowel unit, as in *simple*, of which the structure is VCCV$^{le}$.
- Surrounding letters in the word can help to determine the spelling of final /əl/. For example, if the *-el* ending is used with *angle*, the word becomes *angel*, because the *e* softens the hard *g* from /g/ to /j/. *Circle* would become *circel* /sûr•səl/, the hard final *-c* altered to the soft sound of /s/. (For more on hard and soft *c* and *g*, see Sort 37.)

**Integrating Idioms:** "My brother's **in a real pickle**; he has a party planned for Friday night but just got grounded for failing his math test today." (In a difficult situation or predicament. The phrase may stem from a Dutch use of the word *pickle* in the phrase *sit in the pickle*. As sticky as pickling brine or solution can be, you would certainly be in a troublesome situation if you sat in it!)

**Did You Know?** Browse through any grocery store and you are likely to find a large assortment of pickles: dill, sweet, sour, with garlic, from midget- to giant-sized, sliced or whole. Stories of the word's origins also vary. One story identifies *pickle* as an eponym, a word that is derived from the name of a person, such as the previously described *sandwich* (see Sort 12). As the story goes, the process of pickling started in the 1300s with a Dutchman by the name of Willem Beukelz (**Boi•kĕlz**). The English really liked Beukelz's idea, but when they talked about it, they pronounced his name so that it sounded like "pickles," and the word caught on (Terban, 1988). Another source suggests that *pickle* was likely borrowed into English from the Dutch word *pekel*, meaning a "solution for preserving and flavoring food." When *pickle* was first recorded around 1400, it had a different meaning from the one we think of today. It was a type of spicy gravy that was served with fowl and meat. In time it took on more of the Dutch meaning, referring to the brine or to foods such as cucumbers preserved in the brine (*The American Heritage Dictionary of the English Language*, 1996).

## SORT 36. Unstressed Initial Syllables

### Sorting by Sound and Pattern

| <u>a</u> | <u>e</u> | <u>o</u> | Oddball |
|---|---|---|---|
| **alarm** | **select** | **consume** | **?** |
| against | demand | collect | college |
| another | depend | command | comment |
| attend | develop | pronounce | serious |
| banana | result | protect | |
| canoe | | | |
| garage | | | |
| marine | | | |
| patrol | | | |
| salute | | | |

***Considerations:*** (*Note:* for the introduction to this sort, you will need 5–6 blank note cards for every pair of students and one set of header cards.) In the final sort of this section, attention is shifted to unstressed syllables in the initial position of the word. The focus is not on particular sound-alike patterns, as in the previous sorts, but simply on developing understanding that the infamous schwa can occur in another part of the word and that, because it can be spelled by any of the vowels, it requires careful attention. Differences in dialect are likely to cause some students to question whether certain words really have a schwa sound in the first syllable, as in *demand* (/də•mănd/), which they may pronounce with a stressed first syllable, /dē•mănd/, or with a reduced stress, as in /dē•mănd/. Be sensitive to such differences. Unanimous agreement is not important; what is important is that students become aware of the schwa in the beginning syllable of words and that they realize they need to remember its spelling. As a change of pace, before distributing the template of words, hand out 5–6 blank word cards to pairs or trios of students and send them on a scavenger hunt. Each team will need to find or brainstorm words with a schwa sound ("uh") in the first syllable. Remind them that the "uh" cannot be in a stressed syllable, because then the vowel would be short *u*, as in *drummer*. Advise them to record one word per card. When everyone is finished collecting, bring the group together. Ask each group to read aloud their words; discuss word meanings as needed, and encourage the listeners to attend to which syllable is stressed. Eliminate any inappropriate words. Then place each of the five header cards (*a, e, i, o, u*) in front of the students and, going around the group, ask students to sort their cards according to the schwa pattern (for example, *fatigue* would be placed under *a* and *severe* under *e*.) Continue until all of the cards have been categorized. Discuss the results and any spelling insights. Students will likely collect schwa examples for each of the vowels; if they do not, draw from the following list to illustrate: *marine*, *patrol*, *select*, *severe*, *divide*, *divorce*, *cocoon*, *polite*, *support*, and *supply*. After the scavenger hunt, or at a later time, ask students to sort the words on their templates according to the stressed syllable—first or second. This will result in a list of only three words for first-syllable stress (the oddballs shown in Sort 36) and placement of all the other words under the second-syllable-stress category. Then turn their attention to the lengthy list of unstressed-first-syllable words. Ask them to resort the words in this category according to the schwa pattern: *a, e, i, o, u*. The results should look similar to Sort 36; note that the *i* and *u* categories will be empty. Discuss why *college, comment,* and *serious* are oddballs (the first syllable is stressed; also, *comment* has no unstressed syllable).

### Talking Points

- The schwa sometimes occurs in the first syllables of words; it is just as difficult to spell in the initial position as in the final, because it can be represented by any of the five vowels.
- Notice how the schwa is spelled in an unstressed syllable so you can remember it.

**Integrating Idioms:** "I **go bananas** every time I hear her sing!" (Become very excited and enthusiastic; go crazy—a slang expression. This is a good time to discuss what is meant by *slang*. Slang refers to words and phrases that are coined and used for effect; they are usually short-lived and used mainly in casual and playful speech. Carl Sandburg [1878–1967], a well-known American poet, once shared these thoughts about slang: "*Slang is the language that rolls up its sleeves, spits on its hands and goes to work.*" What do you think he meant by these words? Can you think of other slang expressions? If you are not sure about a phrase, check the dictionary to see if it indicates *slang* in the entry.)

**Did You Know?** The first **canoes** were made by American Indians. Columbus first saw the *canoa*, as the Indians of Haiti referred to their boats, on a trip to the West Indies. These early canoes were made by hollowing out entire large trees with a sharp stone. Although paddling such a big boat may seem challenging, some of these early canoes had space for as many as forty paddlers! Over the centuries canoes have been used widely for travel and have been made of readily available or desirable materials. For example, birch bark was lighter than a whole tree and therefore was able to be carried between rivers or lakes if portage was necessary; buffalo hide was plentiful on the plains, where trees were rare. Today, besides wood, canoes are made of plastic, fiberglass, and aluminum. Regardless of the material, they continue to be streamlined so they can be maneuvered in very shallow or narrow waters.

# SORT 30 Unstressed Final Syllables with Long *a* Patterns

| -ace | -age | -ain |
|------|------|------|
| surface | manage | certain |
| luggage | practice | fountain |
| furnace | villain | courage |
| mountain | message | bargain |
| garbage | obtain | necklace |
| curtain | bandage | engage |
| cabbage | menace | package |
| palace | damage | ? |

# SORT 31 Unstressed Final Syllables with /ən/

| -en | -an | -en | -in | -on |
|-----|-----|-----|-----|-----|

| Verbs | Nouns | ? |
|-------|-------|---|
| darken | slogan | dozen |
| cabin | lemon | tighten |
| woman | robin | siren |
| button | cousin | fasten |
| eleven | sharpen | dragon |
| cotton | awaken | chicken |
| loosen | pardon | urban |
| margin | method | strengthen |

# SORT 32  Unstressed Final Syllables with /ər/

| -er | -or (people) | -er | -or (other) | -ar |
|---|---|---|---|---|
| **People Nouns** | | | **Other Nouns** | |
| brother | doctor | | | finger |
| favor | sugar | | | traitor |
| honor | answer | | | father |
| mother | error | | | swimmer |
| mayor | soldier | | | harbor |
| cover | litter | | | collar |
| mirror | grocer | | | neighbor |
| dollar | drawer | | | sailor |

# SORT 33 More Unstressed Final Syllables with /ər/

| -er (Nouns) | -or | -er (Adjectives) | -ar |
|---|---|---|---|
| **Nouns** | **Adjectives** | | **?** |
| farmer | actor | | younger |
| solar | polar | | governor |
| smarter | regular | | shopper |
| voter | editor | | stellar |
| fewer | miser | | sponsor |
| settler | similar | | smoother |
| sculptor | burglar | | visitor |
| beggar | plumber | | hotter |

# SORT 34 Unstressed Final Syllables with /chər/ and /zhər/

| -cher /chər/ | -ture /chər/ | -sure /zhər/ |
|---|---|---|
| pitcher | nature | measure |
| pasture | torture | teacher |
| capture | treasure | culture |
| danger | catcher | leisure |
| feature | injure | mixture |
| pleasure | posture | rancher |
| stretcher | texture | furniture |
| gesture | creature | ? |

| -le | -al | -el |
| --- | --- | --- |
| angle | rural | angel |
| vowel | fossil | novel |
| cancel | wrinkle | final |
| pickle | nickel | bottle |
| equal | couple | channel |
| little | canal | simple |
| level | model | plural |
| normal | middle | ? |

# SORT 36 Unstressed Initial Syllables

| a | e | i | o | u |
|---|---|---|---|---|

| | | |
|---|---|---|
| alarm | select | consume |
| salute | command | serious |
| another | demand | collect |
| develop | college | attend |
| canoe | marine | depend |
| comment | pronounce | garage |
| protect | result | banana |
| patrol | against | ? |

# Consonant Extensions

The five sorts in this section extend and review patterns with the *complex consonants* feature (see *Word Journeys* [Ganske, 2000] or *Word Sorts and More* [Ganske, 2006]). Hard and soft *c* and *g* and final *k* are revisited in the context of polysyllabic words. New sounds for the *ch* digraph are explored, and *ph* is introduced as a digraph. Use of *gu(e)* and *qu(e)* are also examined. In anticipation of Part 3 word studies, the final investigation looks at environments in which *i* helps to form consonant sounds, as in *ci, si, ti,* and *i(on)*.

*What Is Known:* Although each of the sorts in this section targets different letters or patterns, students will likely have previously studied either the sound or the pattern in one-syllable words at the within word pattern stage. Known concepts relevant to the sorts that follow include hard and soft *c* and *g*; final /k/ spelled *-ck, -ke,* and *-k*; /sh/ spelled *sh*; /qw/ spelled *qu*; and /f/ spelled *f*.

*What Is New:* The context of polysyllabic words is new for all of the patterns. Also, there are several new spellings for known sounds and some new sounds for known spelling patterns, as /k/ can also be spelled with *c* (*topic*), *ch* (*chorus*), and *-que* (*unique*); final /g/ in longer words tends to be spelled *-gue* (*fatigue*); /f/ tends to be spelled with *ph* in polysyllabic words (*trophy*); *i* sometimes sounds like /y/ (*onion*); and in certain word environments /sh/ is spelled with *ch, ci, si,* or *ti*.

## SORT 37. Consonant Extensions with Hard and Soft *c* and *g*

### Sorting by Sound and Pattern

| Hard *c* | Hard *g* | Soft *c* | Soft *g* |
|----------|----------|----------|----------|
| **custom** | **guilty** | **center** | **gentle** |
| camera | gadget | cement | general |
| coffee | goalie | census | genius |
| compass | gossip | cereal | genuine |
| cookie | | circle | gigantic |
| correct | | circus | gymnast |
| | | citizen | |
| | | cycle | |

*Considerations:* (Note that the sort contains several three-syllable words.) Because the same principles guide the use of hard and soft *c* and *g*, the two principles can be taught together. After discussing any unfamiliar words, ask students what they notice about the words. They should mention that all of the words begin with either *c* or *g*. Their comments may reveal much greater understanding, such as that when the letter has a hard sound, /k/ or /g/, it is followed by *a, o,* or *u,* and when it is soft, the following letter is *e, i,* or *y*. If their responses show this type of depth, ask them to sort the words in a manner that demonstrates how *c* and *g* work, such as shown here, or with the letters combined so that there is one hard column and one soft column. If students demonstrate more limited knowledge of the feature, explain that both *c* and *g* can produce more than one sound. Then ask them to sort the words by their initial consonant sound. This will result in four categories. Point to the columns with hard *c* and *g* and explain that in these words the sound of the beginning *c* or *g* is hard. Then point out the two columns of words that begin with soft c and g. Ask students to examine the words with a partner to try to discover what makes the c and g hard sometimes and soft others. Prompt students who need hints to look at the second letter in each word. Discuss and clarify their findings. As part of the discussion, invite students to identify and explain the sounds of g and c in other positions of some of the words (*cycle, circle, circus, gadget,* and *gigantic*). Although the principles or rules that govern spellings with hard and soft c and g are powerful ones that work with most words, there are "rule-breakers," as for instance *cello* and *façade, giggle, geyser,* and *margarine.* Students may be able to think of other exceptions or search for them during word hunts. The etymology section of dictionary word entries can provide insights as to why they are oddballs. *Façade,* for example, is a French borrowing; the small mark beneath the c tells us that the c will have a soft sound, despite the following a. Dictionaries and computer programs often represent the word in English with its French spelling, using the *cedilla* diacritical mark to point out the word's unusual soft c sound. The same mark is often used in garçon, another French borrowing.

### Talking Points

- When followed by *a, o,* or *u,* c and g usually make a hard sound (/k/ and /g/), as in *camera, cookie, custom, gadget, gossip,* and *guilty.*
- When followed by *e, i,* or *y,* c and g usually make a soft sound (/s/ and /j/), as in *center, circle, cycle, gentle, gigantic,* and *gymnast.*

**Integrating Idioms:** "Our game was rained out for the third straight day; I guess **that's the way the cookie crumbles.**" (Just what you have to expect sometimes. Seldom can you bite into or eat a cookie whole without bits and pieces falling off; so, too, in life things do not always go smoothly.)

**Did You Know?** We have the Dutch to thank for **cookie,** which we probably borrowed from their word for "little cake"—*koekje.* The Dutch were not the first to make cookies; the first cookie-like cakes probably came from Persia, which was one of the first places in the world to grow sugar. Many countries have their own names for these little delicacies; for example, in England they are called *biscuits,* in Germany they are *keks,* in Italy they are *biscotti,* and in Spain they are *galletas.* Do you know any other names?

## SORT 38. Consonant Extensions with Final /k/

### Sorting by Pattern

| -ck | -ke | -k | -c | Oddball |
|-----|-----|-----|-----|---------|
| **shamrock** | **cupcake** | **chipmunk** | **topic** | **?** |
| attack | keepsake | crosswalk | arctic | antique |
| cowlick | rebuke | remark | elastic | |
| hammock | turnpike | | fabric | |
| limerick | | | mimic | |
| padlock | | | metric | |
| | | | panic | |
| | | | plastic | |
| | | | specific | |

***Considerations:*** Although *-ck, -ke,* and *-k* are typical spellings for final /k/ in one-syllable words, students will discover as they work with the words in this sort and search for additional examples through word hunts that these patterns occur relatively infrequently in polysyllabic words. Probably the most common of the three is *-ck,* and even it tends to be limited to compound words. The *ck* pattern does occur frequently at the end of other syllables, as in *bicker, cackle, chuckle, freckle.* In polysyllabic words the final /k/ is most often represented with *-c.* Many adjectives, such as the word *polysyllabic,* end in *-ic: angelic, classic, economic,* and so forth. Discuss any unfamiliar words (for some students, words such as *cowlick, rebuke,* and others may need clarifying or explaining). Then introduce the sort by spreading the words in front of the students or displaying them on an overhead. Ask them what they all have in common. If someone suggests that they all have two syllables (actually *limerick* has three, but certain dialects may cause it to be pronounced with two—/lĭm•rĭk/), ask "What else?" Once the focus is on the final /k/ sound, ask them to sort their word cards according to how this sound is spelled. Talk about the results and encourage generalizations that will aid spelling. Brainstorming additional words or searching for more examples through word hunts may be necessary before this can be accomplished. *Antique* is introduced as an oddball in anticipation of Sort 40, which looks at final *-que.* As an extension, ask students to consider which words could have *-ed* added to them to form the past tense. How would the new word be spelled? Record their responses on the board. Discuss the results, which should include *attacked, rebuked, padlocked, remarked, mimicked,* and *panicked.* Some students are likely to misspell the last two. Ask them to hypothesize why *k* was added (to maintain the hard *c* sound).

### Talking Points

- Final /k/ can be represented in many ways (*-ck, -k, -ke, -c,* or *-que*); however, in polysyllabic words, the most common form is *c,* which occurs in many adjectives as *-ic,* such as *classic.*

***Integrating Idioms:*** "Last night my mom **pressed the panic button** and called 911. She thought my grandfather had had a heart attack, but it turned out he was just asleep." (Overreacted to the situation. According to one source [Ammer, 1997], some World War II bombers had bell-warning systems that enabled flight crews to bail out of the plane if it was badly hit; however, pilots sometimes overestimated the damage and pushed the signal unnecessarily. By 1950 use of the term had broadened to mean other types of overreaction.)

***Did You Know?*** The word **panic** comes to us by way of a figure from ancient Greek mythology—Pan. Pan was the god of woods, fields, and flocks. He had the body and head of a human and the legs, ears, and horns of a goat and lived and wandered about in mountains and valleys. He was fond of music and is often shown playing panpipes, an early instrument made of reeds of different lengths, which is played by blowing across the open ends. Greek gods, such as Pan, who dwelt in the forest were feared by those who had reason to pass through the forest at night; the darkness and loneliness of the woods ignited their fears and superstitions, and they attributed the cause to Pan. Consequently, any sudden overpowering terror came to be known as *panic.*

## SORT 39. Consonant Extensions with *ch* and *ph*

### Sorting by Sound and Pattern

| *ch* | | | *ph* |
|------|------|------|------|
| /ch/ | /k/ | /sh/ | /f/ |
| **chimney** | **chorus** | **brochure** | **nephew** |
| attach | chaos | chaperone | alphabet |
| challenge | character | machine | elephant |
| mischief | echo | mustache | pamphlet |
| spinach | schedule | parachute | paragraph |
| | stomach | | phrases |
| | | | physical |
| | | | trophy |

*Considerations:* Talk about any unfamiliar words, such as *chaos*. You might ask students to look up *brochure* and *pamphlet* in a dictionary to determine whether they are synonyms or have somewhat different meanings. Review the meaning of *digraph*, and then explain to students that they will be examining the digraphs *ch* and *ph*. Ask them to sort their words by pattern and sound so that the results reveal the sound or sounds of each of the two patterns. The outcome will resemble Sort 39. Discuss the results and any generalizations that students can draw about reading or spelling words with *ch* and *ph*. *Ph* is a relatively rare spelling for /f/ in common English words; it occurs more often in low-frequency words. A browsing of the *ph* section of the dictionary will quickly show this. Although *ch* makes various sounds, as in *echo*, *attach*, and *machine*, when reading words with *ch*, the best guess is /ch/, which is the most common pronunciation for the pattern. If that does not produce a known word, students need to be flexible and apply the other sounds. More recent borrowings from the French have given us the /sh/ pronunciation, as in *chaperone*, and those from Latin and Greek the sound of hard *c*, as in *chorus*. Because the different pronunciations relate to time and place of borrowing rather than to meaning or surrounding letters, spelling can be a challenge.

### Talking Points

- *Ch* can make several different sounds, including /ch/ as in *attach*, /k/ as in *echo*, and /sh/ as in *machine*; when learning to spell a word with one of the sounds, make note of the pattern to remember it.
- /Ch/ is the most common pronunciation for *ch* and, therefore, your best guess when trying to read an unfamiliar word with the pattern.
- *Ph*, as in *pamphlet*, is a common spelling for /f/, but appears mostly in low-frequency words.

*Integrating Idioms:* "Our neighborhood is having a **white elephant** sale this weekend, so people can get rid of their junk." (A useless or unwanted item. According to *The American Heritage Dictionary of Idioms*, this custom started with the Siamese. An albino or white elephant was rare and considered sacred. Sometimes the king would give a white elephant to a subject he did not like; because the elephant was sacred, the person could not kill the animal, and eventually the cost of feeding the animal ruined the person.)

*Did You Know?* *Parachute* is borrowed from the French *para* (as in the light umbrella, *parasol*, which literally means "shield or protection from the sun") and *chute*, meaning "fall." The parachute indeed offers protection from a fall; its lightweight, umbrella-like structure creates resistance that slows down a fall. The word was coined in the 1780s and demonstrated by an early French balloonist named Blanchard, who attached a parachute to a basket, placed a dog inside, and dropped it from a balloon. A few years later, Blanchard's hot air balloon ruptured, and he had cause to safely use the device himself. Early parachutes were made of canvas; to increase strength and lightness, Blanchard began making them of folded silk. Despite the pioneering efforts of Blanchard and others in the 1700s, documents of the Middle Ages show that people were already experimenting with devices to protect them when falling from a height, and in the 1400s the famous Leonardo da Vinci drew a sketch of a parachute.

## SORT 40. Consonant Extensions with *gu*(e) and *qu*(e)

### Sorting by Sound and Pattern

| *gu* | *-gue* | *qu* | *-que* | Oddball |
|------|--------|------|--------|---------|
| **penguin** | **fatigue** | **question** | **unique** | **?** |
| extinguish | dialogue | frequent | critique | disguise |
| jaguar | league | liquid | opaque | guidance |
| language | prologue | quality | technique | mosquito |
| | vague | require | | |
| | | sequence | | |
| | | squirrel | | |

*Considerations:* Students may need to have the meanings of some words clarified, as perhaps *extinguish*, *jaguar*, *league*, *prologue*, *vague*, *unique*, *critique*, or *opaque*. Spread the words out for students to review and ask them what the words have in common. Most will notice that all of the words include either *gu* or *qu*. Next, gather the cards and place the key words *penguin* and *fatigue*, as well as the "?" card, in front of them. Say each word, emphasizing the portion with *g*. Then read aloud each of the remaining *gu* or *-gue* words (for the time being skip over words with *qu*). Ask students which category the word should be placed in, but do not reveal the word until they have made their selection; then place it in the appropriate category. When complete, discuss possible generalizations to facilitate spelling. *Disguise* and *guidance* are oddballs because they do not have a /gw/ sound, as the *gu* words under *penguin* do. Proceed in the same manner with the *qu* and *que* words, creating two new categories under the key words *question* and *unique*. Exceptions can be added to the oddball list already started. Talk about any observations and generate ideas to aid spelling. Add the headers as the spelling patterns are discussed. Point out to students that *mosquito* is an exception. The unusual pronunciation stems from the word's Spanish ancestry. As a follow-up, ask students to re-sort the words using all four key words to guide them. This approach may be used for the initial sort if students are able to handle the somewhat subtle distinctions in sound. In case students wonder, there are other words in which *u* sometimes produces a /w/ sound (as *cuisine*, *Duane*, *suede*, *suave*, *suite*, *tuille*—a piece of armor for covering the thigh). As in the /gw/ and /qw/ words in this sort, the *u* is preceded by a consonant and followed by another vowel.

### Talking Points

- Sometimes *gu* is pronounced with a hard *g* sound, /g/, as in *disguise*, and sometimes as /gw/, as in *language*; final *-gue* is usually pronounced as a hard *g*, as in *fatigue*, and is a common spelling for final /g/ in polysyllabic words.
- In English, *q* is followed by *u*, and *qu* is pronounced /kw/; final *-que* is pronounced /k/, as in *unique*.

**Integrating Idioms:** "The snowstorm was **a blessing in disguise**: our flight was canceled, but the resort gave everyone two nights of free lodging, so we got to extend our vacation." (Something that seems like a misfortune turns out to be a lucky occurrence.)

**Did You Know?** *Language*, with its current spelling, was first recorded as the word for "talk" in the early 1300s. It evolved from the Latin word for "tongue," *lingua*. Estimates of just how many languages there are vary by the thousands, depending on the definition of *language*. If we define *language* as a "living language," namely one that is used widely by a particular group of people, the estimate is "6,912 known living languages" (*Ethnologue: Languages of the World* at *www.ethnologue.com*). So which language has the greatest number of speakers? Mandarin Chinese, followed by English.

The origin of **penguin** is somewhat of a mystery and perhaps a case of mistaken identity. According to one story, the word originated in Wales, far away from any penguins. In Welsh, *pen* means "chief" or "head," and *gwyn* means "white," resulting in "white head." However, the heads of penguins are mainly black, so what is the explanation? In the late 1500s when explorers were traveling around the world, British sailors visited Newfoundland. The island was crowded with large gray and white flightless birds. Perhaps Welshmen were among the sailors, as both the island and the bird were named *pen gwyn*. Although the birds had large white spots on their heads, they were not white, so perhaps the island (and its flightless inhabitants) got its name because the sailors thought that all or part of the island resembled a white head. No one knows. Still later in the century, when English explorers traveled south of South America, they saw flightless birds that reminded them of the ones in Newfoundland. They called them *penguins*, though these birds were very different from those sighted in Newfoundland. Today we know the birds seen in Newfoundland by the name of *great auk*, a species that soon became extinct because the birds were easily caught.

---

## SORT 41. Consonant Extensions with Vowel *i*

### Sorting by Sound and Pattern

| *ci* /sh/ | *si* /sh/ | *ti* /sh/ | *i* /y/ | Oddball |
|-----------|-----------|-----------|---------|---------|
| **special** | **mansion** | **motion** | **onion** | **?** |
| ancient | session | caption | billion | vision |
| conscience | tension | fiction | junior | |
| conscious | | mention | opinion | |
| crucial | | option | senior | |
| glacier | | patient | | |
| vicious | | station | | |

*Considerations:* This sort introduces *i* as a consonant sound in particular contexts, as in *ancient*, in which it makes the /sh/ sound when combined with *c*. Several of the final syllable patterns found here are the focus of sorts at the beginning of the next stage, in which one aim is to develop the understanding that words related in meaning also tend to be related in spelling, thus *disrupt/disruption*, not *disrupt/disrupsion*. Discuss any unfamiliar words; *conscience* and *conscious* may need clarifying and perhaps *crucial*, *caption*, and *ancient*. More capable students may be able to complete the sound and pattern sort, independently or with a partner, with minimal guidance, using the headers and key words as guides. Others may benefit from more teacher direction and modeling. In either case, go over the key words and headers, emphasizing the targeted portion of the word: /sh/ for *ci*, *si*, *ti* and /y/ for *i*. Remind students to consider both pattern and sound as they sort. When completed, discuss the results.

### Talking Points

- /Sh/ in an unstressed final syllable is often spelled *ci*, *si*, or *ti*, as in *glacier*, *tension*, and *caption*.
- In unstressed final syllables, *i* sometimes sounds like a *y*, /y/, as in *onion* and *senior*.

*Integrating Idioms:*  "When I stay with my grandmother she often asks me how my day went and says that **a clean conscience** makes a good pillow." (Feeling free of guilt makes it easy to sleep. Benjamin Franklin's proverb of "a quiet conscience sleeps in thunder" from *Poor Richard's Almanack* has a similar meaning.)

*Did You Know?*  Anyone who has ever had to make a **crucial** decision has been at a crossroads of having to decide between one option or the other. *Crucial* stems from the Latin word *crux*, meaning "cross." In the 1500s *crux* referred to a guidepost marking directions for a division in the road. A person can encounter many such crossing points—in his or her studies, in a relationship, in deciding how to spend time, and so forth—at which the decision made is a very important one.

  The words **onion** and *one* share more than the first two letters of their spellings. *Onion* actually stems from the Latin word for "oneness" or "union"—*unio*. So what is the meaning connection, you might wonder. The vegetable is made up of many layers that are *united* at the bottom. It is this same layering connotation that led Romans to call pearls by the same name, *unio*.

# SORT 37 Consonant Extensions with Hard and Soft *c* and *g*

| Hard c | Hard g | Soft c | Soft g |
|--------|--------|--------|--------|
| custom | guilty | | center |
| gentle | cement | | compass |
| gossip | gymnast | | gadget |
| gigantic | circle | | coffee |
| camera | genius | | cycle |
| goalie | circus | | correct |
| general | cookie | | cereal |
| citizen | genuine | | census |

# SORT 38  Consonant Extensions with Final /k/

| -ck | -ke | -k | -c |
|-----|-----|-----|-----|
| shamrock | cupcake | | chipmunk |
| topic | antique | | turnpike |
| specific | fabric | | limerick |
| cowlick | hammock | | arctic |
| panic | elastic | | attack |
| crosswalk | keepsake | | plastic |
| metric | mimic | | rebuke |
| padlock | remark | | ? |

# SORT 39  Consonant Extensions with *ch* and *ph*

| ch /ch/ | ch /k/ | ch /sh/ | ph /f/ |
|---|---|---|---|

| | | |
|---|---|---|
| chimney | chorus | brochure |
| nephew | pamphlet | schedule |
| parachute | attach | alphabet |
| stomach | trophy | mischief |
| spinach | chaperone | paragraph |
| chaos | elephant | character |
| physical | challenge | machine |
| echo | mustache | phrases |

# SORT 40 Consonant Extensions with *gu*(*e*) and *qu*(*e*)

| gu | -gue | qu | -que |
|---|---|---|---|
| penguin | fatigue | | question |
| unique | sequence | | prologue |
| opaque | league | | quality |
| jaguar | mosquito | | extinguish |
| technique | frequent | | critique |
| require | disguise | | dialogue |
| guidance | language | | liquid |
| vague | squirrel | | ? |

# SORT 41 Consonant Extensions with Vowel *i*

| ci /sh/ | si /sh/ | ti /sh/ | i /y/ |
|---------|---------|---------|-------|
| special | mansion | | motion |
| onion | conscience | | fiction |
| option | tension | | crucial |
| glacier | vicious | | billion |
| vision | patient | | session |
| junior | conscious | | mention |
| caption | senior | | opinion |
| ancient | station | | ? |

# Prefixes and Suffixes

In this section students explore some of the most common prefixes and suffixes and their affixation to base words. Later in this book, prefixes and suffixes are reexamined in the contexts of more sophisticated base words and word roots. Meaning lies at the heart of the word studies that follow. Students need to understand the meaning changes that prefixes and suffixes bring about, as well as to realize that readers and writers can use their knowledge of these common word parts to break longer words down into more manageable chunks for easier word identification, meaning making, or spelling. To help students understand that prefixes and suffixes add meaning, not just letters, to a word, careful attention has been given to including certain words to encourage students to think about this meaning connection. For example, consider *relish* and *unite* in Sort 42. Even though the words begin with *re-* and *un-*, if the letters are removed what remains is not a base word. *Misspell* in Sort 43 serves a similar purpose. Sometimes adding a prefix to a base word results in a spelling that may not "look right," as for instance *reelect*. Students need to realize that meaning is a very powerful force in English spelling, especially when low-frequency words are involved. This concept is further emphasized in studies at the next stage.

*What Is Known:* It is assumed that students know what a base word is and understand the concept of suffixes through their previous studies of inflectional endings -*ed*, -*ing*, -*s*, -*es*, -*er*, and -*est*.

*What Is New:* The concept of prefixes and suffixes as affixes, nonword parts that alter the meaning of a base word, may be new and should be explained. Although base words are used in the following sorts, let students know that sometimes prefixes and suffixes attach to word parts called *roots* that are not complete words. They will learn about these later.

---

**SORT 42.** Prefixes (*un-* and *re-*)

### Sorting by Pattern and Meaning

| *un-* | *re-* | Oddball |
|-------|-------|---------|
| **unwrap** | **rebuild** | **?** |
| unable | recycle | relish |
| unclear | reelect | unite |
| uneven | remove | |
| unfair | reorder | |
| unhappy | replace | |
| unkind | reread | |
| unsure | return | |
| untied | review | |
| unusual | rewind | |
| | rewrite | |

*Considerations:* Show students the words and discuss any that are unfamiliar; encourage them to share ideas about what the categories may be. Then ask everyone to sort the words according to their thinking. When they are finished, talk about the categories. If students group *relish* and *unite* with the *re-* and *un-* categories, respectively, ask how the words in each column are alike and whether the words might be grouped another way besides words that begin with *un* or *re*. If necessary, suggest that they consider meaning. Students should note that, apart from the oddball category, the *un-* words all add "not" to the meaning of their base words and that those with *re-* have been changed to mean "back" or "again." Explain that the *un-* and the *re-* in these words are *prefixes*. Before ending the session, invite the group to brainstorm more words with *un-* or *re-* beginnings and identify whether and how the spellings affect the words' meanings. If a questionable word is put forward, suggest that the group consult a dictionary.

### Talking Points

- A prefix is a meaningful word part that is sometimes added to the beginning of a word to alter its meaning. The prefixes *un-* and *re-* are very common; the former means "not" and the latter means "back" or "again."
- As with compound words, sometimes a "doesn't-look-right" spelling can result when a prefix is added to a base word, as with *reelect*; writers need to remember that it is meaning that really matters.
- Some words, such as *relish* and *unite*, may look as though they have a prefix attached to a base word, but the meaning connection is lacking.

**Integrating Idioms:** "Hey, guys, we all agree we could have chosen a better topic, but don't you think we're **past the point of no return**?" (Too far into the project to decide on another one. If you had just enough fuel to get to a destination, once you're past the halfway point, you have to keep going; you don't have enough to make the trip back.)

**Did You Know?** We often reread text to increase our understanding, especially if it's difficult. **Read** comes from the Old English word *raedan*, meaning to "advise" or "interpret something difficult that is written." Although many words in English share a common ancestry with words from other Western European languages, this is not the case with the verb *to read*. Italian, French, German, and other language versions stem from the Latin word *legere*. Although *read* did not develop from this word, *legend* and *legible* did. The ancestry of **write** also differs; it stems from an Old English word *writan*, which in turn came from a root meaning "to cut, scratch." It is likely that early writing on parchment involved much scratching with the quill pen. Other Western European languages drew on the Latin word *scribere*, for "to write." Although English did not borrow *to write* from this word, others of our words do stem from it. What do you think they might be? (*Scribe* and *scribble* for example; for others, see Sort 38 in Part 3.)

## SORT 43. Prefixes (*dis-*, *fore-*, *mis-*)

### Sorting by Pattern and Meaning

| *dis-* | *fore-* | *mis-* | Oddball |
|--------|---------|--------|---------|
| **dislike** | **forehead** | **mistrust** | ? |
| disagree | forecast | misjudge | foreign |
| discomfort | foreground | mismatch | forest |
| discover | foremost | misplace | |
| dishonest | foresight | misprint | |
| disobey | forewarn | misspell | |
| disorder | | mistake | |
| distrust | | | |

*Considerations:* This set of words introduces students to three more prefixes: *dis-* ("opposite of"), *fore-* ("before, in front of"), and *mis-* ("to do something wrongly"). First ask students to sort the words according to their prefixes. Then discuss the word meanings by applying the meaning of the prefix to the base word, as "If you *dislike* something or someone, it's the opposite of liking them; you don't like them." In some cases, the connection may be more implied than direct, as, for example, with *forecast*. You might ask students to hypothesize on what is being cast or thrown before. Students should realize that *f-o-r-e* in *forest* and *foreign* are just letters and not meaning units, as evident in the absence of a base word. Ask them if they can think of any other words that could have been included in the sort. If a word such as *distance* is mentioned, let students know that although *dis-* is a prefix in the word, *tance* is not a base word but a word root.

### Talking Points

- *Dis-*, *mis-*, and *fore-* are all prefixes. *Dis-* means "opposite of," *fore-* means "before, in front of," and *mis-* means "to do something wrongly."
- *Forest* and *foreign* are good reminders that words can look as though they have a prefix but do not have the meaning associated with a combined prefix and base word.

*Integrating Idioms:* "Last night when my brother was helping me with my math homework, he became frustrated and said that I **couldn't see the forest for the trees.**" (Let details get in the way of seeing how to solve the problems. You can get so bogged down with details [all the trees] of a situation that you actually lose sight of the big picture.)

*Did You Know?* **Foreign** and **forest** share ancestral beginnings; both come from Latin words for "outside"—*foris*, and *foras*. In ancient times anyone who lived outside and away from the town gates was considered *foreign*. Today we typically associate the word with "outside of a person's native country." The *g* in *foreign* which gives many spellers difficulty was added later and is thought to be the result of confusion with the spelling of either *reign* or *sovereign*. The word *forest* originally had no connection to trees. In medieval times it was a protected area in which royalty kept deer and other game for hunting and sport.

    *Spell,* as in **misspell,** developed from Middle English *spellen*, to "read letter by letter," which in turn came from an Old French word, *espeller*. *Spell* itself was probably first recorded over 600 years ago. The concept of a *spelling bee*, in which everyone's hope is to not *misspell*, came about during the first half of the 1800s and the phrase itself within a few decades. The meaning of *spell* as "a charm or trance" derives from an Old English word for "discourse" or "story." Whether referring to a "trance" or to "correct writing," the root of both words is *spel*. *Spel* comes from a large family of languages that includes most of Europe and parts of Asia. We can still see the root today in *gospel*, which literally means "good tidings" or "discourse." (For a list of common misspellings, check-your-spelling quizzes, and other activities, go to "Miss Spelling's Spelling Center" at *www.alphadictionary.com/articles/misspelling.html*.)

---

## SORT 44. Prefixes (*in-, in-, non-, pre-*)

### Sorting by Pattern and Meaning

| *in-* | *in-* | *non-* | *pre-* | Oddball |
|-------|-------|--------|--------|---------|
| **indent** | **inactive** | **nonstop** | **prepay** | **?** |
| income | incomplete | nonfat | precaution | pretzel |
| indoors | incorrect | nonfiction | preheat | |
| inflamed | indirect | nonsense | prejudge | |
| input | | nonsmoking | preschool | |
| insight | | | preteen | |
| | | | preview | |

*Considerations:* With this set of words, students learn about three more prefixes: *in-*, *non-*, and *pre-*. *Non-* means "not" and *pre-* means "before." Because *in-* can mean "in, into" as well as "not," the two meanings are treated as separate categories, so actually students will be working with four categories besides oddballs. *In-* is a common prefix, especially in lower frequency words, in which it often attaches to a root rather than to a base word; it is revisited at the next stage. Ask students to sort their words according to prefix and then to carefully consider meaning in order to subdivide the list of *in-* words. Next initiate a discussion of the words; encourage students to make meaning connections between the prefix and base words. By now students should readily recognize a word such as *pretzel* as an oddball, included to make sure they are thinking.

### Talking Points

- *In-, fore-,* and *non-* are three more prefixes. *Non-* means "not," *fore-* means "before, in front of," and *in-* can mean "in, into" but also "not."
- Because prefixes can have multiple meanings and more than one prefix can carry the same meaning, it's important to interpret and use them correctly. For example, *inactive* means "not active" rather than something that is actually "in action," and a room in which smoking is prohibited is a *nonsmoking* room, not an *insmoking* room.

*Integrating Idioms:* "You should have exercised precaution instead of **throwing caution to the wind**." (Being very careless. If you throw something to the wind, you're likely to lose it, because it will blow away and you won't be able to find it. It would be a very careless act.)

*Did You Know?* **Pretzel** has an interesting history or story behind it. The pretzel as we know it was likely first introduced in the United States during the 1800s by German immigrants. It (the *brezel*) had been enjoyed in German countries as a food item for several centuries before that, and its origins are even older. The knot-shaped pretzel probably goes back to medieval Latin and to a story that suggests that a monk first created the shape to symbolize arms folded in prayer. The word derives from *bracchiatus*, meaning "having branches," which in turn comes from a word for "branch," or "arm." Estimates of the average annual per person consumption of pretzels range from 2 pounds per year to 20 pounds. What might account for the large range (size of pretzel and person, where one lives, taste, etc.)?

## SORT 45. Suffixes (*-ful, -less, -ly, -ness*)

### Sorting by Pattern and Meaning

| *-ful* | *-less* | *-ly* | *-ness* |
|---|---|---|---|
| **careful** | **careless** | **loudly** | **illness** |
| cheerful | breathless | finally | darkness |
| colorful | helpless | friendly | coolness |
| painful | homeless | really | openness |
| peaceful | priceless | safely | stillness |
| thoughtful | | smoothly | weakness |
| useful | | | |

*Considerations:* This word study builds on previous suffix work with inflectional endings (*-ed, -ing, -er, -est, -s, -es*). The new suffixes are *-ful*, meaning "full of"; *-less*, meaning "without"; *-ness*, meaning "state of being"; and *-ly*, meaning "in a particular manner." Unlike earlier studies, which dealt with suffixes that begin with a vowel and require dropping the final *-e* or doubling the final consonant of the base word, here the suffix begins with a consonant and requires no change. This is an important concept for students to gain from their work. Inclusion of the words *peaceful, useful, homeless, priceless,* and *safely* illustrate this principle. Base words that end with the same consonant with which the suffix begins (*finally, really, openness*) help students to realize that double consonants can occur for reasons other than application of the doubling principle and that though they may not look right, meaning dictates their inclusion. Ask students to sort their words by suffix or guide them through the sort with modeling as needed. Discuss word meanings in light of the suffix and base word meanings. As part of the discussion, you might write *chilly* on the board or overhead and ask students to consider where it would be categorized. They should reason that it would be an oddball, because if you take away the base word *chill*, all that would remain is *-y*, a suffix but not one currently being examined. If desired, extend the sort with a review of parts of speech by asking students to categorize the words according to adjective, adverb, and noun, as follows:

## Sorting by Meaning

| Noun | Adjective | Adverb |
|------|-----------|--------|
| darkness | breathless | loudly |
| coolness | careful | finally |
| illness | careless | (friendly) |
| openness | cheerful | really |
| stillness | colorful | safely |
| weakness | (friendly) | smoothly |
| | helpless | |
| | homeless | |
| | painful | |
| | peaceful | |
| | priceless | |
| | thoughtful | |
| | useful | |

### Talking Points

- A *suffix* is a meaningful word part attached to the end of a base word to alter its meaning; knowing the meaning of suffixes can help you better understand words: *-ful* means "full of," *-less* means "without," *-ness* means "a state of being," and *-ly* means "in a certain way."
- Unlike previously studied suffixes that began with a vowel and usually required dropping a final *-e* or doubling a final consonant (such as *-ing*, *-ed*, and *-es*), suffixes that begin with a consonant do not require a change.

**Integrating Idioms:** "Dad says not to **hold my breath** on going to the movies Friday night." (Count on it. If you tried to hold your breath until something that was unlikely to occur happened, you would end up breathless.)

**Did You Know?** The adjective form of **coolness**, *cool*, has evolved with numerous meanings. Its original temperature-related meaning dates to well before the 1400s, when the word was spelled *col*. During Shakespeare's time (the 1500s) the idea of coolness was applied to less than enthusiastic feelings expressed about people, events, and so forth, as "He was pretty cool to my idea of turning in my project late." It was applied to money in the sense of a lot, "a cool million," during the 1700s. In the 1900s jazz, a type of music, was described as "cool," and people began to use the word to express the ideas of "good," "excellent," or "great" (the "coolest"). What other meanings might be added to the word in the new millennium?

War is a time of conflict; peace is the opposite, a state of harmony with an absence of hostility. When there is peace, there tends to be fairness, respect, and kindness. Both concepts have spawned scores of books, including at least one that features both words in its title—Tolstoy's *War and Peace*—and have given rise to numerous related words and phrases: *warlike, warlord, warrior, warplane, warship, wartime,* and *war chest* and **peaceful,** *peaceable, peacekeeper, peacemaker, peacenik, peacetime, Peace Corps, peace officer, peace offering, peace pipe, peace sign,* and others. The *Nobel Peace Prize* is awarded annually to individuals considered to have done the best job in promoting world peace. *Peace,* which was first recorded in the mid-1300s, was borrowed from Old French (*pais*), which came from the Latin words *pax* and *pac,* meaning "tranquility" and "absence of war." *Pacific Ocean* and *pacifier* also derive from the latter root (for further discussion of this root, see Part 3, Sort 48). What might the meaning connection be (*calm*)? The word *war* stems from a root meaning "mixed up" or "confused" (*liverwurst*, which is a type of sausage made up of a meat mixture, shares the same root and the meaning connection of "mixed up").

---

## SORT 46. Adding Suffix *-y* to Words with No Change, *E*-Drop, and Double

### Sorting by Pattern (and thinking about meaning—the base word)

| No Change | *E*-Drop | Double | Oddball |
|---|---|---|---|
| **grouchy** | **shady** | **sunny** | **?** |
| bossy | breezy | baggy | angrily |
| curly | crumbly | foggy | many |
| lengthy | drizzly | furry | |
| silvery | greasy | skinny | |
| squeaky | juicy | starry | |
| | noisy | | |
| | scary | | |
| | tasty | | |

*Considerations:* With their knowledge of base words and the no-change, *e*-drop, and doubling principles, many students will be able to approach this set of words as an open sort. Others will likely be able to categorize the words with minimal support; provide the headers and key words and possibly model one or two words. Go over any unfamiliar words at the onset and follow up the sorting with a discussion of the categories and oddball words and a review of the base words. You might ask students to record the base word at the bottom of each of the cards; for the oddballs, *many* is the base word rather than *man*, and *angrily* includes the suffix *-ly* affixed to *angry*. In addition to becoming aware of the different ways to add *-y*, students should recognize that adding the letter changes the part of speech; in most cases, the change is from noun to adjective. (Students may notice that some of the words, such as *taste, scare, crumble,* and *drizzle,* can or do function as verbs.) Nouns are not the only parts of speech that can become adjectives; though unusual, even a conjunction can: *if* → *iffy.* Invite students to choose nouns to change into adjectives by adding *-y: flowery, thorny, tinny,* and so forth. Students may enjoy learning that adjectives can also become nouns (but often ending in *-ie*), as in *soft* → *softy/softie, pink* → *pinky/pinkie, good* → *goody/goodie, brown* → *brownie, old* → *oldie, quick* → *quickie, sweet* → *sweetie.* Their usage is usually informal.

### Talking Points

• Adjectives ending in *-y* can be formed from many nouns by following the *e*-drop, doubling, and no-change principles for *-ed* and *-ing:* Drop the final *-e* before adding *-y;* double the final consonant and then add *-y,* if the noun ends in a VC pattern; and just add *-y* if the word includes a team of vowels or ends in more than one consonant.

*Integrating Idioms:* "I've only got a few minutes to **shoot the breeze.**" (Chat; engage in idle conversation. Even on a breezy day, to take aim at the gusts would not be a very productive use of time.)

*Did You Know?* Have you ever been in a situation in which you became sick of a noise? *Noise,* from which we get **noisy,** has long been associated with sickness. The word stems from *nausea,* a word that usually conjures up images of being sick and ready to vomit. *Nausea* derives from the Greek root for "ship," *naus,* and is related to other sea words—*naval* and *nautical* (see also Part 3, Sort 36).

Being on a ship often made people sick, and this in turn would lead to lots of crying out and complaints, giving rise to the word *noise*.

### Literature Link

Heller, R. (1989). *Many luscious lollipops: A book about adjectives*. New York: Grosset & Dunlap. Colorful, informative, and full of an exciting array of adjectives.

---

## SORT 47. Putting It All Together: Prefixes and Suffixes with Base Words

### Sorting by Meaning

| Prefix Only | Suffix Only | Prefix and Suffix | Suffix and Suffix | Prefix, Suffix, and Suffix |
|---|---|---|---|---|
| **redirect** | **wonderful** | **disrespectful** | **noisiest** | **unknowingly** |
| disqualify | beautiful | indebted | annoyingly | reassuringly |
| research | frequently | misleading | carelessness | unexpectedly |
| uncommon | happiness | unfriendly | fuzziness | |
| | heavily | | playfulness | |
| | ususally | | usefulness | |
| | worried | | | |

**Considerations:** This sort encourages students to pull together their understandings about prefixes and suffixes. You might introduce the sort and talk about word meanings by analyzing the words with students in a manner similar to the following, being sure to keep the focus on the gist of the meaning rather than exact wording.

*dis* ("the opposite of") + *respect* ("think highly of, regard") + *ful* ("full of") = "lack of regard for someone"

As you talk about each word, you might ask students to underline prefixes in one color and suffixes in another. Categorize each word after it is discussed according to the additions: *prefix only, suffix only; prefix and suffix; suffix and suffix; or prefix, suffix*, and *suffix*. Encourage students to collect and record more words throughout the week. Ask them to try to identify other category combinations besides those used in this sort and suggest that they create a listing, including the meaning, of the various prefixes and suffixes they come across.

**Integrating Idioms:** "She's a star and looks great, but I met her last summer, and she may be beautiful, but her **beauty is only skin deep**." (Superficial, on the surface. Once you get beyond a person's outward appearance and get to know the individual, you can find that the person acts in a way that is not so appealing.)

**Did You Know? Indebted** means "obligated to" or "in debt to" some other person. The tricky-to-spell silent letter *b* in *debt* was not always there. Its early spelling of *dette* (the end of the 13th century) was borrowed from an Old French word, *dete*; neither word included the letter *b*. However, a couple of hundred years later scholars added the *b* to both the French and English words to show that the word originally came from the Latin word *debitum*. The *b* was never pronounced and has been eliminated from the French but is maintained in English. Can you think of other words with silent letters? Might they have a similar story? How could you find out?

# SORT 42 Prefixes (*un-* and *re-*)

| un- | | re- |
|:---:|:---:|:---:|
| unwrap | rebuild | untied |
| rewrite | relish | unclear |
| return | unite | replace |
| unfair | rewind | unkind |
| remove | unsure | review |
| unhappy | reread | reorder |
| unable | recycle | unusual |
| reelect | uneven | ? |

# SORT 43 Prefixes (*dis-*, *fore-*, *mis-*)

| dis- | fore- | mis- |
|------|-------|------|
| dislike | forehead | mistrust |
| forest | forewarn | distrust |
| discover | misjudge | foresight |
| foreground | disorder | misprint |
| misplace | foremost | discomfort |
| disobey | misspell | mistake |
| forecast | mismatch | dishonest |
| disagree | foreign | ? |

# SORT 44 Prefixes (*in-*, *in-*, *non-*, *pre-*)

| in- | in- | non- | pre- |
|---|---|---|---|
| indent | inactive | | nonstop |
| prepay | incomplete | | preteen |
| insight | preview | | incorrect |
| nonfat | indirect | | nonsense |
| preheat | indoors | | pretzel |
| income | precaution | | inflamed |
| nonfiction | input | | prejudge |
| preschool | nonsmoking | | ? |

# SORT 45 Suffixes (*-ful*, *-less*, *-ly*, *-ness*)

| -ful | -less | -ly | -ness |
|------|-------|-----|-------|
| careful | careless | | loudly |
| illness | cheerful | | homeless |
| darkness | safely | | colorful |
| thoughtful | finally | | coolness |
| really | weakness | | painful |
| helpless | smoothly | | breathless |
| peaceful | stillness | | friendly |
| priceless | useful | | openness |

# SORT 46 Adding Suffix -y to Words with No Change, *E*-Drop, and Double

| No Change | E-Drop | Double |
|-----------|--------|--------|
| grouchy | shady | sunny |
| angrily | skinny | tasty |
| squeaky | greasy | scary |
| many | foggy | crumbly |
| curly | drizzly | breezy |
| juicy | starry | lengthy |
| furry | bossy | baggy |
| silvery | noisy | ? |

| Prefix | Suffix | Prefix & Suffix | Suffix & Suffix | Prefix, Suffix, & Suffix |
|---|---|---|---|---|
| redirect | | wonderful | | disrespectful |
| noisiest | | unknowingly | | worried |
| misleading | | usefulness | | usually |
| frequently | | disqualify | | playfulness |
| unexpectedly | | fuzziness | | indebted |
| annoyingly | | happiness | | research |
| beautiful | | unfriendly | | uncommon |
| carelessness | | heavily | | reassuringly |

# Additional Sorts

The sorts in this section address multisyllabic homophones and less common single-syllable homophones, homographs, and other compounds. For the studies of homophones (same sound–different spelling) and homographs (same spelling–different sound), game-like activities are used to encourage repeated reinforcement of spelling–meaning or pronunciation–meaning connections. Ten additional sorts focusing on compound words, including hyphenated compounds, are also included. They may be used as typical word sorts, or they may be introduced and then placed at a learning station.

## Homophones

*What Is Known:* By the end of the syllable juncture stage, students have examined the structures within and across syllables; vowel patterns in both stressed and unstressed syllables; consonant patterns; and various meaning units, including compound words, prefixes, and suffixes. They have been exposed to a few *homophones* (sound-alike words with different meanings) in earlier sorts and have likely dealt with single-syllable homophones at the within word pattern stage. Homophones used in previous sorts are asterisked.

*What Is New:* In homophones of more than one syllable, the spelling variation can occur in either a stressed or unstressed syllable, as in *morning/mourning* or *council/counsel*. Several homophones used in the following sorts are likely to have unfamiliar meanings.

---

**SORT 48.** Additional Sorts: Homophones Set 1

| | Sorting by Sound | |
|---|---|---|
| 1st Syllable Stressed | 2nd Syllable Stressed | Single-Syllable Trios (no stress) |
| **boarder/border** | **allowed*/aloud** | **cent/scent/sent** |
| berry/bury | ascent/assent | flew/flu/flue |
| ceiling/sealing | | rain/reign/rein |
| choral/coral | | vain/vane/vein |
| colonel/kernel | | |
| desert/dessert | | |
| fairy/ferry | | |
| marry/merry | | |
| morning/mourning | | |
| weather*/whether | | |

## SORT 49. Additional Sorts: Homophones Set 2

### Sorting by Sound

| 1st Syllable Unstressed | 2nd Syllable Unstressed | Single-Syllable Trios (no stress) |
|---|---|---|
| **accept/except** | **title/tidal** | **seas/seize/sees** |
| affect/effect | council/counsel | frees/freeze/frieze |
| | currant/current | peak/peek/pique |
| | dual/duel | raise/rays/raze |
| | hangar/hanger | |
| | lessen/lesson | |
| | manner/manor | |
| | miner/minor | |
| | muscle/mussel | |
| | patience/patients* | |

## SORT 50. Additional Sorts: Homophones Set 3

### Sorting by Sound

| Two-Syllable Pairs | Three-Syllable Pairs | Two-Syllable Trios |
|---|---|---|
| **cellar/seller** | **addition/edition** | **pedal/peddle/petal** |
| bazaar/bizarre | capital/capitol | carat/caret/carrot* |
| borough/burrow | cereal*/serial | medal/meddle/metal |
| cymbals/symbols* | complement/compliment | palate/palette/pallet |
| profit/prophet | principal/principle | |
| roomer/rumor | stationary/stationery | |

*Notes.* In Set 3, *mettle*, meaning "courage, spirit," could also be included with the *medal* group of homophones, and *burro*, a "small donkey," could be added to make a trio with *borough* and *burrow*.

**Considerations:** *Homophones* (sound-alike words with different meanings), sometimes called *homonyms*, are sources of numerous spelling confusions, largely because the spelling of one homophone is confused with the meaning of another. Because meaning plays such a critical role in correctly spelling homophones, the primary aim of the homophone studies that follow is to clarify and develop the vocabulary of students as means for helping them learn to spell the words. The categories serve to assist students as they talk about the words and, in some cases, to focus their attention on the part of the word with the spelling variation. Several single-syllable homophones of lower frequency are included in Set 1. A different format is used for the cards in these sorts to accommodate reinforcement through Homophone Rummy, a game that will enable students to become familiar with the word meanings and spellings and encourage repeated practice. Begin by reviewing what a homophone is. Then ask the students to make pairs or trios of the various homophones in order to discuss their meanings. Elaborate or clarify as needed, and suggest a dictionary to settle any disputes. Next, invite students to help group the words. (See answer keys for possibilities.) Discuss the results. For follow-up practice, make sets of the cards available for Homophone Rummy; each set will accommodate 3–4 players. One more person may be designated as a "judge" to determine whether or not a response is correct. A reproducible answer key with sentence examples is provided in Appendix F. Although the 108 words included in this section have been divided into three sets, words from one set can be mixed with another after students have studied the words. If desired, more common single-syllable homophones can be mixed in for review (see *Word Sorts and More*, Ganske, 2006), or they can be used as a separate set for students at the within word pattern stage. Directions for the activity follow.

## Homophonic Rummy

Scramble the cards and distribute them one at a time to each of the players until everyone has six cards. Place the remaining cards face down in a draw pile. Turn over the top card and place it next to the pile. Before turn taking begins, players identify any pairs or trios of homophones they may have, place them on the table, and provide a definition for each of the words or use the words in sentences. If the meanings are correct, the cards remain on the table; if not, the player must pick them up again. Turn taking then begins.

Player 1 has the choice of taking the top card from the draw pile or selecting the face-up card next to it. If the latter decision is made, the card must be playable, that is, must complete a pair (or trio) in the player's hand. Player 1 lays any newly formed pairs (or trios) on the table and demonstrates understanding of the words, as described. Player 1 then discards by placing an unwanted card face up next to the already started line of discards; if that card has been picked up and used, the card is laid in its place to begin a new line of discards. Play then passes to Player 2, who has several options: (1) to draw from the draw pile, (2) to pick up the last card from the discard line, if it is playable, or (3) to select one of the other cards in the discard line, as long as it is playable. In this last instance, the player must also pick up all of the cards that follow the one chosen, even if they are not playable. Rotations of play continue until either someone runs out of cards (one way to end the game) or until no one can play any more cards (another way to end it). The decision about how to end the game should be determined at the onset of the game. In either case, the winner is the person who played the most cards. Note that trios of words may be played all at once by a single player, or the third card may be played by the same or another player at a later time, as long as the two related words have already been played. In either case, the player must demonstrate an understanding of the word's meaning.

### Talking Points

- *Homophones* are words that sound alike but have different meanings, *marry* and *merry*; they are sometimes called *homonyms*. Because homophones are the cause of many spelling errors, caution is needed when spelling this type of word.

***Integrating Idioms:*** "It doesn't work to **bury your head in the sand**; you need to face up to the matter. If you don't start completing the work, you're not going to pass the class." (Ignore a problem or sign of danger. This expression stems from the mistaken belief that because ostriches cannot fly, they burrow in the sand in order to hide. Actually, ostriches, like other fowl, take in sand or gravel to help digest their food.)

***Did You Know?*** **Muscle** and **mussel** not only sound alike but also share a common ancestry. Both words derive from the Latin word *musculus*, which means "little mouse." What, you might wonder, does a mouse have to do with bodily tissues that help our bodies to move or with a sea creature? If you ever watched someone with a well-developed arm muscle flex it, you will get a hint. As the muscle moves it resembles a small mouse, the tendons serving as the tail. The meaning connection of *mussel* is less clear. It may also relate to "mouse," as the basic outline of a mussel in its shell is similar to that of a mouse, or the connection may relate to "muscle." After all, in its shell a mollusk appears to be not much more than a muscle. Although it may seem like a tall tale to think that both *muscle* and *mussel* are named after a small rodent, it is interesting to note that the two words are also related in Greek: the Greek word *mys* came to mean both "mouse" and "mussel."

| boarder | allowed | fairy | whether |
|---------|---------|-------|---------|
| **boarder** | **allowed** | **fairy** | **whether** |
| weather | dessert | merry | ferry |
| **weather** | **dessert** | **merry** | **ferry** |
| desert | marry | aloud | border |
| **desert** | **marry** | **aloud** | **border** |

| morning | sealing | colonel | berry |
|---|---|---|---|
| morning | sealing | colonel | berry |
| assent | ceiling | bury | ascent |
| assent | ceiling | bury | ascent |
| coral | choral | kernel | mourning |
| coral | choral | kernel | mourning |

| | | | |
|---|---|---|---|
| cent | vane | reign | flu |
| **cent** | **vane** | **reign** | **flu** |
| flue | sent | vein | rain |
| **flue** | **sent** | **vein** | **rain** |
| rein | flew | vain | scent |
| **rein** | **flew** | **vain** | **scent** |

| accept | title | mussel | lessen |
|---|---|---|---|
| accept | title | mussel | lessen |
| miner | effect | lesson | minor |
| miner | effect | lesson | minor |
| except | muscle | affect | tidal |
| except | muscle | affect | tidal |

| manner | current | patients | hanger |
|---|---|---|---|
| manner | current | patients | hanger |
| duel | counsel | hangar | dual |
| duel | counsel | hangar | dual |
| council | patience | currant | manor |
| council | patience | currant | manor |

| | | | |
|---|---|---|---|
| seas | raze | frees | rays |
| **seas** | **raze** | **frees** | **rays** |
| frieze | peak | raise | pique |
| **frieze** | **peak** | **raise** | **pique** |
| seize | peek | freeze | sees |
| **seize** | **peek** | **freeze** | **sees** |

| cellar | addition | cereal | roomer |
|--------|----------|--------|--------|
| cellar | addition | cereal | roomer |

| cymbals | serial | symbols | capitol |
|---------|--------|---------|---------|
| cymbals | serial | symbols | capitol |

| capital | rumor | edition | seller |
|---------|-------|---------|--------|
| capital | rumor | edition | seller |

| profit | principal | borough | complement |
|--------|-----------|---------|------------|
| profit | principal | borough | complement |

| stationery | burrow | bazaar | stationary |
|------------|--------|--------|------------|
| stationery | burrow | bazaar | stationary |

| bizarre | compliment | principle | prophet |
|---------|------------|-----------|---------|
| bizarre | compliment | principle | prophet |

| | | | |
|---|---|---|---|
| pedal | carrot | medal | palate |
| pedal | carrot | medal | palate |
| caret | peddle | pallet | metal |
| caret | peddle | pallet | metal |
| palette | meddle | carat | petal |
| palette | meddle | carat | petal |

## Homographs

This section includes two sorts to increase students' understanding of *homographs*, words that have the same spelling but are pronounced differently and have different meanings. A sort may be used to introduce the words, but for follow-up practice, games such as Concentration or Export/Import, described later, are recommended. These will encourage repeated practice and add enjoyment to the study. Shifting the stress to come up with an alternative pronunciation will help students to be more flexible in their approach to reading homographs and other unfamiliar words encountered in text. For the games, a second template is included with sentence examples for the homographs. This template is formatted so that by cutting out the word card template and the sentence template, the two can be photocopied back-to-back for the Import/Export game.

*What Is Known:* Students have likely encountered homographs in their reading and spelling (e.g., *read*), but may not know the term for the concept. They should have a working knowledge of the patterns involved and be able to identify the stressed syllable. A few of the words have previously been studied (see asterisked words).

*What Is New:* Understanding that stress in a homograph relates to part of speech.

## SORT 51. Additional Sorts: Homographs Set 1

### Sorting by Sound and Meaning

| 1st Stress | 2nd Stress | Oddball |
|------------|------------|---------|
| Nouns | Verbs | ? |
| **ad**dress | ad**dress** | |
| **con**flict | con**flict** | |
| **des**ert* | de**sert*** | |
| **min**ute* | | mi**nute** (adjective)* |
| **ob**ject | ob**ject** | |
| **per**mit | per**mit** | |
| **pres**ent | pre**sent** | |
| **pro**duce | pro**duce** | |
| **proj**ect | pro**ject** | |
| **reb**el | re**bel** | |
| **rec**ord | re**cord** | |
| **ref**use | re**fuse** | |

## SORT 52. Additional Sorts: Homographs Set 2

### Sorting by Sound and Meaning

| 1st Stress | 2nd Stress | Oddball |
|---|---|---|
| Nouns | Verbs | ? |
| **con**tract | con**tract** | lead /lēd/ (n., v.) |
| **con**duct | con**duct** | lead /lĕd/* (n., adj.) |
| **in**crease | in**crease** | |
| **in**sert | in**sert** | |
| **in**sult | in**sult** | |
| **re**ject | re**ject** | |
| row /rou/ | row /rō/ | |
| **sub**ject | sub**ject** | |
| **sur**vey | sur**vey** | |
| tear /tîr/ | tear /târ/ | |
| wound /woond/ | wound /wound/ | |

*Considerations:* Because the spellings of homographs do not differ, Sorts 51–52 may be combined (24 different spellings will result), or they may be used separately. All of the words in Sort 51 have two syllables; Sort 52 includes both single-syllable and polysyllabic words. The stressed syllable is the source of pronunciation differences in polysyllabic homographs; this syllable is in bold type (in their work, students can underline or circle the stressed syllable). For other homographs, the pronunciation is recorded underneath the word. Before distributing the templates of words, begin by writing the following sentences on the board or overhead:

"The doctors and nurse showed a lot of **patience** toward their **patients**."
"If we **record** the conversation, we'll both have a **record** of the interview."

Ask students to read each of the sentences and then turn to a partner to talk about their observations. After a minute or two, ask them to tell what they noticed. They should realize that the first sentence contains a pair of homophones and that the second sentence includes two words that are spelled the same but sound different and have different meanings. Point out that just as we call the first pair *homophones* (write the word after the sentence) because they have the "same sound," so we call the second pair *homographs* (write this word also) because they have the "same writing" or spelling. Explain to students that most of the homographs they will be working with have two syllables, like those in the sentence. Because differences in pronunciation and meaning for these words relate to differences in stress, the stressed syllable is in bold print on their word cards. Refer back to *record* and *record* and ask students which syllable is stressed in each; underline it. Lay down the category headers Noun, Verb, and ?, and, beginning with the two words from the sentence, ask students to say the words, discuss their meanings, and determine their categories. When the sorting is complete, encourage students to share talking points with a partner. *Minute*, with a second-syllable stress, is an adjective and therefore an oddball; *lead* is also an oddball. When pronounced with a short vowel, it can be either a noun (*The lead in my pencil broke*) or an adjective (*The book said he died of lead poisoning*). As part of the discussion, you might remind students that the past tense verb is *led*, not *lead*.

To reinforce pronunciation–meaning connections with the homographs in this sort, as previously noted, a second page of sentence examples with the homographs is included for the games of Concentration and Import/Export, described next.

## Concentration

Students will likely have experience with this activity, though they may know it as Memory. For this homograph variation, they will need one complete set of word cards and sentence cards (namely, pages 1 and 2 of Sorts 51 or 52, except the following five cards: Noun, Verb, ?, Import, and Export, which are not needed in this game). Photocopy the set of homographs on one color of paper and the sentences on another color. Scramble the cards from each template. Place the homographs face down in a 6 × 4 array; next to this array make another 6 × 4 array, using the sentence cards. Player 1 begins by turning over one word from each array and reading aloud the word and sentence. If the two cards make a match (correct pronunciation and meaning), they are set aside, and Player 2 takes a turn. If the two cards do not make a match, the cards are returned to the array face down, and Player 2 takes a turn. Back and forth turn taking continues until all of the cards in the arrays have been used. The winner is the person with the most cards. A dictionary or expert can be used to settle disputes.

## Import/Export

This game is a variation of the OH NO! game included in *Word Sorts and More* (Ganske, 2006). It will be more challenging if words from both sorts, 51 and 52, are used. This will make a total of 48 words. Every pair or trio of students in the group will need a set of playing cards with the word photocopied on one side and the sentence on the other, as described at the onset of this section. Students should bear in mind that the sentences are merely examples to aid in verifying responses. Although the Noun, Verb, and ? cards will not be used in the game, the two gray cards (or four if both sets are used) labeled Import and Export will be used. Nothing should be printed on the back side of these cards. Determine playing order for the game; then place the cards in scrambled order, word-side up, as a stack on the table. If an Import or Export card chances to be on top, hide it randomly in the middle of the pile. The object of this game is to accumulate the most cards (one point is awarded for each card, plus a bonus point for each pair of homographs). To begin the game, Player 1 takes the top card from the pile, reads the word, and provides a definition or sentence for the word. Correct use of the word is verified by reviewing the sentence on the back of the card. If correct, Player 1 keeps the card, starting a points pile of cards. If incorrect, the card is returned to the bottom of the stack, word-side up. (Sentences on the cards are just examples; if in doubt about the correctness of a response, consult a dictionary or expert.) Player 2 then takes a turn and follows the same process. If Player 2, or any other player, draws an Import card, Player 2 earns the right to "import" or select a card from each of the other players' accumulated cards to add to his or her own collection of cards. As long as Player 2 can pronounce the word and provide a correct meaning for it, Player 2 may keep the card. Otherwise the card is returned to the bottom of the draw pile. Players who have not accumulated cards are passed over in the importing process. A similar but opposite procedure is followed when an Export card is drawn. In this case, the player must give each of the other players an accumulated card to add to their collections. When exporting cards, if the player does not have enough cards for each of the other players, the player distributes the card(s) in a clockwise manner until they are used up. In order to keep an exported card, the receiving player must correctly identify the word and its meaning. Otherwise, it is returned to the bottom of the card pile. Turn taking continues in like manner until all of the cards have been correctly identified. Import and Export cards are set aside after being drawn; they are not reused and do not count in the final scoring. The game ends when there are no more cards to be drawn; cards and pairs of homographs are counted and totaled to determine the winner.

*Integrating Idioms:* "First I couldn't find my homework, then I missed the bus because of looking for it, and then to **add insult to injury** I got in trouble for coming to class late." (To worsen an already bad situation. If you were suffering from an injury and someone came along and insulted you about something, it would just make the situation worse.)

*Did You Know?* When you **survey** something or distribute a survey to people to find out their views on a matter, you are taking a very close look at whatever it is. So it is not surprising that *survey* stems from a Latin word, meaning "super look."

Although the origins of **row** /rō/ as a line of people or objects, or as an action for forwarding a boat are known and directly relate to the meaning, the origin of *row* /rou/ as a noisy disturbance is unknown. What do you think the story of this word might be?

| | | |
|---|---|---|
| **ad**dress | ad**dress** | **min**ute |
| mi**nute** | ob**ject** | **des**ert |
| **pro**duce | **con**flict | re**cord** |
| re**fuse** | de**sert** | **ob**ject |
| pro**duce** | **ref**use | pre**sent** |
| **rec**ord | con**flict** | **proj**ect |
| per**mit** | pro**ject** | **reb**el |
| **pres**ent | re**bel** | **per**mit |
| **Noun** | **Verb** | **?** |

| | | |
|---|---|---|
| I'll be with you in just a **minute**. | Please help me to **address** these envelopes. | What is the **address** of the company? |
| The **desert** is a hot, dry place. | I **object** to walking all the way home. | There was a **minute** particle of dirt in her eye. |
| Will you help me to **record** a CD? | They must resolve the **conflict** between the two countries. | The corner market always has lots of fresh **produce**. |
| We need to move that **object** off the table. | I am surprised he was willing to **desert** his friend. | I **refuse** to clean up my brother's room. |
| They will **present** the trophy during halftime. | Trash collection is tomorrow, so I took the **refuse** out. | They're going to **produce** a movie here next year. |
| I've finished the **project**, and it's not due until next week. | The play and game schedules **conflict**. | She broke the **record** for running the quarter mile. |
| My little sister's a **rebel**; she never does what you ask. | Can you **project** your pictures onto the screen? | She'll **permit** me to use her calculator for the project. |
| You need a **permit** before you can drive the car. | If we have peas one more time for dinner, I'm going to **rebel**. | I have never seen such a big and beautiful **present**. |
| **Export** | **Import** | |

| wound /woond/ | **con**duct | in**crease** |
|---|---|---|
| in**sert** | row /rō/ | **sub**ject |
| sur**vey** | **re**ject | tear /tîr/ |
| tear /târ/ | con**tract** | **in**sert |
| in**sult** | row /rou/ | con**duct** |
| lead /lĕd/ | sub**ject** | **in**sult |
| **in**crease | wound /wound/ | **con**tract |
| **sur**vey | re**ject** | lead /lēd/ |
| **Noun** | **Verb** | **?** |

From *Mindful of Words* by Kathy Ganske. Copyright 2008 by The Guilford Press. Permission to photocopy this form is granted to purchasers of this book for personal use only (see copyright page for details). Enlarge 135% to fill page.

| | | |
|---|---|---|
| We need to **increase** environmental awareness. | The child's **conduct** was unacceptable. | The nurse came to bandage the man's **wound.** |
| My favorite **subject** is science. | Stand in the front **row** so you can see them **row** past. | Please **insert** these flyers into the newspapers. |
| A **tear** fell from her eye as she listened to the sad story. | I don't want the shirt; it's a **reject**. | We had to **survey** the class about their favorite books. |
| That store always has an **insert** in the Sunday paper. | Muscles **contract** in the cold. | Be careful when you turn the pages so you don't **tear** them. |
| Some metals **conduct** electricity better than others. | There was quite a **row** at the bus stop today. | Mom says if you **insult** people they won't be your friends. |
| After the **insult** the clerk apologized. | Why **subject** us to the torture of memorizing dates? | The **lead** of my pencil broke, *or* This is a **lead** pipe. |
| They signed a **contract** when they bought the house. | She **wound** the string into a ball. | Scientists say there is an **increase** in volcanic activity. |
| He will **lead** the group this time. | If you **reject** the invitation, you may not be asked again. | The telephone **survey** was about shopping interests. |
| **Import** | **Export** | |

## More Compound Words

Each of the 10 sorts that follow is themed; in other words, the categories all relate to a particular topic. For instance, in the Space sort each of the compounds includes one of the following words as part of the compound: *sun, moon, star,* or *sky*. The sorts may be introduced as open sorts with an aim that students determine a theme that unifies the categories. It is not necessary for students to formally work with each of the compound sorts. Select those that seem most appropriate for particular content areas or for the students' needs or use them as a break from other features being studied or to simplify planning when you need to be absent. You might also include some of the sorts in station activities after briefly discussing the meaning connections. If word hunts are incorporated as part of the study of compounds, allow students to search for other compound words, and then group their findings into categories of their own choosing. Searching for the particular categories included in each of the following sorts may be too limiting and may lead to a frustrating experience for students. You might also ask students to illustrate the individual words in found compounds and then invite peers to try to guess the entire word.

**What Is Known:** For the following compound-word sorts students should be quite confident in their use of letter name and within word pattern features. Depending on when the sorts are used, they may also know features at the syllable juncture stage.

**What Is New:** The sorts in this section review compound words as two words put together to make a new word, while providing opportunities to expand vocabulary and consider the meaning of words and their word parts. The final two sorts, with hyphenated compounds, will likely be the most challenging for students.

---

## SORT 53. Compounds with Substance Words

### Sorting by Meaning

| *air* | *fire* | *land* | *water* |
|---|---|---|---|
| **airplane** | **fireplace** | **landmark** | **waterfall** |
| airborne | firearm | landfill | watercolor |
| aircraft | firecracker | landlady | waterlog |
| airline | firefly | landlord | watermark |
| airport | fireproof | landmass | watermelon |
| | fireworks | landscape | waterproof |
| | | landslide | |

**Considerations:** Be sure to discuss word meanings, as several of the words may be unfamiliar to some students; in particular, *airborne* (*borne* is the past participle of *to bear*, meaning "to carry"), *firearm, landfill, landmass,* and *landscape*. Ask students to explain the relationship of the two words to the compound as a whole. Students may brainstorm compounds with word parts similar in meaning to those used in the sort, such as *earth* and *sea*, as in *earthquake, earthworm, seashell, seacoast, seafood, seaport, seashore,* and *seasick*.

*Talking Points*

- Compound words are two words put together to make a new word. Thinking about the meanings of each of the smaller words can help to determine the meaning of the compound.

*Integrating Idioms:* "The candidate **won by a landslide**." (Won by a lot of votes. Sometimes in a real landslide, the whole side of a mountain comes sliding down.)

*Did You Know?* The first **watermark** was made in 1282 in Bologna, Italy. This impression is made by pressing a metal stamp or a wire design on a roller against freshly made paper before most of the water has been removed. Watermarked paper serves a variety of purposes. It discourages counterfeiting, identifies a product, and makes stationery and other paper more impressive by showing an institution's logo or seal. Does your school office use watermarked paper?

When we think of the word **landscape**, we are likely to think of an expansive natural scene that we can take in all at once (or perhaps of the horizontal paper placement for printing, as opposed to the vertical placement known as *portrait*). However, the word, which was first recorded in 1598, began as a term in the art world. Dutch painters of the time were perfecting a genre of painting known as *landscape*, which the English considered to mean "a picture showing scenery on land." Over 30 years passed before the English used the word to describe a scene in the world around them. Today we have other related words, such as *cityscape* and *landscape architect*. What do you think these words mean? (To show students examples of 16th-century Dutch landscapes, such as the work of Pieter Bruegel the Elder or his son Pieter, or other landscapes, try an art-related website, such as *www.allthemasters.com*, or search online for a virtual museum tour.)

## SORT 54. Compounds with Space Words

### Sorting by Meaning

| *sun* | *moon* | *star* | *sky* |
|---|---|---|---|
| **sunburn** | **moonbeam** | **starfish** | **skyline** |
| sunbathe | moonlight | starboard | skydive |
| Sunday | moonrise | starburst | skyrocket |
| sundial | moonscape | stargazing | skyscraper |
| sundown | moonwalk | starlit | skywriting |
| sunflower | | | |
| sunglasses | | | |
| sunlight | | | |
| sunstroke | | | |

*Considerations:* This sort contains several words whose meanings may be unfamiliar to some students: *sundial, sunstroke, moonrise, moonscape, starboard, starburst, skyline, skydive,* and *skywriting*. Thinking about the meanings of similar words, such as *moonscape–landscape* and *skywriting–handwriting*, or illustrating such words can help students with the vocabulary. (For an illustration of skywriting, see the work of Gritch the Witch in Margie Palatini's delightful tale *Piggie Pie!* The book contains numerous compound words as well.) After investigating the meaning of *starburst*, students might create their own with pastels or colored pencils. Students may benefit from a review of the *e*-drop principle that is at work in *stargaz(e)ing* and *skywrit(e)ing*. While discussing the various *moon* words, invite students to ponder the meanings of *earthlight* or *earthshine* and *earthrise*. The meanings are similar to their *moon* counterparts but with a different perspective. *Earthrise* refers to the rising of the earth above the moon's horizon and *earthlight* to the sunlight reflected from the earth's surface that lights up part of the moon.

### Talking Points

- Knowledge of a known compound word can often be used to understand an unfamiliar one, as in *landscape* for *moonscape* or *handwriting* for *skywriting*.

***Integrating Idioms:*** "We haven't had extra recess time **in a month of Sundays**." (A very long time. Suppose there are 30 days in a month; a month of Sundays would be 30 weeks, or about 7½ months!)

***Did You Know?*** The word **skyscraper** was first used in the late 1800s to describe a tall ornament on the top of a building rather than the building itself. In more recent times *skyscraper* has come to mean a "very tall building." But just how tall does a building have to be to be called a *skyscraper*? It is really a matter of perspective: After all, is our idea of a very tall building the same as that of our grandparents and great-grandparents? Over time greater and greater heights have earned the distinction of *skyscraper*. In 1873 the tallest building was 142 feet high and had 6 floors. By 1890, the tallest building included 15 stories. Though staggering for its time, the building was soon dwarfed in 1913 by the Woolworth Building in New York City, which had 60 stories. The well-known Empire State Building in New York became the tallest building in 1931 with 102 stories and a height of 1,250 feet, plus its spire. It remained the tallest building for some 40 years, when it was surpassed by the 1,454-foot, 110-floor Sears Tower in Chicago. Although the Sears Tower remains the tallest building in the United States, taller buildings are found in Malaysia (1,883 feet) and Taiwan (1,671 feet). As taller and taller buildings are planned and constructed, what will the limiting factors be?

   **Skywriting**, first recognized as a word in 1923, was developed by an English aviator in 1922. Skywriting creates words by releasing visible vapor from an airplane. How long the image lasts depends on the wind, but it typically disappears within a few minutes. Skywriting usually consists of one or two words used as an advertisement or other message, such as the warning "Surrender, Dorothy" written by the Wicked Witch of the West in the 1939 movie version of *The Wizard of Oz*. A more advanced form of skywriting called *skytyping* relies on a fleet of 5–7 specially equipped planes that electronically type out a message composed of little dots, similar to a dot-matrix printer. Messages created this way can be 15 miles long, seen for 40 miles, and last up to about 30 minutes. Although some people may be fascinated by skywriting and skytyping, others regard this form of media as a type of pollution. What are your thoughts about it?

## SORT 55. Compounds with Opposite Words

### Sorting by Meaning

| work | play | day | night | Oddball |
|------|------|-----|-------|---------|
| **workshop** | **playground** | **daylight** | **nightmare** | **?** |
| workbench | playbill | birthday | (fortnight) | (fortnight) |
| workbook | playhouse | daybreak | nightfall | (playwright) |
| workman | playroom | daydream | nightgown | |
| workout | (playwright) | daylily | nighttime | |
| workroom | | daytime | | |
| | | today | | |

**Considerations:** *Nighttime* may present a spelling challenge for some students who find that the double *t*'s "don't look right." This provides a great opportunity to emphasize that compound words are composed of two or more words and that without the double *t*'s that meaning element is lost. You will likely need to discuss the meaning of *fortnight* (a period of two weeks, or 14 days), which will probably be unfamiliar to students. Although the word looks as though it is connected to our word *fort*, it is really an altered spelling of the Old English word for "fourteen." Also, while discussing the meaning of *playhouse*, call students' attention to the word's meaning as *a theater* if they do not suggest it. This meaning also occurs in *playbill* (a theater program) and *playwright* (one who writes plays). Some students will likely be unfamiliar with the meaning of *bill* (a public notice) and *wright* (one who makes or repairs something, as in *shipwright* and *wheelwright*). They may not even consider *wright* a word and think it should be classified as an oddball; this is fine. Students might enjoy being "wordwrights" and coining other possible "wright" words. Note that the meaning of *smith* is similar to that of *wright* but usually refers to one who works with or makes things from metals, as in *blacksmith, goldsmith, locksmith, silversmith, tinsmith.* An exception, *wordsmith,* is often used to describe a person who is good at using words or is knowledgeable about them. Students are likely to become wordsmiths through their word studies. Some students may prefer to place *birthday* and *today* in the oddball category because the targeted word part appears in the second syllable rather than the first.

### Talking Points

- The spelling of a compound word may not "look right," but it is important to keep in mind the meaning connection, as in *nighttime,* not *nightime.*

**Integrating Idioms:** "After working on the project for a week, we could begin to **see daylight.**" (See the end of the project approaching. If you were moving through a long tunnel, it would seem very dark until almost at the end.)

**Did You Know?** The common **daylily** has flowers that last only one day. Each plant gets many buds, so each day there are new flowers to see. There are about 60,000 different kinds of daylilies and nearly every color but blue. Some daylilies are even scented. Although daylilies originated in Eurasia, they are very adaptable and are found in very cold, as well as very warm, climates. Another flower also has ties to the word *day.* Although the word *daisy* does not contain the *d-a-y* spelling, it does relate in meaning. The word comes from the Old English name, *daeges-eages,* meaning "day's eye," and is pronounced similar to *daisy.* The meaning connection stems from the flower's tendency to close its petals at night and reopen during the day to reveal its round center.

## SORT 56. Compounds with Around the Home Words

### Sorting by Meaning

| *home* | *bed* | *bath* | *table* | *door* |
|---|---|---|---|---|
| **homemade** | **bedtime** | **bathtub** | **tabletop** | **doorbell** |
| homebody | bedbugs | bathhouse | tablecloth | doorkeeper |
| homecoming | bedroll | bathrobe | tablespoon | doorknob |
| homeland | bedside | bathroom | tableware | doorstep |
| homesick | bedspread | bathwater | | |
| homework | | | | |

*Considerations:* Discuss word meanings as needed. *Bathhouse*, like *nighttime* in the previous sort, provides opportunity for students to see that even though a spelling may not look right, as in the case of the double *h*'s, meaning dictates that both letters be included.

*Talking Points:* The word *bathhouse*, with its double consonants, is a good reminder that meaning dictates the spelling of compounds.

*Integrating Idioms:* "Hey, just because we know one idea doesn't work, let's not **throw the baby out with the bathwater**." (Get rid of the good in the process of getting rid of something bad. What a loss it would be if, in throwing out the dirty bathwater, the baby was cast out also.)

*Did You Know?* Students might enjoy speculating on the meaning of the well-known phrase "Sleep tight and don't let the **bedbugs** bite." Although they are likely to realize that the intention is to sleep well, they may never have given consideration to the word *tight*. Before the days of bedsprings, mattresses were placed on ropes tightly stretched across the length of the bed. A saggy bed would not lead to good sleep; thus the wish to "sleep tight." As for bedbugs, no one back then or now wants those around for a restful night. Bedbugs are flat, reddish brown in color, and about ¼ inch long. They hide out during the day and come out at night to feed on human blood. (For further information on this and similar creatures, see the article "Body Beasts" in *National Geographic*'s Spring 2007 issue of *Extreme Explorer*.)

## SORT 57. Compounds with Position Words

### Sorting by Meaning

| *down* | *up* | *over* | *out* | *under* |
|---|---|---|---|---|
| **download** | **upset** | **overcoat** | **outdoors** | **underline** |
| downcast | upbeat | overcast | outbreak | underbrush |
| downpour | upcoming | overgrown | outcast | underground |
| downspout | upkeep | overheard | outgoing | understand |
| downstairs | | overlook | (outrage) | |
| | | | outside | |

*Considerations:* The words that form part of each of the compound words in this sort are found in many other words. You may wish to include or substitute other possibilities, such as *downfall, downhill, downstream, downtown, update, upend, uphold, uphill, upright, uproar, uproot, upscale, upside down, overbite, overflow, overhang, overload, oversleep, overthrow, outcome, outcry, outfield, outlaw, outline, underdog, understate,* or *underwear.* Note that the word *outrage* looks like a compound, but as its "Did You Know?" story relates, it really is not. Although no "?" card is included, students may choose to place it to the side after hearing its story. For this and other compound word studies, consider providing students with opportunities to write riddles using the compound in the question or the answer. For example, here is one from a wonderful website (*www.rickwalton.com/curricul/ comprid.htm*) with numerous activity ideas for compounds:

Q:  We know that sometimes it rains cats and dogs, but what do we call it when it rains ducks?

A:  A downpour.

*Talking Points:* Sometimes the meaning connection of a compound to its individual parts is unclear, as with *understand.* (*Under* used to mean "among" or "between"; perhaps if you stood among or between people, plants, animals, or objects, your on-the-spot vantage point would enable you to clearly grasp or *understand* the situation.)

*Integrating Idioms:* "If we're going to solve this problem, you've got to **think outside the box.**" (Consider atypical possibilities. A box is used to contain something; its insides are all the same and usually quite blank. Solving problems often requires considering various possibilities and thinking creatively.)

*Did You Know?* Although today we commonly associate **outrage** with *rage,* as though the word were formed by *out + rage,* the word is actually a borrowing from the French *outrage* (*outré* meaning "beyond") plus the Latin ending *-age.* To understand the meaning connection, consider that when something is an outrage, it is so bad that it is beyond our ability to think of it occurring, especially in this day and age.

## SORT 58. Compounds with Weather Words

### Sorting by Meaning

| *rain* | *wind* | *snow* | *thunder* | Oddball |
|---|---|---|---|---|
| **raindrop** | **windburn** | **snowball** | **thunderbolt** | ? |
| rainbow | windbreak | snowdrift | thundercloud | hailstone |
| raincoat | windfall | snowflake | thunderhead | |
| rainproof | windmill | snowmobile | thunderstorm | |
| rainstorm | windpipe | snowshoe | | |
| | windshield | snowstorm | | |
| | windstorm | | | |

*Considerations:* Discuss the meanings of *windbreak, windfall, windpipe, snowshoe, thunderhead, hailstone,* and any other words that may be unfamiliar. For some of the words, using a picture may be the easiest way to build understanding of the word's meaning. When discussing *snowshoe*, you might ask students to consider why a particular rabbit found in the northern part of North America is called the *snowshoe rabbit*. An online search could be used to validate their thoughts. Students may suggest placing the *-storm* words in a separate category. If they do, ask them to consider the meaning connection to *brainstorm*.

## Talking Points

- Sometimes the meaning of a compound is unclear from its parts because the meaning is figurative rather than literal, as in *windfall*. (If something fell from the wind, it would likely be sudden and unexpected; the connotation of a *windfall* as something of benefit was added later.)

*Integrating Idioms:* "I hope Mr. Eeger doesn't assign another book and paper today; I'm **snowed under** right now with projects." (Overwhelmed. Just as a snowstorm can deeply bury plants and objects [see Did You Know? below], work sometimes piles up, making people feel like they are buried.)

*Did You Know?* **Wind** is a word that we have had since the middle of the 700s, and it has the same spelling today that it had back then. When we think of **thunder** we may not associate it with wind, but we usually do with a recent flash of lightning. Because light and sound travel at different speeds, the amount of time between the flash and the thunder depends on how far away the lightning occurred. If the lightning bolt is a mile away, it will be about 5 seconds before we hear the thunder. If it is 10 miles away, it will take nearly a minute. If it is more than 15, we will not even hear it. When lightning strikes nearby, the thunder is extremely loud.

Weather that extends beyond the norm often catches our attention; for instance, consider the wettest place on earth, a mountain in Hawaii, where for the past 20 years the average annual rainfall has been 460 inches! Or how about the greatest annual snowfall—a whopping 1,140 inches recorded at a ski area in Bellingham, Washington, during 1998–1999. Or the 318 miles per hour winds, the highest ever recorded by the U.S. Weather Service, that occurred during a 1999 tornado in Oklahoma. What other extreme weather situations are you aware of?

## Literature Links

Barrett, J. (1978). *Cloudy with a chance of meatballs*. New York: Scholastic. The unusual weather in the town of Chewandswallow is sure to engage students across the grades in this longtime favorite picture book; or try the sequel, *Pickles to Pittsburg* (1997).

Libbrecht, K. (2007). *The art of the snowflake: A photographic album*. St. Paul, MN: Voyageur Press. View pages and pages of incredible macrophotography that has captured snowflakes in color with all their beauty, detail, and uniqueness.

Martin, J. B. (1998). *Snowflake Bentley*. Boston: Houghton Mifflin Company. This Caldecott award-winning picture-book describes the story of Wilson Bentley, a scientist who first photographed snowflakes.

**SORT 59.** Compounds with Food Words

Sorting by Meaning

| *corn* | *bean* | *pea* | *butter* | *egg* |
|--------|--------|-------|----------|-------|
| **corncob** | **beanbag** | **peanut** | **butterfly** | **eggshell** |
| cornflower | beanpole | peacock | butterball | eggbeater |
| cornhusk | beanstalk | peashooter | buttercup | egghead |
| cornmeal | | | butternut | eggnog |
| cornrows | | | butterscotch | eggplant |
| cornstalk | | | | |
| cornstarch | | | | |
| popcorn | | | | |

*Considerations:* When possible, use illustrations, photographs, or real objects to help explain word meanings; otherwise students may draw inaccurate conclusions. For example, students may mistakenly think of a wire whisk when considering what an eggbeater is. Also, ask the students to speculate on the meaning connections of such words as *cornrows, peacock, butterfly, egghead,* and *eggnog.* Students who wish to may consider *popcorn* an oddball word, because *corn* is at the end of the word. They may also wonder about *nog* as a word. *Nog,* a strong alcoholic beverage, was often added to the eggs, milk, and sugar mixture we think of as *eggnog.*

### Talking Points

- Words that are found in numerous compounds sometimes appear at the beginning of the word and sometimes at the end, as in *cornmeal* and *popcorn.*

*Integrating Idioms:* "Before a test I always **get butterflies** in my stomach." (Feel nervous. If you really had butterflies in your stomach fluttering around, they would give you a very uneasy feeling.)

*Did You Know?* Students may or may not have heard **corn** used to describe a horny hardening of the skin on a person's toe, but this meaning, which derives from a different source than the corn you eat, is related to both unicorn ("one horn") and to the cornucopia of Thanksgiving ("horn of plenty"). The edible *corn* comes from an Old English word meaning "grain" and often referred to the most common type of grain. In the United States the word refers to the eared grain—*Indian corn* or *maize.* In England it refers to wheat, in Scotland and Ireland to oats, and in Germany *korn* refers to rye. Corn or maize comes from Central America and Mexico. The United States grows a lot of corn. How much is *a lot?* According to the National Corn Growers of America website (*www.ncga.com*), over the past several years the United States has produced nearly 11 billion bushels of corn each year; considering that each bushel weighs about 56 pounds that means about 28,000,000 tons of corn are produced. Most of that (around 50%) is used to feed livestock in this country; only about 11% is used for breakfast cereal, starch, sugar, and other food items. In recent years corn has been increasingly used (currently about 18%) to produce a type of fuel known as ethanol. Why do you think there is an interest in producing this type of fuel? What might be the pros and cons? Is ethanol available at gas stations in your area?

The origins of **butterfly** are unclear, but *The American Heritage Dictionary of the English Language* (3rd ed., 1996) offers two colorful possibilities: (1) An early Dutch name for *butterfly* suggests that this flying creature may have been named after the color of its excrement, and (2) it was believed to be a mischievous witch transformed into a flying insect who liked to steal milk and butter. What do you think? For more information on butterflies, see one of the many books written on the topic, such as *Butterflies!* (2006) by the editors of *Time for Kids* or *Amazing Butterflies and Moths* (Still, 1991), a book in the Eyewitness Junior series.

### Literature Links

U'Ren, A. (2003). *Mary Smith*. New York: Farrar, Straus & Giroux. A picture-book story based on the life of Mary Smith, who lived in London in the early 20th century and who had an usual way of waking people up before the days of reliable and affordable alarm clocks: a peashooter.

---

## SORT 60. Compounds with Color Words

### Sorting by Meaning

| *black* | *white* | *blue* | *green* | *red* |
|---|---|---|---|---|
| **blacktop** | **whitecap** | **bluebird** | **greenhouse** | **redhead** |
| blackball | whiteout | bluebell | greenbelt | redwood |
| blackberry | whitewash | blueberry | greenhorn | |
| blackbird | | bluegill | Greenland | |
| blackboard | | bluegrass | greenroom | |
| blackmail | | blueprint | | |
| blackout | | | | |
| blacksmith | | | | |

*Considerations:* Several words in this sort may be unfamiliar to students. Be sure to discuss the meanings thoroughly and in multiple ways. Pictures and artifacts may be of help in enabling students to comprehend the concepts. Depending on the geographic area, students may be more or less knowledgeable about a particular word. For example, students living in mountainous regions may have firsthand experience with a *whiteout*, and children in the urban northeast areas may understand *blackout*. Similarly, few students from Kentucky will likely need assistance with *bluegrass*. Some students may know a *blackberry* only as a fruit or only in an electronic sense, *BlackBerry*. *Greenland*, the largest island in the world, can be located on a map; students might search to discover why it is named as it is. After all, nearly all of Greenland lies in the Arctic Circle. You might also play a game of Would You . . . ? using some of the words. Provide students with clues such as: Would you whitewash a blackboard; why or why not? Would you be more likely to find an environmentalist or an actor in a greenroom? Would your rather smell a bluebell or a bluegill? Would you find a greenbelt in a closet or outside a town?

### Talking Points

• Spoken compounds can have very different meanings, as in *blackberry* and *BlackBerry*.

*Integrating Idioms:* Following are explanations of several common idioms with color-related words. The words are not in this sort because they are compounded either through hyphenation or by writing the words separately:

"The thief was **caught red-handed** with the vase." (Caught in the act of doing something wrong, as though with the blood of a terrible deed still on the criminal's hands.) "His report card so impressed his parents that they gave him the **red-carpet treatment**." (Treated him very special. The phrase refers to the fact that a red carpet is sometimes unrolled for an important person to walk on.) "It says here **in black and white** that your journal is due every Tuesday." (Written down. The expression refers to black type on white newsprint or other paper.)

*Did You Know?*  The word *blackmail* has nothing to do with the post office. In Scotland during the 1500s, farmers were treated unfairly. Besides working hard, they also had to deal with outlaws who forced them to pay a fee to have their land protected. If the fee was not paid, their crops were destroyed. The word *blackmail* comes from a Scottish word meaning *rent* or *tax* and from the common association of dark or bad with the word *black*, as in *blackball*.

One story about the origin of **greenhorn** relates to a type of 17th- and 18th-century jewelry making. Certain decorative pieces were made from brown-colored animal horn and set in silver. The horn was impressed with a figure, often a head, and heated to complete the process. If temperatures too high were used, the horn turned green. Because apprentices were often the cause of this, the word came to refer to any inexperienced person.

On a brief and final color note, ask students who are familiar with BlackBerry technology to speculate on the name's origin. According to Wikipedia, a sort of collaborative, online encyclopedia (*wiki* = Hawaiian for "quick" + *pedia* = short for "encyclopedia"), when name experts were considering possibilities, someone noted that the miniature buttons looked like the seeds of a strawberry. The idea of calling the tool a *StrawBerry* was not popular because the word *straw* didn't seem to have the right flow when said. Someone else soon suggested *BlackBerry*, and the name stuck.

### Literature Links

Macaulay, D. (1990). *Black and white.* New York: Houghton Mifflin. Four stories or one story? A cleverly written book that can be enjoyed on various levels.
O'Neill, M. (1989). *Hailstones and halibut bones.* New York: Doubleday. Twelve poems that reveal how various colors look, sound, feel, smell, and taste.

---

## SORT 61. Hyphenated Compounds

| Sorting by Meaning | | | | |
|---|---|---|---|---|
| Body | Numbers | Sports | Heat/Cold | Oddball |
| **hands-on** | **first-class** | **all-star** | **warm-blooded** | **?** |
| dog-ear | fifty-fifty | out-of-bounds | freeze-dried | hot dog |
| empty-handed | forty-five | runner-up | ice-cold | ice cream |
| head-on | one-sided | time-out | red-hot | |
| left-handed | twenty-one | | | |
| right-handed | two-faced | | | |
| tongue-tied | | | | |

*Considerations:* Discuss the meanings of any unfamiliar words. When possible, demonstrate the meaning or have students act it out, especially words such as *dog-ear, tongue-tied,* and *two-faced.* You might ask students to illustrate the literal and figurative meanings of these particular words. Also, remind students that numbers are consistently hyphenated but to beware of other words or phrases that sound like compounds, because compounds can be joined into one word, hyphenated, or even written as two separate words, such as *hot dog* and *ice cream*. What is more, one form of the word may be used one time and another the next time, depending on the context of the sentence and the meaning of the word. Also, a few words may be correctly spelled in several ways. For example, all of the following are correct:

> I ate a hot dog for lunch.
> I ate a hotdog for lunch.
> My little brother likes to hot-dog on his skateboard.
> What's your favorite kind of ice cream?
> Shall we get an ice-cream cone before we leave?

Notice in the previous sentence that *ice cream* is acting like an adjective instead of a noun. When that is the case, the word or phrase is usually hyphenated, as in *She is in fifth grade* versus *A fifth-grade boy just moved into our neighborhood*. Writers sometimes create their own hyphenated compounds to add interest to a story, as Margie Palatini (see also Sort 54, "Considerations") has done in *Piggie Pie!* with the phrases *dragon-tongue pudding* and *still-smoking tootsies*. *Such hyphenated compounds may consist of two tied-together words or a whole string, as in never-to-be-completed homework*. You might invite students to try their hands at creating hyphenated compounds to describe one of the following nouns or a noun of their own choosing:

> *fence     clothes     house     book*

### Talking Points
- When two or more words describing a noun seem to work together, they should probably be hyphenated as a compound word.

*Integrating Idioms:* "You can't **be two-faced** and expect people to like you." (Be insincere. The person acts like two different people by saying one thing but acting in a different way.)

*Did You Know?* Americans are ice-cream lovers. Each of us eats about 15 quarts of **ice cream** each year. Just think of how many cows it takes to supply the milk and cream for the population of a large city! Though the word was first recorded in 1744, for more than 70 years before that, it was called *iced cream*, just like our *iced tea* and *iced coffee* of today. For all of our love of this tasty treat, its origins go back much farther than 17th-century England, to ancient Rome, China, and India.

## SORT 62. Hyphenated Compounds with Repeated Elements

### Sorting by Meaning

| Noun | Verb | Adjective/Adverb |
|---|---|---|
| **eager-beaver** | **dilly-dally** | **itty-bitty** |
| bow-wow | (fiddle-faddle) | (harum-scarum) |
| fender-bender | (hurry-scurry) | helter-skelter |
| (fiddle-faddle) | (pitter-patter) | lovey-dovey |
| flip-flop | (shilly-shally) | pell-mell |
| fuddy-duddy | (teeter-totter) | rinky-dink |
| heebie-jeebies | | (shilly-shally) |
| (hurry-scurry) | | teeny-weeny |
| hocus-pocus | | willy-nilly |
| nitty-gritty | | wishy-washy |
| (pitter-patter) | | |
| razzle-dazzle | | |
| (shilly-shally) | | |
| (teeter-totter) | | |

*Note.* Words that act as multiple parts of speech are shown in parentheses.

*Considerations:* Compound words are not always composed of two words, as in the previous sorts. Although some of the words in this set follow that pattern (*eager-beaver* and *flip-flop*, for instance), others do not. This sort includes many *reduplications*, words formed with doubled parts that differ in only a single element of the word, such as *flip-flop* and *wishy-washy*. (Meanings for all of the words in this sort are included at the end of this discussion.) Ability to spell the words may or may not be an aim of this sort; fostering appreciation for language, as well as building vocabulary, are goals. The sort can be used whenever teachers believe students are ready to handle it. The words may be categorized in ways other than by part of speech, if desired, such as changed part (e.g., vowel or consonant). Students might also classify the words as "can define," "have heard," and "unknown." The Would You . . . ? activity described in Sort 60 might also be used, as, for example: *If your family had a* **fender-bender***, would you be more likely to go home in a taxi or in the family car? If your teacher is about to explain the* **nitty-gritty** *of tonight's math homework, would you likely listen carefully or think about a weekend trip? If you were promised a chance to see your favorite movie, which of the following would you do:* **shilly-shally, dilly-dally***, or* **hurry-scurry***? Would you be more likely to regard a new baby brother or sister or a grandparent as a* **fuddy-duddy***? If a dog gave you the* **heebie-jeebies***, would your reaction to it be* **lovey-dovey** *or* **wishy-washy***?*

## Word Meanings

*Bow-wow*, bark of a dog; *dilly-dally*, dawdle; *eager-beaver* (slang/informal), person who is very, or overly, industrious; *fender-bender* (informal), a car accident involving minor damage; *fiddle-faddle*, nonsense, to waste time; *flip-flop*, a flapping sound or (when used informally) a reversal; *fuddy-duddy*, old-fashioned; *harum-scarum*, lacking sense, in a reckless manner; *heebie-jeebies* (old slang), jitters; *helter-skelter*, in a hurried manner, confused; *hocus-pocus*, foolishness, trickery; *hurry-scurry*, hurrying and confusion; *itty-bitty*, very small; also, *itsy-bitsy*; *lovey-dovey* (informal), very affectionate; *nitty-gritty* (informal), details; *pell-mell*, in a reckless manner, headlong; also *pellmell*; *pitter-patter*, light tapping sound, to make such a sound; *razzle-dazzle* (informal), dazzling excitement; *rinky-dink* (slang), old-fashioned, shoddy; *shilly-shally*, indecision, vacillation; *teeny-weeny* (informal), tiny; also *teensy-weensy*; *teeter-totter*, seesaw; *willy-nilly*, whether it is wished for or not; *wishy-washy*, weak, indecisive.

**Integrating Idioms:** "My sister's a real **eager-beaver**; she's sure to help us get the project started." (Hard working and enthusiastic. We often associate beavers with hard work, as they build dams and lodges and cut down trees in preparation for their construction projects.)

**Did You Know? Teeter-totter:** Depending on the region of the country, other terms may be used for this outdoor play equipment. *Teeter-totter* is common in the Midwest and western United States. *Seesaw* is also common. In New England, there are many possibilities, including *tilt*, *tilting board*, *dandle*, *dandle board*, *teeter*, and *teeterboard*. One term is not better than another; they are just different.

### Literature Link

Clements, A. (1997). *Double trouble in Walla Walla*. Brookfield, CT: Millbrook Press. Words for this sort were chosen from Clements's delightful book.

## States Stress Break

This sort may be used to provide students with practice in identifying stressed syllables before they begin the study of Vowel Patterns in Stressed Syllables (Sorts 16–29). Due to the many and varied spellings in the words, if they are used at that time, limit the focus to detecting the stressed syllable, the one said with greater emphasis. Toward the end of the stage, or even as part of studies at the next stage (derivational constancy), the words may be reviewed with the expectation that students learn their spellings. If the aim is to practice listening for the stressed syllable, use both of the States Stress Break pages. If spelling is an aim, provide opportunity for students to work with one page at a time.

To focus just on stress, lay out the headers and read the words aloud one at a time while students listen without seeing the words. Model and think aloud to classify a few of the words; be sure to slightly emphasize the syllable that is accented. Then invite student participation. For state names that consist of two words, determine the stress for the polysyllabic word. Discuss the results. The same approach may be used when spelling is also an aim. To encourage repeated practice, offer students several game-like options for working with the words. The cards could be used for Concentration (a "pair" would be any two words that share the same stressed syllable). They could also be used with a folder game; each time the stressed syllable of one of the words is correctly identified, the player advances along a path. The cards could also be formed into a draw pile, with two or three additional cards labeled "Stressed Out." As students take turns drawing cards and identifying the accented syllable, they keep those they correctly identify and return to the bottom of the stack the ones they miss. A player who draws a Stressed Out card must return all accumulated cards to the bottom of the draw pile. For many states-related activities, maps, and printables, see edHelper.com's United States Theme Unit—50 States at *www.edhelper.com/geography/Fifty_States.htm*.

## SORT 63. States Stress Break

### Sorting by Sound

| Syllable 1 | Syllable 2 | Syllable 3 | Oddball |
|---|---|---|---|
| **Arkansas** | **Alaska** | **Alabama** | **?** |
| Delaware | Connecticut | Arizona | (Louisiana*) |
| Florida | Hawaii | California | Maine |
| Georgia | Kentucky | Colorado | New York |
| Idaho | Missouri | Illinois | |
| Iowa | Montana | Indiana | |
| Kansas | Nebraska | (Louisiana*) | |
| Oregon | Nevada | Massachusetts | |
| Maryland | North Dakota | Minnesota | |
| Michigan | Ohio | Mississippi | |
| New Hampshire | South Dakota | North Carolina | |
| New Jersey | Vermont | Oklahoma | |
| New Mexico | Virginia | Pennsylvania | |
| Rhode Island | West Virginia | South Carolina | |
| (Tennessee)** | Wisconsin | (Tennessee)** | |
| Texas | Wyoming | | |
| Utah | | | |
| Washington | | | |

*Note*. For state names comprised of two words, use the polysyllabic word to determine the stress.

*Louisiana* may be pronounced with either four or five syllables; in the former instance, the first two are combined and the primary stress is then on the third syllable rather than the fourth.

**Tennessee* may be pronounced with either a first- or a third-syllable primary stress.

# SORT 53  Compounds with Substance Words

| air | fire | land | water |
|-----|------|------|-------|
| airplane | fireplace | landmark | |
| waterfall | airline | waterproof | |
| landmass | watercolor | firefly | |
| waterlog | firearm | landslide | |
| landlady | airborne | landscape | |
| aircraft | landlord | fireworks | |
| firecracker | watermark | airport | |
| landfill | fireproof | watermelon | |

# SORT 54  Compounds with Space Words

| sun | moon | star | sky |
|-----|------|------|-----|

| sunburn | moonbeam | starfish |
|---------|----------|----------|
| skyline | stargazing | sunlight |
| skyrocket | sunflower | starboard |
| sunglasses | moonrise | sunstroke |
| skyscraper | Sunday | skywriting |
| moonwalk | skydive | sundown |
| sundial | starlit | moonlight |
| moonscape | sunbathe | starburst |

# SORT 55  Compounds with Opposite Words

| work | play | day | night |
|------|------|-----|-------|
| workshop | playground | daylight | |
| nightmare | daydream | birthday | |
| playhouse | workbook | nighttime | |
| daytime | playroom | workbench | |
| workout | nightfall | playwright | |
| nightgown | daylily | workman | |
| fortnight | workroom | playbill | |
| daybreak | today | ? | |

# SORT 56  Compounds with Around the Home Words

| home | bed | bath | table | door |
|------|-----|------|-------|------|

| | | |
|---|---|---|
| homemade | bedtime | bathtub |
| tabletop | doorbell | bedroll |
| tableware | bathroom | homebody |
| bedbugs | bathwater | doorkeeper |
| homecoming | doorstep | bathrobe |
| tablecloth | bedspread | homeland |
| doorknob | homework | tablespoon |
| homesick | bathhouse | bedside |

# SORT 57 Compounds with Position Words

| down | up | over | out | under |
|------|-----|------|-----|-------|

| | | |
|---|---|---|
| download | upset | overcoat |
| outdoors | underline | outrage |
| underground | overlook | downcast |
| downstairs | outgoing | understand |
| overcast | downpour | overgrown |
| downspout | outbreak | upbeat |
| overheard | upkeep | outside |
| upcoming | outcast | underbrush |

# SORT 58 Compounds with Weather Words

| rain | wind | snow | thunder |
|------|------|------|---------|
| raindrop | windburn | snowball | |
| thunderbolt | snowstorm | rainproof | |
| windshield | thunderhead | windmill | |
| snowflake | hailstone | thunderstorm | |
| snowdrift | windfall | raincoat | |
| rainbow | thundercloud | windpipe | |
| snowshoe | windstorm | rainstorm | |
| windbreak | snowmobile | ? | |

# SORT 59 Compounds with Food Words

| corn | bean | pea | butter | egg |
|------|------|-----|--------|-----|

| | | |
|---|---|---|
| corncob | beanbag | peanut |
| butterfly | eggshell | butternut |
| cornrows | buttercup | beanstalk |
| peacock | cornhusk | egghead |
| eggplant | cornstalk | peashooter |
| cornflower | butterscotch | popcorn |
| eggnog | beanpole | butterball |
| cornstarch | eggbeater | cornmeal |

# SORT 60 Compounds with Color Words

| black | white | blue | green | red |
|-------|-------|------|-------|-----|

| | | |
|---|---|---|
| blacktop | whitecap | bluebird |
| greenhouse | redhead | bluegrass |
| greenhorn | whiteout | blackberry |
| blacksmith | greenroom | bluegill |
| bluebell | redwood | greenbelt |
| blackball | blueberry | blackmail |
| Greenland | blackboard | blueprint |
| blackbird | whitewash | blackout |

# SORT 61 Hyphenated Compounds

| Body | Numbers | Sports | Heat/Cold |
|------|---------|--------|-----------|
| hands-on | first-class | | all-star |
| warm-blooded | runner-up | | two-faced |
| red-hot | twenty-one | | left-handed |
| forty-five | dog-ear | | freeze-dried |
| time-out | hot dog | | tongue-tied |
| empty-handed | out-of-bounds | | one-sided |
| ice cream | fifty-fifty | | head-on |
| right-handed | ice-cold | | ? |

# SORT 62  Hyphenated Compounds with Repeated Elements

| Noun | Verb | Adjective/ Adverb |
|------|------|-------------------|
| eager-beaver | dilly-dally | itty-bitty |
| fiddle-faddle | helter-skelter | teeny-weeny |
| nitty-gritty | pitter-patter | hocus-pocus |
| pell-mell | fender-bender | harum-scarum |
| razzle-dazzle | shilly-shally | heebie-jeebies |
| flip-flop | lovey-dovey | hurry-scurry |
| willy-nilly | wishy-washy | teeter-totter |
| fuddy-duddy | bow-wow | rinky-dink |

| 1st-Syllable Stress | 2nd-Syllable Stress | 3rd-Syllable Stress |
|---|---|---|
| ? | Kansas | Alaska |
| Alabama | Louisiana | Florida |
| Missouri | Ohio | Kentucky |
| South Carolina | Colorado | Pennsylvania |
| Hawaii | Iowa | North Carolina |
| Delaware | Virginia | Georgia |
| California | New Jersey | New York |
| Maryland | Wyoming | Nevada |

| Arkansas | Vermont | Illinois |
|---|---|---|
| Minnesota | Washington | Michigan |
| Oklahoma | Idaho | North Dakota |
| New Hampshire | Arizona | Texas |
| Connecticut | Wisconsin | New Mexico |
| South Dakota | Indiana | Massachusetts |
| Montana | Mississippi | Utah |
| Maine | Oregon | West Virginia |
| Tennessee | Nebraska | Rhode Island |

# Part 3

# Word Study for Derivational Constancy Spellers

Students at the derivational constancy stage of spelling development (also known as the derivational relations stage) are likely to be proficient readers and to have considerable knowledge about spelling various one- and two-syllable words. They are also likely to be students in the upper elementary grades, middle school, or beyond. As students work with words at this stage, they gradually gain confidence in dealing with what appears on the surface to be an erratic spelling system, in which sounds of letters fluctuate from word to word, as /k/ for the final -c in *critic* but /s/ for the same *c* in *criticize*. Students come to realize that it is not what is on the surface that matters in spelling such words but what lies underneath. For, though complex, the system governing the spelling of the lower frequency words studied at this stage is stable and orderly at a deeper level, a level that preserves the meaning of derived or related words. Thus, though the sound of the letter *c* has shifted or alternated in the words *critic* and *criticize*, the spelling that carries the meaning is retained. This would not be the case if the words were spelled as they sound, as, for instance, *critic* and *critisize*. The same applies to many other words, as in *discuss/discussion*, not *discuss/discushon* and *democratic/democracy*, not *demacratic/democracy*. The principle at work here—*words that are related in meaning also tend to be related in spelling, despite changes in sound* (Templeton, 1983)—is a powerful one and one that has importance for understanding vocabulary, as well as for spelling words. There are 58 sorts in this part; the first 25 examine spelling–meaning patterns, and the next 33 explore meaning relationships among families of words derived from Greek and Latin roots. (For additional information related to understanding and teaching the features associated with the first 25 sorts, see *Word Journeys*, Chapter 7, Ganske, 2000.) Specific talking points are not included for the Greek and Latin roots section of this part. The understandings that students need to take away relate to associating specific roots with particular meanings and to realizing that families of words can share the same root. This information is integrated into the answer key for each sort. Idioms are included for some, but not all, of the sorts at this stage. Expect students to continue to reflect on understandings they gain from each sort about how words work and to discuss these understandings and/or record them in their word study notebooks.

# Revisiting Prefixes and Suffixes

This section includes seven sorts that extend and review knowledge of prefixes and suffixes. The issue of when and when not to double the final consonant of a base word is reexamined with poly-syllabic base words, several new prefixes are introduced, and y-to-i changes are revisited.

**What Is Known:** At the syllable juncture stage, students worked with the principles of doubling, e-drop, and no change using one-syllable words. They worked with various prefixes and suffixes and how they attach to base words, including suffixes involving y-to-i changes.

**What Is New:** Affixing suffixes to polysyllabic base words is a new concept. Also, although some of the prefixes were introduced at the previous stage, others are new here.

---

## SORT 1. *E*-Drop and No Change with *-ed* and *-ing*

### Sorting by Pattern

| *E*-Drop | No Change | *Y* to *I* | Oddball |
|---|---|---|---|
| **becoming** | **returning** | **hurried** | **?** |
| balanced | concerned | buried | carrying |
| continued | followed | emptied | studying |
| dividing | functioning | replied | |
| exciting | interesting | | |
| imagined | published | | |
| involved | surrounding | | |
| measuring | | | |
| realized | | | |
| surprising | | | |

**Considerations:** This sort reviews e-drop, no-change, and y-to-i principles for adding inflected end-ings and extends the concepts to base words of more than one syllable. Begin by explaining to stu-dents that they will be examining how endings such as -ed and -ing are added to longer words in this and other sorts. Make clear that just as with one-syllable words, how the ending is attached depends on the spelling of the base word. As you discuss any unfamiliar words, go over the base-word spell-ing for each of the words. Tell students to record the spelling somewhere on the card, as for instance *realized/realize.* Then ask students to work with a partner to sort the words under the appropriate category headers. Remind them to consider the base word as they make their category decisions. Discuss the results. Students may have placed *carrying* and *studying* under the no-change category. This is fine, because no change is actually involved. However, they are placed as oddballs in the answer key because, contrary to the other base words ending in -y, the y did not change to i. Prompt students to consider why this might be. They should come to realize that the principle for changing y-to-i does not usually apply when adding -ing (*buried* and *emptied*, but *burying* and *emptying*). Though not evident from this sort, the same is true when adding -ed to words in which the final -y is part of the vowel pattern, as -oy, -ay, and -ey in *destroyed, displayed* and *conveyed.*

*Talking Points*

- As with one-syllable words, drop the final -*e* of a polysyllabic word before adding -*ed* or -*ing*, as in *realized* and *measuring*.
- As with single-syllable words, change final -*y* to *i* before adding -*ed* unless the -*y* is part of a vowel pattern, for example, *carried* and *displayed*.
- Do not change the base word when adding -*ing* to words ending in -*y*, such as *carrying*.

*Integrating Idioms:* "I'm **following in my uncle's footsteps**; I plan to be an artist one day, too." (Be like someone else. If you literally walked in the footsteps of somebody else, you would do exactly the same things and be just like that person.)

*Did You Know?* Why is **bury** pronounced like *berry* instead of like *fury* and *jury*? The answer goes back to the early days of the English language (more than 1,000 years ago) and to the influence of dialect. The Old English form of *bury* was *brygan*, which was pronounced as /**bür•**yən/. Sometime between the 1100s and 1400s pronunciation of the *u* changed; however, due to dialect, the change varied from region to region of England. The spelling tended to remain consistent and reflected the pronunciation of people around London, which was the capital of England and therefore influential. People in that area pronounced *u* with the sound you hear in *foot*, which when put with *r* sounded like the *ur* in *burn*. However, the pronunciation that became the dominant one was from a different region; this mismatch of a spelling from one region but a pronunciation from another is why *bury* is different from *fury* and *jury*. *Busy* has a similar history. Regional dialects are common in the United States and often affect the pronunciation of words. Sometimes in different regions even different words are used for a particular concept, such as *pop–soda, bag–paper sack, green beans–string beans–snap beans, earthworm–angleworm, skillet–frying pan*, and so forth. Dialect differences are often noticeable on television shows or in movies. Have you noticed any differences in dialect?

## SORT 2. Doubling and No Change with -*ed* and -*ing*

### Sorting by Pattern and Sound

| Double | No Change |
| --- | --- |
| **permitted** | **edited** |
| concurred | angered |
| conferred | considered |
| controlling | benefiting |
| equipped | entered |
| forgetting | exhibited |
| inferring | exited |
| occurred | gossiping |
| preferred | happened |
| regretted | inhabited |
| submitting | offering |
| | suffering |
| | visited |

*Considerations:* Doubling is called for in single-syllable words when the word ends with a VC pattern, as in *tap/tapping*, not *tap/taping*; the doubled consonant preserves the short vowel sound. When dealing with words of more than one syllable, standards similar to the one vowel and one final consonant (VC pattern) criteria apply. However, just the last syllable of the word is considered. An additional stress-related criterion must also be met, and this, too, applies to the final syllable. Thus, when the last syllable of a base word ends with a single vowel and consonant *and* is stressed, double the consonant before adding the ending. There are various ways to introduce the concept of doubling with polysyllabic base words. For an alternative to the one that follows, see *Word Journeys*, Chapter 7.

Start by telling students that they will be exploring the doubling principle with base words of more than one syllable (known as *polysyllabic* base words). Review the process with a single-syllable word; then explain that doubling works a little differently with polysyllabic words, as they will learn. Go over the words together and ask students to identify and underline each base word. Then prompt students to begin by categorizing the words according to doubled final consonant or no change. Discuss the results, which should be as shown in Sort 2. Point to each of the base words, and note that they all end in VC, yet only some require doubling. Prompt students to examine the columns of words to try to figure out what else is involved in doubling besides a final VC pattern. After a few moments, if no one mentions syllable stress, suggest that they underline the stressed syllable in each word. With guidance, they should notice that all of the "double" words have a stress on the final syllable of the base word. They may initially describe the words as having a stressed second syllable. If so, point out *considered*, *inhabited*, and *exhibited*, which do not have a doubled final consonant, although their stress is on the second syllable. After some discussion, ask students to agree on talking points to describe the doubling principle for polysyllabic words. Discuss their ideas and the following talking points:

### Talking Points

- When adding *-ed* or *-ing* to a polysyllabic word, if the final syllable ends in a VC pattern and the syllable is stressed, double the final consonant, as in *preferred*, but not in **suffering** or *considered*.

*Integrating Idioms:* "My mother reminded me not to **forget myself** at the wedding reception." (Forget my manners. It is important to consider your behavior or an embarrassing situation may result.)

*Did You Know?* It is likely no surprise that **gossip** is a word with a long history, as it seems probable that people have long been engaged in the practice. The word *godsibb* first appeared in the 11th century. It was formed of *sibb*, an Old English word meaning "kinship," and modern English *god*. The word *sibling* ("having one or more parents in common") is a descendant of *sibb*. *Godsibb* referred to someone who was spiritually related to another, such as godparents ("sponsors at a baptism"). Over time, the spelling evolved, first into *gossib* and then into *gossip*. The meaning also broadened to include close friends, as well as godparents. These people likely engaged in idle talk at times, perhaps even about the godchild or the child's parents. Soon the word came to mean "someone who engages in spreading bits of rumor."

## SORT 3. Doubling and No Change with Various Suffixes

### Sorting by Pattern and Sound

| Double | No Change | Oddball |
|--------|-----------|---------|
| **beginner** | **piloted** | ? |
| abhorrent | canceled | equipment |
| committee | conference | regretful |
| compelled | developing | |
| deferred | honored | |
| patrolling | limited | |
| propeller | orbiting | |
| referral | profited | |
| repellent | quarreled | |
| | reference | |
| | wandered | |
| | whispered | |

*Considerations:* Explain to students that in this sort they will be learning more about doubling when adding suffixes. Introduce the sort by going over any unfamiliar words and identifying each of the base words. Then, as with the previous sort, ask students to categorize the words under the header cards Double and No Change. Review the categories and discuss the results, which will be as shown in Sort 3, except that the two oddballs will be included under the no-change category. Then ask students to underline the stressed syllable in each word. Remind them of the previous sort in which the double words were stressed on the final syllable of the base word, whereas for other words, stress was on one of the other syllables. Ask if that is the case here. Move any words that do not fit this principle (*equipment* and *regretful*) under the "?" card. Then ask students to turn to a partner to talk about why these words are oddballs. Discuss their ideas and the following talking points, being sure to highlight the fact that doubling does not apply to adding suffixes that begin with a consonant. Some students may question the spelling of *canceled* or mention having seen the word spelled another way. *Cancelled* is the way the word is spelled in British English and is acceptable in American English, although the single *l* is more common. It may also be easier to remember considering the doubling principle: The final syllable is not stressed so doubling is not expected. Students who live in snowy regions of the country may see both spellings in use: for instance TV stations announcing school closings sometimes differ in which one they post. Other words ending in -el also have alternative spellings, as in *traveling/travelling, leveled/levelled, labeled/labelled*, and so forth. Unlike *cancelled*, computer spell checkers reject the double consonants of these words.

### Talking Points

- The final consonant of a polysyllabic base word is doubled if the suffix begins with a vowel and if the base word ends with a VC pattern that is stressed, as in *propell̲er* and *repell̲ent*, but not *devel̲oping* and *equip̲ment*.

*Did You Know?* **Repel** is made up of *re-*, meaning "back," and *pel*, meaning "to drive." If you are repelled by something, you literally are driven back from it. *Repellent*, which includes the same word parts, is often used to drive back mosquitoes. **Compel** is also part of the *pel* family of words. The *com-* in this word means "with," so *compel* means "with drive" or force. If you are compelled to do something, you are driven to do it. *Propeller* comes from the same root. The prefix *pro-* means "in front of," so to *propel* is "to drive in front of," which is just what the propeller of an airplane does; it drives the plane forward. *Compel, repel,* and *propel* have been part of the English language since the 1300s and 1400s. However, *repellent* as a substance for driving away insects is much more recent; it was first recorded in 1908. *Propellers,* referring to devices used on ships and flying machines, was first recorded during the early 1800s.

## SORT 4. Suffixes with Final *-y* (*-ier, -iness, -ious, -ily, -ied*)

### Sorting by Meaning

| *-ier* | *-iness* | *-ious* | *-ily* | *-ied* |
| --- | --- | --- | --- | --- |
| **heavier** | **happiness** | **various** | **luckily** | **multiplied** |
| cloudier | business | envious | angrily | magnified |
| healthier | friendliness | furious | necessarily | occupied |
| livelier | loneliness | mysterious | ordinarily | qualified |
| | uneasiness | studious | readily | satisfied |

**Considerations:** This sort, which reviews *y*-to-*i* changes before suffixes, is fairly straightforward. Only the *-ous* suffix is new. To increase the level of challenge, omit the headers and invite students to sort the words according to the suffix. When they are finished, ask them to identify the base words; they might record the spellings on the word cards. Discuss the results and any unfamiliar words. You might point out that *busy* can also be added to *-ness* without a spelling change. Whereas *business* refers to "work," *busyness* refers to "a state of being busy," as in *My busyness kept me from attending the movie.* As you discuss the students' observations and the talking point, remind them that the principle for changing *y*-to-*i* does not hold true when the suffix begins with *i* (see Sort 1 of this part).

### Talking Points

- Usually final *-y* changes to *i* when adding a suffix, regardless of whether the suffix begins with a consonant or a vowel (excepting *i*), as in *lonely → loneliness* and *vary → various,* but *vary → varying,* not *variing.*

**Integrating Idioms:** "Wednesday night we won our first game in two years, but Thursday when the coach taught our government class it was **business as usual**." (The routine was normal. Some students may have thought there should be some discussion about the game, as the coach was the teacher, but the class stayed on topic.)

**Did You Know? Multiply,** *multiplication, multiplicand,* and *multiplicity* are all related to *multiplex* ("a movie theater or other building with separate units"). Their meanings derive from *multi-,* which means "many," and *plex* or *plic,* which means "folds." Just as a blanket has many layers folded in, when you multiply, you increase or "fold in" a number multiple times. A multiplex theater has several theaters "folded" into one building. We can think of something that is *complicated* as being "with folds." When you *duplicate* something and make an identical copy, you have "two folds." Can you think of other words with the *plic* or *plex* pattern, in which the pattern is a root that means "fold"?

---

## SORT 5. Prefixes (*un-*, *dis-*, *in-*)

### Sorting by Meaning

| *un-* | *dis-* | *in-* | Oddball |
|---|---|---|---|
| **uncertain** | **disbelief** | **incapable** | **?** |
| unafraid | disapprove | inaccurate | indentured |
| unfamiliar | disclose | inadequate | |
| unimportant | discolor | indistinct | |
| unnatural | disconnect | infamous | |
| unsuccessful | discount | injustice | |
| | discourage | insecure | |
| | disease | insincere | |

**Considerations:** This sort is straightforward. It reviews prefixes introduced at the syllable juncture stage. Students may not know the meaning of *indentured*, although it is often used in intermediate-grade social studies texts (see the "Did You Know?" story for this word). Review the meaning of each prefix: *un-* and *dis-* both mean "not" or "the opposite of"; although *in-* can mean "in, into," here it means "not" in all of the words except *indentured*. As you go over the words, ask students to apply the prefix meaning to the word, as *uncertain* means "not certain." Draw attention to the word *unnatural*, which has a double consonant due to affixation; the spelling may look strange, but the double consonants are needed to maintain meaning. At this time, you might distribute copies to students of the Understanding Prefixes handout included in Appendix G. It can be attached to their word study notebooks for future reference.

### Talking Points

- *Un-* and *dis-* are prefixes that mean "not," or "the opposite of"; *in-* can mean "in, into" as well as "not."
- When prefixes are added to words, double consonants can result, as in *unnatural*. Though they may look peculiar, they are needed for meaning.

**Integrating Idioms:** "I told my sister **in no uncertain terms** to stay out of my room." (Specifically and directly. If something is said very clearly, there can be no question as to what is meant by it; the statement emphasizes how serious the person saying it really is.)

**Did You Know?** In early America people sometimes bound themselves to work for another person for a period of time (usually 7 years) in exchange for something, such as passage on a ship. The practice of indenturing servants was outlawed under the United States Constitution. **Indenture** refers to the document or contract of agreement. *Indent-* literally means "in tooth" in Latin. So why was the agreement given this name? The document was cut or torn in two with ragged or serrated edges, and each party received a half. The toothed edges allowed the document to be put together to prove their agreement.

## SORT 6. Prefixes (*mis-, en-, de-, anti-*)

### Sorting by Meaning

| *mis-* | *en-* | *de-* | *anti-* | Oddball |
|---|---|---|---|---|
| **misbehave** | **enlarge** | **defrost** | **antisocial** | **?** |
| miscalculate | enable | decompose | anticrime | English |
| misfortune | encircle | dehumidify | antifreeze | envelope |
| mismanage | encourage | deodorant | antigravity | |
| mispronounce | enrage | dethrone | antismoking | |
| | | devalue | | |

*Considerations:* Like the previous sort, this sort is straightforward and can be completed by students without teacher direction. However, there should be follow-up discussion. Unfamiliar words should be discussed, as should the meanings of the prefixes. Although *mis-* ("badly" or "wrongly") is a review for students, the other three prefixes are new. *En-* means "to put into" or "cause to"; its spelling sometimes alters to *em*, as in *empower*. *De-* has several meanings: "out," "off," "apart," and "away"; and *anti-* means "against" or "opposing." If students miscategorize *envelope* with the *en-* words, ask them to identify the base word. Because there is none, it is considered an oddball in this sort. Then point out that *en-* does function as a prefix in the word. However, instead of attaching to a base word, it is affixed to a word root, something they will learn more about later on. *English* is an intact word; it has no prefix. Remind students that it is always capitalized, whether it refers to the language, to people, or to a course of study. Be sure students have a copy of the Understanding Prefixes handout from Appendix G as a reference.

### Talking Points

- *Mis-, en-* (also *em-*), *de-*, and *anti-* are all prefixes; *mis-* means "wrongly," *en-* means "cause to," *de-* means "away," and *anti-* means "against."
- *English* is always capitalized.

*Integrating Idioms:* "Just **tell me in plain English** why you had to stay after school." (Simply, clearly, and straightforwardly. Sometimes excitement or concern can cause someone to ramble in a way that is unclear, or the person might be using technical language; in this case you might say "Just tell me in plain English what is wrong with my computer.")

*Did You Know?* English has sometimes been called a *living language*, because it is not static but ever-changing, just like other living things. Old words become obsolete and disappear from the language; new words and new meanings (*neologisms*) are added as they are coined or borrowed from other languages. It is difficult to determine just how many words there are in English because of the changes that take place and because different forms of words may not be counted the same way. For example, how many different words follow: *record, recording, recorded, records, accord,* and *discord*? These are decisions that lexicographers who compile dictionaries must make, as well as deciding what to do about scientific and technical terms; do you include some . . . or all?

English has changed considerably over the centuries. Old English (middle of the 5th to the 12th centuries) is for the most part unreadable without benefit of a translation. The alphabet then was even somewhat different; it included letters we no longer use and did not include letters we do use. (To see what Old English is like, you might search online or ask at a library to borrow a copy of

Seamus Heaney's [2000] bilingual translation of *Beowulf*, a poem written sometime between the 8th and 10th centuries. It shows Old English on one page and the modern translation on the facing page.) We have Old English to thank for many of our basic words, such as *the, and, in, is, I, wife, father, man, child, house,* and *work*. An invasion by the Normans in 1066 led to the borrowing of many French words. Sometimes the borrowing resulted in multiple words for the same concept. The Old English is usually identifiable as a shorter, simpler word, as in *come/arrive, eat/devour,* and *sight/vision*. It is interesting to note that animal names tend to come from the Old English, whereas the foods made from them derive from the French, as in *sheep/mutton, cow/beef,* and *pig/pork*. Why might this be? Since the Norman Conquest, words have been added to the English language from countries all over the world.

## SORT 7. Prefixes (*inter-, mid-, sub-, super-*)

### Sorting by Meaning

| *inter-* | *mid-* | *sub-* | *super-* | Oddball |
|---|---|---|---|---|
| **interstate** | **midnight** | **subway** | **supermarket** | **?** |
| interact | midair | subconscious | superpower | interfere |
| interchange | midday | subheading | superman | |
| international | midpoint | sublease | supernatural | |
| interview | midstream | subsoil | superstar | |
| | midsummer | substandard | | |

*Considerations:* As with the previous two sorts, this sort is straightforward, but all of the prefixes are new. After students have sorted the words, discuss the word meanings. Give them an opportunity to identify the meaning of each prefix before you tell them. Talking with a partner may help them to generate ideas. Remind students that the meaning they identify must apply to all of the words in the category. Discuss their ideas and clarify as needed. *Inter-* means "between" or "within"; when you *interact* with someone, there is action going on between you. An *interchange* is "a change between roads"; it allows you to move from one to another. *International* activities are "between nations," and an *interview* is literally a "seeing between," in other words, coming to understand a person or an issue. Although the prefix *inter-* is part of *interfere*, as with *envelope* in the previous sort, it is affixed to a root rather than to a base word. *Mid-* means "middle." Something in *midair* is in the "middle of the air"; *midpoint* is at "a point in the middle" of something, as in *the midpoint of the semester* or the *midpoint of a line; midstream* is in the "middle of the stream"; and *midsummer* is about "halfway through summer." *Sub-* usually means "below" or "under." A *subway* is a "way underground"; *subsoil* is "soil below the topsoil"; *subconscious* is "below the level of conscious thought"; *subheading* is "a heading below the main heading"; a *sublease* is a "lease under" in that the original renter, who still has a lease on the property, leases it to someone else; and *substandard* is "below standard" in quality. *Super-* means "above" or "over." In the words for this sort, it carries the connotation of exceeding the usual, as in *superstar*. As part of the discussion, draw students' attention to the double consonants in *midday*. You might also explain that another prefix, *intra-* (meaning "within"), is sometimes confused with *inter-*, as in *interstate* ("between or among states") *commerce is on the rise* versus *intrastate* ("within a state") *commerce is on the rise*.

*Talking Points*

- *Inter-* often means "between, among," *mid-* means "middle," *sub-* usually means "under," and *super* means "above, beyond."

*Integrating Idioms:* "Every time you tell a story, you **leave me hanging in midair**." (Stop without completing the story. Because humans spend their time on the ground except when assisted by artificial means such as an airplane or glider, to be left hanging in midair would be distressing.)

*Did You Know?* The story of *superman* begins with a German philosopher by the name of Nietzsche (nē•chə), who wrote about his concept of an ideal human, whom he called Ubermensch. *Ubermensch* was translated into English in 1895 as *Overman* and in 1896 as *Beyondman*. It was not until 1903 that the word was translated as *Superman* by playwright George Bernard Shaw. Superman as a man of extraordinary abilities and power was first recorded in 1925, and the nearly invincible superhero, capable of flying, was introduced to America through a comic strip in 1938. Do you think Superman would have evolved as a superhero at all if the name had remained *Overman* or *Beyondman*? Just imagine people reporting "*It's a bird; it's a plane; it's Overman!*" on seeing the superhero in flight!

# SORT 1 *E*-Drop and No Change with *-ed* and *-ing*

| E-Drop | No Change | Y to I |
|--------|-----------|--------|
| becoming | returning | hurried |
| emptied | imagined | functioning |
| involved | buried | dividing |
| measuring | followed | published |
| studying | balanced | exciting |
| replied | surrounding | continued |
| surprising | concerned | carrying |
| realized | interesting | ? |

# SORT 2  Doubling and No Change with *-ed* and *-ing*

| No Change | | Double |
|---|---|---|
| edited | permitted | offering |
| forgetting | preferred | benefiting |
| suffering | equipped | considered |
| conferred | angered | occurred |
| gossiping | submitting | exited |
| regretted | concurred | exhibited |
| entered | inferring | happened |
| controlling | visited | inhabited |

# SORT 3  Doubling and No Change with Various Suffixes

| No Change | | Double |
|---|---|---|
| piloted | beginner | equipment |
| compelled | orbiting | repellent |
| honored | patrolling | canceled |
| regretful | propeller | reference |
| limited | conference | committee |
| profited | referral | developing |
| deferred | abhorrent | whispered |
| wandered | quarreled | ? |

# SORT 4  Suffixes with Final -y (-ier, -iness, -ious, -ily, -ied)

| -ier | -iness | -ious | -ily | -ied |
|------|--------|-------|------|------|

| | | |
|---|---|---|
| heavier | happiness | various |
| luckily | multiplied | readily |
| furious | satisfied | friendliness |
| cloudier | angrily | occupied |
| envious | loneliness | healthier |
| necessarily | studious | qualified |
| magnified | livelier | mysterious |
| business | ordinarily | uneasiness |

# SORT 5  Prefixes (*un-*, *dis-*, *in-*)

| un- | dis- | in- |
|---|---|---|
| uncertain | disbelief | incapable |
| indistinct | unfamiliar | disconnect |
| disclose | insincere | indentured |
| unsuccessful | disease | infamous |
| discourage | inaccurate | disapprove |
| insecure | unimportant | discount |
| discolor | injustice | unnatural |
| inadequate | unafraid | ? |

# SORT 6 Prefixes (*mis-, en-, de-, anti-*)

| mis- | en- | de- | anti- |
|------|-----|-----|-------|
| misbehave | enlarge | defrost | |
| antisocial | English | enrage | |
| encircle | dehumidify | mispronounce | |
| misfortune | antifreeze | devalue | |
| encourage | miscalculate | envelope | |
| antismoking | dethrone | antigravity | |
| mismanage | anticrime | decompose | |
| deodorant | enable | ? | |

# SORT 7 Prefixes (*inter-*, *mid-*, *sub-*, *super-*)

| inter- | mid- | sub- | super- |
|---|---|---|---|
| interstate | midnight | | subway |
| supermarket | substandard | | midstream |
| midsummer | subsoil | | midair |
| superpower | interact | | sublease |
| international | superman | | midpoint |
| superstar | subconscious | | interfere |
| interchange | supernatural | | midday |
| subheading | interview | | ? |

# Consonant Alternations
## (DSA Features P and Q)

This section, which includes Sorts 8–12, examines the concept of *consonant alternations*. When suffixes are added to words, the sounds of certain consonants often change or alternate, though their spellings may remain intact; as, for example, the silent-to-sounded change that occurs from *sign* to *signal*, or the final-consonant sound change in *construct* when the suffix *-ion* is added, *construction*. Adding a suffix does not always mean a change, as we see in *constructive*. Sometimes when a suffix is added not only a change in sound but also a change in spelling occurs. Such changes tend to be predictable because they often occur in families of words, as in *admit/admission*, *commit/commission*, and *permit/permission*. Many related words involve a consonant alternation, and probably most common among them are words with the /shən/ ending. When spelling words with /shən/, writers must consider not only that the spelling may not correspond to the sound but also that there are multiple ways to spell the ending, including *-tion*, *-sion*, and *-ian*. These and other issues are the focus of the sorts in this section.

**What Is Known:** Students should be familiar with many of the base words used in the sorts of this section. Also, they have worked with affixation of suffixes in this part and the previous one on syllable juncture spelling.

**What Is New:** The concept of consonant alternations is new, as is the principle that words related in meaning tend to be related in spelling despite changes in sound.

---

## **SORT 8.** Silent and Sounded Consonants

|  Sorting by Sound ||
| Silent | Sounded |
| --- | --- |
| **muscle** | **muscular** |
| autumn | autumnal |
| bomb | bombard |
| column | columnist |
| design | designate |
| hasten | haste |
| moisten | moist |
| resign | resignation |
| sign | signature |
| soften | soft |
| solemn | solemnity |
| wrestle | wrest |

**Considerations:** Although there are few words with sounded-to-silent alternations, their study can segue to the study of other alternations. Students will likely already know how to spell several of the silent-consonant words in this sort from their studies at the previous stage. Introduce the sort by placing *muscle* and *muscular* in front of the students. Inform them that the sort they will be working with is the first of many that will include pairs or families of words that are related in meaning, such as *muscle* and *muscular*. Sometimes they may know how to spell one of the words but have difficulty spelling a related word. As they work with the pairs or families of words, they will learn ways to make the spelling easier. Ask them to talk about the easier and more difficult aspects of the words *muscle* and *muscular*. They will likely mention the silent *c*; if not, bring this to their attention by placing the appropriate header card above each word. Point out that because it is silent, spellers sometimes omit the *c* in *muscle* but not in *muscular*, where the sound of the *c* is a reminder that it needs to be included. Thinking of the *c* in *muscular* can be a reminder that a *c* is also needed in the related word *muscle*. Ask students to sort the remaining words according to whether the word has a silent consonant or just sounded consonants. Discuss the results and clarify the meanings of any unfamiliar words, such as *wrest*, which means "to take something forcibly by twisting," as for example in *We had to wrest the bone from the dog's mouth*. This same sense of "twisting" is apparent in the related word, *wrestle*. The meanings of *solemn* and *solemnity* as having to do with "serious" and "sober" may also need clarifying. Students may not perceive a relationship between *design* and *designate*, other than their shared spellings. Point out that both words literally have to do with "marking out." A design marks out an artistic work or the plan of a building, and when something is designated, it is marked out or selected for some purpose, as to *designate an area of sidewalk for repair* or *designate a person as the group leader*. Write the spelling–meaning principle on the board (see the first talking point) and discuss it in relation to the sort. Ask students to record it in their notebooks. Note that due to the limited pool of words, word hunts are not appropriate for this sort.

### Talking Points

- Words related in meaning tend to be related in spelling, despite differences in sound, as in *haste* and *hasten*.
- Sometimes thinking of a related word can help with spelling, as in *moist* for *moisten*.

***Integrating Idioms:*** "We **can never move a muscle** in that class." (Must be very still. Because the heart is a muscle, the idea of not moving a muscle points to the extreme quiet that is expected.)

***Did You Know?*** Could the silent *n* in **autumn** and the spelling difficulties associated with it be the reason we have two synonyms for this season, *fall* and *harvest*? More likely it is characteristics of the season that give these words their synonymous status with *autumn*. Autumn is the season when agricultural products are harvested and leaves fall. As long ago as 1545 the seasons were referred to as *spring time*, *sommer*, *fall of the leaf*, and *winter*. The expression was shortened to just *fall* more than 300 years ago and today is commonly used in the United States.

## SORT 9. Adding *-ion* to Base Words with No Spelling Change

### Sorting by Sound and Pattern

| -ct | -ct + ion | -ss | -ss + ion |
|-----|-----------|-----|-----------|
| **direct** | **direction** | **express** | **expression** |
| connect | connection | confess | confession |
| detect | detection | discuss | discussion |
| elect | election | impress | impression |
| infect | infection | possess | possession |
| predict | prediction | | |
| react | reaction | | |

*Considerations:* Introduce the sort by showing students the template of words (without the headers) and asking them what they notice. After their work with silent and sounded consonants, they will likely mention that the sort comprises pairs of related words and that many of the words end in *-ion*. Tell them that they will be learning to add the suffix *-ion* to words as part of this and later word studies. Ask them to partner the words by making two columns, one for the base word and one for the related word, as in *direct/direction*. When they are finished, ask students to examine the two lists to see whether they can be subdivided while keeping pairs of words together. If necessary, guide them to the four categories designated by the headers in Sort 9. Discuss their observations; students will likely notice that words in one category end in *-ct* and in another with *-ss*. They may not grasp the changes in sound that occur from the base word to the related form with *-ion* (the *t* in *direct* changes from /t/ to /sh/ in *direction*, and the final *-s* in *express* changes to /sh/ in *expression*). Draw their attention to this, using the key words as examples; underline the consonant alternation (*-ct* or *-ss*). Place the header cards above their appropriate categories. Explain to students that /shən/ can be confusing to spell, because *-tion*, *-sion*, and *-ian* are all appropriate for certain words. However, thinking about the base word can make the spelling obvious, because usually for words that end in *-ct* or *-ss*, you simply add *-ion*. There is no spelling change, just a change in sound. Before ending the lesson discuss any unfamiliar word meanings. (Note that words with final *-ct* are somewhat less consistent than those with *-ss* in how *-ion* is added. For a few words, *-ation* is added, as in *expect/expectation*.)

### Talking Points

• For most base words that end in *-ct* or *-ss*, just add *-ion*, as in *direction* or *expression*.

*Integrating Idioms:* "I heard him speak at an assembly, and he **made a real impression on me**." (Had a lasting effect on the person. When something is pressed into a substance, it stays there for a long time, even permanently; e.g., the fossilized footprints of dinosaurs.)

*Did You Know?* Just as the final consonant sound alters when the suffix *-ion* is added to *connect* (from /t/ to /sh/ to form **connection**), so, too, the story of *connection* is one involving changes, but not of sound, of spelling. Although the word evolved from the Latin word *conectere*, meaning "to bind together," its early spelling did not clearly reflect this heritage. In the late 1300s the word was spelled *conneccion*, and in the mid-1400s it was *connexioun*. The *-ction* spelling was not common, especially in America, until the 1700s, when other words (such as *direction* and *collection*), already spelled with final *-tion*, influenced its spelling.

Many **discussions** live up to their dictionary definition of being "earnest conversations"; some may even become heated debates, in which one person attempts to shake up things by squashing the ideas of another through rational argument. Someone else may have it in mind to clear the air, shake out the tensions, and rescue the situation, objectively pointing out the merits and faulty logic of both parties. Considering this scenario, it may not be so surprising that *discussion* evolved from the Latin for "shaking apart" or "striking asunder" and that *squash* and *rescue* derive from the same "shaking"-related root.

---

## SORT 10. Adding *-ion* and *-ian* to Base Words with No Spelling Change

### Sorting by Sound and Pattern

| -t | -t + ion | -ic | -ic + ian | Oddball |
|---|---|---|---|---|
| **digest** | **digestion** | **magic** | **magician** | **?*** |
| adopt | adoption | clinic | clinician | present/ |
| assert | assertion | electric | electrician | presentation |
| except | exception | music | musician | |
| invent | invention | optic | optician | |
| suggest | suggestion | | | |

**Considerations:** Although no Oddball card is included in this sort, there are exceptions. Students need to be guided by their examination of the words and categories to determine whether or not there is an exception, not be led by the presence of a "?" card. This sort builds on the previous one through an examination of words ending in other consonants plus *t* (designated as *-t* rather than *-ct*). It also introduces a new concept for words with /shən/, namely that *-ian*, rather than *-ion* is used to identify people. The use of *-ian* for people is true of many words, even words without /shə n/: *librarian*, *guardian*, *Indian*, *custodian*, *Egyptian*, and *historian*, to name a few.

Begin the sort in a manner similar to the previous one, withholding the header cards until the categories have been discussed. If students are confounded by the absence of an Oddball card as they sort, remind them that they can always set aside words that don't fit the categories. Students should again realize that there is no spelling change when the suffix is added, except in the case of *present/presentation*. Discuss this pair of oddballs; numerous words that end in consonant-*t* do require *-ation*, such as *tempt/temptation*, *indent/indentation*, *protest/protestation*. Remind students that consonant alternations or changes can cause spellers confusion unless the base word is kept in mind. Go over unfamiliar word meanings before ending the sort. Be sure students have a clear understanding that *-ian* is used when the word refers to a person.

### Talking Points

- For most base words that end in consonant-*t* just add *-ion*, as in *digest/digestion*.
- For base words that end in *-ic*, add *-ian* to designate a person, as in *magician*.

**Integrating Idioms:** "I know I have to **face the music** for the broken window, but it's hard to take grounding *and* paying for it." (Accept the consequences of your actions. There is uncertainty as to the origins of this expression; some believe it to relate to an actor facing the orchestra pit with a hostile audience behind it during a poor performance; others believe it refers to a formal and disgraceful dismissal from the military, which would be accompanied by music.)

***Did You Know?*** ***Music***, like the days of the week and many other words, has its origins in the world of the ancients and their beliefs. Music was an essential component of everyday life for the ancient Greeks. The word *music* originated from *Mousa*, which is Greek for *Muse*. The Muses were goddesses, and originally there were three of them. Over time, the myth expanded until there were nine Muses, each having purview or charge over a particular area of the arts or sciences, including various types of poetry, song, dance, drama, history, and astronomy. Ancient Greeks often called on them for inspiration. The Greek word *musike* referred to any of the areas presided over by the Muses. Music often evokes strong feelings. What do you think the following authors were trying to say about music?

> "Music washes away from the soul the dust of everyday life."
> —Berthold Auerbach

> "Music expresses that which cannot be said and on which it is impossible to be silent."
> —Victor Hugo

---

## SORT 11. Adding *-ion* to Base Words with *E*-Drop

### Sorting by Sound and Pattern

| *-te* | *E*-Drop + *ion* | *-se* | *E*-Drop + *ion* |
|---|---|---|---|
| **educate** | **education** | **confuse** | **confusion** |
| celebrate | celebration | averse | aversion |
| communicate | communication | immerse | immersion |
| cooperate | cooperation | precise | precision |
| evaporate | evaporation | | |
| exaggerate | exaggeration | | |
| illustrate | illustration | | |
| pollute | pollution | | |

***Considerations:*** Up to this point /shən/ has been formed by simply adding *-ion* or *-ian* directly to the base word. In this sort students must apply their understandings of final *-e* when adding *-ion*. As with other instances of e-dropping, the change is predictable, except in a few cases; for example, some *-se* words require the addition of *a*, as in *converse/conversation*. If discussing this with students, point out that without the *a* the result is *conversion*, an entirely different word.

   Introduce the sort in a manner similar to that used with the two previous sorts. Discuss the results and talking points, as well as any unfamiliar meanings. Because many of the words in this sort (and in later sorts) involve a change in stress when *-ion* is added (***celebrate/celebration***), before ending the session or at a later time, ask the group to re-sort their words according to whether or not there is a stress change, as shown in the following sound sort. Discuss their observations.

## Sorting by Sound: Stress Change

| Stress Change | No Stress Change |
|---|---|
| **cel**ebrate/cele**bra**tion | a**verse**/a**ver**sion |
| com**mu**nicate/communi**ca**tion | con**fuse**/con**fu**sion |
| co**op**erate/coope**ra**tion | im**merse**/im**mer**sion |
| **ed**ucate/edu**ca**tion | pol**lute**/pol**lu**tion |
| e**vap**orate/evapo**ra**tion | pre**cise**/pre**ci**sion |
| ex**ag**gerate/exagge**ra**tion | |
| **il**lustrate/illu**stra**tion OR | |
| il**lus**trate/illu**stra**tion | |

### Talking Points

- Base words that end in *-te* or *-se* drop the final *-e* before the *-ion* suffix is added, as in *celebrate/celebration* and *confuse/confusion*.
- Sometimes adding a suffix changes the stress, as in ***educate/education***

***Did You Know? Pollution*** can result from many different types of activity, such as agriculture, energy, industry, and transportation, and can affect air, soil, and water. Polluted areas are often considered "dirty," and indeed the words *pollute* and *pollution* derive from a Latin word meaning "to soil or defile." Although *pollute* as a word meaning "to dirty" or "to make foul" has been around since about the mid-1500s, its general use to describe dirtying of the atmosphere or environment is fairly recent, since 1954. Why do you suppose it took so long for this sense to come into use? Is pollution a problem in your area? If so, what, if anything, is being done about it?

---

## SORT 12. Adding *-ion* to Base Words with Predictable Spelling Changes

### Sorting by Sound and Pattern

| *-de* → *-sion* | *-d* → *-sion* | *-mit* → *-mission* |
|---|---|---|
| **conclude/conclusion** | **extend/extension** | **admit/admission** |
| erode/erosion | comprehend/comprehension | omit/omission |
| explode/explosion | expand/expansion | permit/permission |
| invade/invasion | suspend/suspension | |
| persuade/persuasion | | |

***Considerations:*** The last sort in this section goes well beyond simply dropping a final *-e* before adding *-ion*; here some letters are dropped and others are substituted. Although at first glance the changes may seem complex, they are predictable. The *-mit* category, in particular, involves a family of words, words that derive or stem from the Latin root *mit*, meaning "to send." As is evident from Sort 12, significant changes occur in words of this type when *-ion* is added, but the same changes are made to all words in the family. Examples of other word families that require multiple changes when adding *-ion* are *describe/description* and *prescribe/prescription, produce/production* and *reduce/reduction, receive/reception* and *deceive/deception*.

Introduce the sort by asking students to pair the base words with their derived forms. Then ask them to review the list and look for ways to subdivide it that will help them to understand how to add the *-ion* suffix. They may arrive at two categories: *-sion* and *-ssion*. If so, ask if the same type of change was used with all of the words. With guidance they should arrive at the three groupings shown in Sort 12. Discuss their observations and thoughts. Remind students again that considering the base word can help with the spelling of words ending in *-ion*. Also, point out that sometimes, as with the *-mit* family, thinking of another word in the family and how its *-ion* form is spelled can aid spelling of a different word in the family.

### Talking Points

- Base words that end in *-de* or *-d* drop the letters and add *-sion*, as in *erode/erosion* and *expand/expansion*.
- Base words that end in *-mit*, drop the *-t* and add *-ssion*, as in *omit/omission*.
- Although some spelling changes that occur when adding *-ion* are complex, they tend to be consistent across a whole family of words, and therefore predictable.

**Did You Know?**  What possible connection could there be between animals such as beavers, gerbils, gophers, guinea pigs, hamsters, mice, muskrats, porcupines, rats, and squirrels and **erosion**? The animals listed are all *rodents*, mammals with upper and lower incisors that grow continuously. The word *rodent* shares a common ancestry with *erode*. Both derive from the Latin word for "to gnaw." Rodents must constantly gnaw in order to keep their ever-growing teeth from getting out of control, and erosion is a kind of "gnawing" or "eating away," of the earth's surface. It is not teeth that cause the wearing down though; it is forces such as wind, moving water, gravity, and ice. Given enough time, these forces can erode just about anything (consider the Grand Canyon or compare the heights of the older Appalachian Mountains to the younger Rocky Mountains).

# SORT 8 Silent and Sounded Consonants

| Silent Consonant | | Sounded Consonant |
|---|---|---|
| muscle | muscular | bombard |
| column | resign | haste |
| signature | autumn | wrest |
| bomb | solemn | resignation |
| moisten | design | soft |
| sign | hasten | columnist |
| autumnal | moist | designate |
| wrestle | soften | solemnity |

# SORT 9
### Adding *-ion* to Base Words with No Spelling Change

| -ct | -ct + ion | -ss | -ss + ion |
|---|---|---|---|
| direct | direction | express | |
| expression | infection | react | |
| impress | confession | detection | |
| reaction | possession | infect | |
| predict | connect | discussion | |
| election | possess | confess | |
| discuss | impression | detect | |
| connection | elect | prediction | |

# SORT 10

Adding *-ion* and *-ian* to Base Words with No Spelling Change

| -t | -t + ion | -ic | -ic + ian |
|---|---|---|---|
| digest | digestion | | magic |
| magician | electric | | invention |
| except | assertion | | adopt |
| clinician | invent | | musician |
| music | electrician | | present |
| presentation | optic | | suggestion |
| exception | assert | | optician |
| suggest | adoption | | clinic |

# SORT 11  Adding -ion to Base Words with E-Drop

| -te | E-Drop + ion | -se | E-Drop + ion |
|---|---|---|---|
| educate | education | confuse | |
| confusion | averse | precision | |
| celebration | evaporation | cooperate | |
| exaggeration | pollute | communicate | |
| illustration | immerse | celebrate | |
| communication | pollution | cooperation | |
| precise | aversion | evaporate | |
| immersion | illustrate | exaggerate | |

# SORT 12 Adding *-ion* to Base Words with Predictable Spelling Changes

| -de → -sion | -d → -sion | -mit → -mission |
|---|---|---|
| conclude | conclusion | extend |
| extension | admit | admission |
| comprehend | expansion | erode |
| persuade | omission | invasion |
| permit | explode | expand |
| erosion | persuasion | suspend |
| suspension | omit | permission |
| invade | comprehension | explosion |

# Vowel Alternations
### (DSA Feature R)

This section introduces students to another type of alternation, vowel alternations. As with consonant changes, the sound of a vowel pattern shifts from the base word to a derived form. Changes in stress sometimes occur, as well. There are three types of vowel alternations: long to short, long to schwa, and short to schwa. Usually the base word has the more obvious spelling, and the derived form the more obscure, as in *deprive/deprivation*. However, sometimes it is the derived form that is pronounced in a way that makes the spelling pattern obvious, as in *vitality* versus *vital*. As with consonant alternations, vowel alternations sometimes also involve predictable spelling changes.

*What Is Known:* Students have thoroughly examined basic vowel patterns by the time they reach the derivational constancy stage, including the schwa. They have also worked with stressed syllables and with affixation of suffixes. At this point in time, they likely have the additional advantage of having worked with one type of alternation, those involving consonants.

*What Is New:* The concept of vowel alternations and the types of changes that can occur.

---

## SORT 13. Long to Short Vowel Changes

|  Sorting by Sound ||
| --- | --- |
| Long | Short |
| **cave** | **cavity** |
| assume | assumption |
| athlete | athletic |
| crime | criminal |
| decide | decision |
| divide | division |
| humane | humanity |
| introduce | introduction |
| revise | revision |
| suffice | sufficient |
| type | typical |
| volcano | volcanic |

*Considerations:* This is a good time to observe the level of sophistication with which individual students approach the examination of words by asking them to complete an open sort (reserve the header words until the categories have been discussed). Do students begin by pairing the words, as that is how the last several sorts have been introduced? Or do they approach the words in some other manner? What do they do next? When they are finished sorting, ask for volunteers to share their results. Then, if no one has noticed the changes in vowel sound, which is likely, suggest that everyone pair up base words with their related forms in order to better examine the words. This may elicit ideas about vowel alternations, especially if you suggest that they pay attention to the vowel sounds in each word. Guide the students to the realization that each base word includes a long vowel that alternates to a short vowel in the derived form, as in *cave* and *cavity*. Ask them to identify the vowel alternation in each pair of words by underlining it. Add the headers and discuss the results, pointing out that just as with the consonant alternations, knowledge of vowel changes can help in spelling words. There are multiple ways to spell vowel sounds, but the spelling pattern tends to remain constant despite changes in sound. Therefore, knowing how to spell *please* helps to ensure *pleasant* as the correct spelling of the adjective, rather than *plesant*. Discuss any unfamiliar word meanings before closing the lesson. As an extension, you might assist students in identifying the various suffixes that have been added to the sort words, though without concern for how they were added.

### Talking Points

- When a suffix is added to a base word, the sound of a vowel may change, but the spelling is likely to remain constant, as in *divide/division* and *crime/criminal*.

**Did You Know?** *Volcano* takes its name from Vulcan, who was the Roman god of fire and metalworking. His forge was thought to be inside of Mount Etna (located on the island of Sicily off the coast of Italy), which periodically belched fire and flames. Over time, this and other erupting mountains came to be named *volcanoes*, after Vulcan.

   *Athlete* is derived from the Greek word *athlos*, meaning "prize," and *athlein*, "to compete for a prize." The word entered English in the 1500s. For a discussion of types of athletic competitions involving multiple events, see Sorts 26 and 27.

---

## SORT 14. Long to Schwa Vowel Changes

### Sorting by Sound

| Long | Schwa |
|------|-------|
| **invite** | **invitation** |
| admire | admiration |
| combine | combination |
| compete | competition |
| define | definition |
| deprive | deprivation |
| hesitate | hesitant |
| ignore | ignorant |
| narrate | narrative |
| organize | organization |
| relate | relative |
| social | society |

**Considerations:** As a check on students' ability to transfer understandings of long-to-short vowel alternations to long-to-schwa alternations and as an attention-getting way to introduce this sort, you might begin with a soft or ungraded quiz. Dictate five to seven of the words from the "schwa" category. Go over the spellings and discuss the results. Then, with the students' help, sort the words into "long" and "schwa" categories, using the header cards as a guide. Underline and discuss the vowel alternations of each pair and review the talking points.

### Talking Points

- Knowledge of related words can be especially helpful when spelling words with the schwa, as in *divide/dividend*, because despite changes in sound, the spelling is likely to remain constant.

*Did You Know?* **Define** is made up of two meaning units, or *morphemes*: the prefix, *de-*, and the word root, *fin*. Although *de-* has several meanings, here it acts as an intensifier; it emphasizes the meaning of the root, which is "boundary" or "limit." When we define something, we are setting limits on how people should think of the word. Imagine what our communication would be like if we did not define words! We find *fin* as a root in numerous other words, and it carries the same meaning—as, for example, in *confine*, which means "with boundaries," as when a person is confined to a hospital bed or an animal is confined to a cage. *Finish* and *finally* suggest that a person or thing has reached the limit, the end. Something that is *finite* has a limit. It does not go on forever, whereas something that is *infinite* (prefix *in-*, which means "no, not" + *fin*, which means "limit") has no limits. The etymologies of words provide this information; they tell the story or history of each word. An unabridged dictionary includes the information as part of the entry for the word.

---

## SORT 15. Long and Short Vowel Changes with Schwa

### Sorting by Pattern

| Base Word | Derived Word |
|---|---|
| **symbol** | **symbolic** |
| contribute | contribution |
| declare | declaration |
| distribute | distribution |
| habit | habitual |
| incline | inclination |
| mandate | mandatory |
| migrate | migratory |
| mobile | mobility |
| preside | president |
| prohibit | prohibition |
| reside | resident |

### Sorting by Sound (Vowel Change)

| Long | Schwa | Short | Schwa |
|---|---|---|---|
| **migrate** | **migratory** | **symbolic** | **symbol** |
| declare | declaration | contribute | contribution |
| incline | inclination | distribute | distribution |
| mandate | mandatory | habit | habitual |
| preside | president | mobility | mobile |
| reside | resident | prohibit | prohibition |

*Considerations:* Because the schwa vowel is so confusing to spell, this sort extends concepts from the previous sort. Here both long and short alternations with schwa are explored. Begin by asking students to sort the words into two categories, base words and derived words, as shown in the pattern sort. Then tell students that in addition to long-to-short and long-to-schwa alternations, there is another way that vowel sounds change when a suffix is added. Draw attention to the change in *migrate/migratory* in the sort just completed. Underline the vowel *a* in each word, and identify the sound it makes (long *a* in *migrate* and schwa in *migratory*). Set the pair of words aside, as shown in the sound sort. Follow the same process with *declare/declaration*, being sure to underline vowel *a* in each word and discuss the change in sound. Place the words under *migrate* and *migratory*. (If students wonder why it is not being called an *r*-controlled vowel, explain that when a vowel-plus-*r* pattern is in an unstressed syllable, as it is here, it is called a schwa.) Then place *symbolic* and *symbol* to the side of the other cards. Ask students to consider how the sound of the vowel changes. They should notice that it alters from a short *o* in *symbolic* to a schwa in *symbol*. Add the header cards and proceed with the remaining words in a similar manner. Discuss the talking points and clarify word meanings as needed. As an extension or follow-up, help students to identify the stressed syllable of each word (highlighting it is one way). Addition of the suffix causes the stress to shift, often turning a stressed syllable into an unstressed one and, therefore, a long or short vowel into a schwa.

### Talking Points

- Although suffixes sometimes cause a short or long vowel to become a schwa, thinking of the base word can clarify the spelling, as in *distribute/distribution*.

*Did You Know?* **Migrate** stems from a root meaning "to change one's place of living." The move is generally from one country or region to another; migrations are made by humans, birds, fish, and insects. Monarch butterflies, for example, migrate from their summer home in southern Canada to a winter range in central Mexico; many birds follow a similar pattern of behavior, often following similar routes, called *flyways*. Some fish migrate from one area of water to another or, as salmon do, from fresh water to salt water and back again. At times, over the centuries and millennia large numbers of humans have migrated. Sometimes the migrations have been brought about because people were forced away, at other times because they were seeking a better life. Migrant workers move for yet another reason. Their moves are often cyclical: They move according to where there is work, such as crops to harvest, and often return to the same locations the following year. *Emigrate* and *immigrate* are two related words that are sometimes confused. They describe the permanent moves of people. *Emigrate* refers to the departure point, the place from which the person is exiting, and *immigrate* considers the place to which the person is coming. Other related words include *emigrant*, *immigrant*, and *émigré*, one who left a native country, especially for political reasons. Were your ancestors immigrants at one time? From what country did they emigrate?

### Literature Links

Lawrence, J. (Illustrator). (1995). *The great migration: An American story*. New York: Harper Trophy. Chronicles the African-American migration north in the early 20th century through a sequence of 60 paintings and accompanying captions.

## SORT 16. Vowel Alternations with Predictable Spelling Changes

Sorting by Pattern

| Vowel Spelling Change | No Vowel Spelling Change |
| --- | --- |
| exclaim/exclamation | analyze/analysis* |
| explain/explanation | emphasize/emphasis |
| proclaim/proclamation | synthesize/synthesis |
| | |
| clarify/clarification | |
| justify/justification | |
| qualify/qualification | |
| | |
| deceive/deception | |
| perceive/perception | |
| receive/reception | |

*Considerations:* The purpose of this sort is to familiarize students with some of the predictable spelling changes that can occur with vowel alternations. After discussing any unfamiliar words, introduce the sort by informing students that just as consonant alternations sometimes entail a predictable spelling change, some vowel alternations do, also. Ask students to work with a partner to categorize pairs of words under the header categories: vowel spelling change and no vowel spelling change. Explain that there may be consonant spelling changes in some of the words, also, but that their focus is on the vowel pattern. Suggest that they underline or highlight letters that are involved in the spelling changes. When they are finished, discuss their results. Although all of the words involve vowel alternations, there is no spelling change for six of the words. Those that do change tend to do so in predictable ways: If you know how to spell one word in the family, you will likely be able to spell others. If students think about the words as four word families, each with common characteristics, learning to spell the words will be easier. Before ending the session, discuss any unfamiliar words.

*Note.* Although spelling is consistent in *analyze* and *analysis*, because the vowel is *y* rather than *i*, students may choose to classify the words as oddballs.

### Talking Points

- Some vowel alternations require a spelling change; however, these tend to be predictable, as in *deceive, perceive, receive* and *deception, perception, reception.*

*Did You Know?* Syn- is a prefix that means "like" or "together." It combines with roots of Greek origin, and when the combining root begins with *b, m,* or *p,* an alternative spelling for the prefix is used, *sym-,* as in *symbol, symmetry,* or *symphony.* **Synthesis** and *synthesize,* from the sort, literally mean "put together" (*thesis,* meaning "to put" + *syn-,* meaning "together"). Similarly, *synonym* means "like name" (*syn-,* meaning "like" + *-onym,* meaning "name"), and *synergy* means "work together" (*-ergy,* meaning "to work" + *syn-,* meaning "together"). Although *synthetic,* a related word, has been used for more than 300 years, the sense of something made artificially through a chemical process was not recorded until 1874. A few words carry the meaning of "synthetic" in the prefix, as, for example, *synfuel.*

## SORT 17. Syllable Stress and Vowel Alternations

### Sorting by Sound

| No Stress Change | Stress Change |
|---|---|
| (de**rive**)/deriv**a**tive | a**cad**emy/aca**dem**ic |
| (**la**bor)/**lab**oratory | **com**edy/co**me**dian |
| se**rene**/se**ren**ity | (de**rive**)/deri**va**tion |
| | di**plo**macy/diplo**mat**ic |
| | in**di**cate/in**dic**ative |
| | (**la**bor)/la**bor**ious |
| | **ma**jor/ma**jor**ity |
| | op**pose**/**op**posite |
| | per**spire**/perspi**ra**tion |
| | **pol**itics/po**lit**ical |

**Considerations:** This sort focuses on syllable stress with vowel alternations. Clarify the meanings of any unfamiliar words, then ask students to pair related words. Explain to them that you will be sorting the words according to whether there is a change in stress from the base word to the derived word. In Sort 17 *labor* and *derive* are shown in parentheses because the cards for these words will need to be used twice, as there are two derived words for each; students can simply move them from one category to another as the words are discussed. When they are finished sorting, discuss the vowel alternations. There are many, as most of the words involve more than one alternation, and the *academy/academic* pair involves three: *academic/academy*, *academy/academic*, and *academic/academy*! Using red, green, and blue crayons or markers, you might invite students to identify an alternation and underline or circle the involved letter in each word. Color coding will allow long-to-short, long-to-schwa, and short-to-schwa alternations to be marked in different colors. Finding all of the changes should not be an aim; awareness that multiple alternations can occur within a word should be. (Sort 17 shows sample responses.) Because a primary purpose of this sort is to increase awareness, repeated sorting of the words by students is unnecessary.

### Talking Points
• Some words include multiple vowel alternations, as in *academy/academic*.

**Did You Know?** Derivational constancy (this spelling phase) is a period of spelling development that focuses on derived words, words that come from the same source. We often associate the word *source* with rivers, as the place where they begin. The words **derive, derivation,** and **derivative** are actually developed from the Latin word *derivare*, which literally means to "draw off stream" (*de-*, meaning to "draw off" + *rivare*, meaning "stream"); in other words, something that is derived comes from a flowing or common source. Words that stem from the same word are said to *derive* from that word. They are *derivatives* of the word, as *labor, laborious,* and *laboratory* have all derived from the Latin word *labor;* they are derivatives of the word. *Rivulet* ("small stream") and *rival* ("one using the same stream as another") share *derive's* ancestry.

## **SORT 18.** Consonant, Vowel, and Stress Changes with *c*

### Sorting by Sound and Pattern (Consonant Alternations)

| /k/ → /s/ | /s/ → /sh/ |
|---|---|
| authentic/authenticity | commerce/commercial |
| eccentric/eccentricity | finance/financial |
| public/publicity | office/official |
| | prejudice/prejudicial |
| critic/criticize | |
| italic/italicize | audacity/audacious |
| | ferocity/ferocious |
| | tenacity/tenacious |

*Considerations:* This particular sort is reserved for the end because it involves stress changes and both vowel and consonant alternations. Also, the several suffixes involved will segue to some final work with suffixes and prefixes in the next section. The sort is intended to expand students' concept of a consonant alternation. Previous sorts with consonant changes dealt with the /shən/ ending, whereas this sort involves suffixes *-ize, -ity, -ial,* and *-ious.* Although the categories target alternations with *c,* addition of the suffix also brings about vowel and/or stress changes. Begin by discussing any unfamiliar words. Then ask students to pair related words. (Reserve the headers for later.) Once this is completed, give them an opportunity to review the paired list, speculate on the focus of the sort, and talk about their ideas with a partner before sharing them with the whole group. Then explain that this set of words involves more consonant alternations, and ask students to sort the words in a way that will highlight them. Let students know that there may be more than one way to group the words. When they are finished, discuss their results; accept any groupings that are reasonably justified. Then guide students to notice that some of the words alter from /k/ to/s/ and others from /s/ to /sh/ and that the words under each type of consonant alternation may be grouped by families. Discuss each family of words and any spelling consistencies. As an extension, you might ask students to look for examples of vowel and stress changes in the sort.

### Talking Points

- Other suffixes besides *-ion* can lead to consonant alternations; thinking of a related word can help with spelling, as with *critic/criticize, public/publicity,* and others.
- Adding a suffix can cause vowel and stress changes, as well as consonant alternations, as in *office/official.*

*Did You Know?* In ancient Rome, the word for **office** originally meant "a kind or helpful act." It then became synonymous with *job,* and in the 1300s Chaucer used it in his *Canterbury Tales* in the sense we commonly associate it with today: a place of work. A related word, *officious,* when borrowed into English was used to describe someone eager to help or serve. However, as sometimes happens, it began taking on a negative connotation, describing the volunteering and involvement of a person whose services were neither asked for nor needed. In time, this negative meaning of "meddling" became the primary meaning. The original meaning is still recorded in dictionaries, but it is identified as *archaic,* which means its use is rare. So though someday you may want to work as an official in an office, it probably would be best to avoid being officious.

# SORT 13 Long to Short Vowel Changes

| Long Vowel | | Short Vowel |
|---|---|---|
| cave | cavity | division |
| revision | humanity | provide |
| crime | typical | athletic |
| extremity | volcanic | decide |
| volcano | divide | introduction |
| athlete | type | revise |
| introduce | provision | criminal |
| decision | humane | extreme |

# SORT 14 Long to Schwa Vowel Changes

| Long Vowel | | Schwa Vowel |
|---|---|---|
| invite | invitation | deprivation |
| ignorant | organize | combine |
| admiration | define | hesitant |
| compete | narrate | society |
| relate | combination | definition |
| hesitate | social | admire |
| narrative | deprive | organization |
| competition | relative | ignore |

# SORT 15 Long and Short Vowel Changes with Schwa

| Long Vowel | Schwa Vowel | Short Vowel | Schwa Vowel |
|------------|-------------|-------------|-------------|
| migrate | migratory | symbol | |
| symbolic | distribute | president | |
| declaration | mandate | prohibit | |
| mobile | habitual | contribution | |
| distribution | preside | inclination | |
| habit | mandatory | declare | |
| contribute | reside | prohibition | |
| resident | incline | mobility | |

| Spelling Change | | No Spelling Change |
|---|---|---|
| exclaim | exclamation | deceive |
| reception | emphasis | qualify |
| justify | perception | synthesize |
| analyze | clarification | proclamation |
| qualification | explain | receive |
| proclaim | synthesis | clarify |
| emphasize | justification | deception |
| perceive | analysis | explanation |

# SORT 17 Syllable Stress and Vowel Alternations

| No Stress Change | | Stress Change |
|---|---|---|
| derive | derivative | comedian |
| comedy | academic | academy |
| diplomacy | perspiration | political |
| indicate | majority | opposite |
| serene | labor | perspire |
| laborious | indication | politics |
| oppose | diplomatic | laboratory |
| derivation | major | serenity |

# SORT 18 Consonant, Vowel, and Stress Changes with *c*

| /k/ → /s/ | | /s/ → /sh/ |
|---|---|---|
| authentic | authenticity | office |
| official | tenacity | commercial |
| prejudicial | critic | eccentric |
| tenacious | financial | ferocity |
| finance | audacious | public |
| publicity | criticize | ferocious |
| audacity | italic | prejudice |
| eccentricity | commerce | italicize |

# A Further Look at Suffixes and Prefixes
(DSA Features S and T)

This final section related to the study of patterns and meaning extends students' understanding of suffixes by examining several new ones: *-able* and *-ible*, *-ant* and *-ance*, as well as *-ent* and *-ence*, and provides a deeper investigation of *-ity* as a suffix (see Sort 18). Prefixes are also returned to in the context of *assimilated* or absorbed prefixes. Prefixes of this type lose the spellings we typically associate with them and take on new, sometimes unrecognizable spellings as they are absorbed into the letters that follow. Consider for example, the prefixes *in-* and *sub-* in *inactive* and *subway* compared with their spelling in *illiterate* and *supplanted*. This final study is especially important because the remainder of this book deals with Greek and Latin roots, which often have several affixes attached to form longer, lower frequency words.

## SORT 19. Examining Suffixes (*-able* and *-ible*)

### Sorting by Pattern and Meaning

| *-able* | *-ible* | Oddball |
|---|---|---|
| **acceptable** | **edible** | **?** |
| avoidable | audible | digestible |
| comfortable | compatible | |
| dependable | feasible | |
| fashionable | horrible | |
| favorable | incredible | |
| laughable | indelible | |
| perishable | irascible | |
| predictable | plausible | |
| preferable | | |
| questionable | | |
| reasonable | | |
| remarkable | | |

*Considerations:* Although this sort may be introduced as a structured sort with strong teacher guidance, you might try the following alternative: Introduce the sort with a soft (ungraded) quiz. Ask students to spell five to seven of the words. Be sure to include both *-able* and *-ible* words, but avoid the oddball for this purpose. After the dictation, distribute the template of words, including the headers. Students can use this to check their performance on the quiz. They will likely have confused suffixes and misspelled some of the words. Ask them to sort the words under the headers and generate a hypothesis to explain when we should use the *-ible* suffix and when *-able*. Encourage them to team up with a partner or two, and make it clear that their theory needs to work with every word in a given category. Any problem words should be placed as oddballs. Let them know that after a reasonable time they will have a chance to test their theory. As students work with the words, circulate and prompt their thinking. After adequate time, you might ask a volunteering team to explain their theory for when to use which suffix. Expand and clarify their thinking as needed. Once students understand the idea that *-able* usually attaches to base words and *-ible* to roots that cannot stand alone, give them an opportunity to write down the spelling of a transfer word, letting them know that your concern is with the suffix and not whether they can spell the entire word right. Alternatively, you might let each team collectively determine a spelling for the word. *Mandible* or *ostensible* are two possible transfer words, as are other *-ible* words not included in the sort. Discuss the word's spelling and strategies used to determine the correct suffix.

## Talking Points

- Base words usually require *-able* and roots *-ible*, as in *favorable* and *feasible*.

**Did You Know?**  Let's consider two of the *-ible* words: *irascible* and *horrible*. **Irascible** means "easily angered" and derives from the Latin word for *anger*. Other related words are *ire* and *irate*. The former refers to "anger" and the latter to being "extremely angry or enraged." **Horrible** was borrowed from the Latin word meaning "to bristle with fear, shudder." It is related to *horror, horrid, horrific, horrify, horrendous,* and *abhor,* which means to "regard something with loathing," to "shun" it (*ab-,* meaning "away" + *hor,* meaning "shudder"). If you've ever felt goosebumps or had your hair stand on end from fear, you've experienced *horipilation,* another member of this family.

---

## SORT 20. Taking a Closer Look (*-able*)

| Sorting by Pattern and Meaning | | |
| --- | --- | --- |
| Base + *able* | E-Drop + *able* | Oddball |
| **agreeable** | **valuable** | **?** |
| accountable | adorable | amiable |
| affordable | admirable | |
| commendable | advisable | |
| considerable | believable | |
| noticeable | comparable | |
| knowledgeable | debatable | |
| manageable | desirable | |
| rechargeable | disposable | |
| replaceable | excusable | |
| | recognizable | |
| | reusable | |

**Considerations:** As with the previous sort, begin with a soft quiz. Ask students to spell the following words: *considerable, advisable, knowledgeable, manageable, believable, affordable,* and *reusable.* Then distribute the template of words and allow time for students to check their spellings. Because they likely misspelled some of the words, tell them that adding *-able* to base words can be confusing but, as they will discover, clues in the words themselves can help with the spelling. Discuss any unfamiliar words, then ask the group to categorize the words under the appropriate headers. When they are finished, discuss each category, and be sure to talk about the spelling of the base word. This is especially important for a word such as *amiable,* which has no base word but is spelled with *-able* to avoid the situation of double *i*'s that would otherwise result—*amiible.* Point out the five words that retain the final *-e,* and ask students to consider why this is the case when normally the final *-e* is dropped. Provide time for them to discuss the possibilities with a partner and to share their ideas. If it is not mentioned, point out that in all of the words that kept the e, a c or g immediately precedes it. If the e was dropped, the a in -able would cause the soft sound of c or g to become hard. (For more on hard and soft c and g, see Sort 37 of Part 2.)

### Talking Points

- Base words drop the final -e before the -able suffix is added unless this will cause a soft c or g sound to be hardened; in this case the e is kept, as in *knowledgeable* and *noticeable*.

**Did You Know? Amiable,** which means "friendly, good-natured," stems from *amicus,* the Latin word for "friend." Because of its Latin origins we find words from other languages that also derived from *amicus,* with similar meanings and spellings. For example, *friend* in French is *ami,* in Italian it is *amico,* and in Portuguese and Spanish it is *amigo.* These words are examples of *cognates,* words related across languages (see Sort 58). There are many cognates. Other English words related to *amiable* include *amicable,* which means "showing good will, friendliness"; *amity,* which means "peaceful relations" (such as between countries); and the legal term *amicus curiae,* which literally means "friend of the court" and refers to a person asked to provide expertise on a topic affecting a court case but who is not actually involved in the case itself. As a friendly end note to this word story, consider the following anonymous quote: "The best vitamin for making friends is B-1." Perhaps the person was thinking of the importance of being amiable as one of the ingredients.

## SORT 21. Examining Suffixes (-ant, -ance, -ent, -ence)

### Sorting by Pattern and Meaning

| -ant | -ance | -ent | -ence |
|------|-------|------|-------|
| **attendant** | **attendance** | **different** | **difference** |
| important | importance | adolescent | adolescence |
| reluctant | reluctance | competent | competence |
| tolerant | tolerance | convenient | convenience |
| | | independent | independence |
| | | innocent | innocence |
| | | negligent | negligence |
| | | obedient | obedience |

*Considerations:* By now, students have considerable experience working with longer, more complex, and lower frequency words. If they need a slower entry into the concepts of this sort, you might introduce the -ant/-ance words first and then add in the others. Otherwise, introduce the sort by dictating three to five words for the students to spell. Some students will likely misspell one or more of the endings. Explain that words with /ənt/ and /əns/ can be confusing to spell because there is more than one way to represent the ending. This sort will provide some clues for choosing the correct ending. Distribute the template of words, and discuss any unfamiliar words. Be sure students understand the multiple meanings of tolerance: the "ability to put up with pain" and "respect for the beliefs and practices of others." (For ideas on teaching the latter see *www.teachingtolerance.org.* The site offers a free magazine and other excellent materials for teachers.) Ask students to pair related words—*attendant/attendance, different/difference*, and so forth. Then ask them to examine the pairs for clues and share their observations. Words with *-ant* also use *-ance*, and words with *-ent* use *-ence*. This is an important observation and a good talking point.

## Talking Points

- When trying to spell words ending in /ənt/ and /əns/, if you know how to spell one of the words, you can spell the other; thus *tolerant* becomes *tolerance*, not *tolerence*.

**Did You Know?** *Adolescent* and **adolescence** are both somewhat difficult words to spell due to their homophonic final syllables, which sound suggests could be spelled *-scent, -sent,* or *-cent* and *-scence, -sense,* or *-cents*. Although spellings of *adolesent* and *adolecents* might seem easier than the correct spellings, they completely obscure the meaning connection. Although *adolescent* has nothing to do with a sense of smell, it has everything to do with becoming an adult. *Adolescent* and *adult* come from the same Latin word, just different forms of it. So the one literally means "growing up," whereas the other means "grown up." Numerous other words carry this sense of "growing"; we can tell this by their *-escence* endings, for example, *convalescence*, which means "growing with strength" and *senescence*, which means "growing old." (See Sort 53 for other *-sen* words.)

---

## SORT 22. Taking a Closer Look (*-ant, -ance, -ent, -ence*)

### Sorting by Pattern and Meaning

| -ant | -ance | -ent | -ence | Oddball |
|------|-------|------|-------|---------|
| **relevant** | **relevance** | **excellent** | **excellence** | **?** |
| abundant | abundance | diligent | diligence | efficiency |
| assistant | assistance | equivalent | equivalence | relevancy |
| significant | significance | insistent | insistence | |
| | | persistent | persistence | |
| | | prominent | prominence | |
| | | efficient | | |

**Considerations:** This sort provides further exposure to *-ant, -ance, -ent,* and *-ence* and introduces students to a third member of these word families, namely *-ancy* and *-ency*. In some cases all three forms exist, as in *relevant, relevance,* and *relevancy* and *equivalent, equivalence,* and *equivalency*. In others, just two; for example, there is no such word as *efficience*, just *efficient* and *efficiency*. There are many words with these endings; as students collect them in their notebooks and encounter them in their reading, they may realize that the e-family is more common. This realization is important in developing a best guess strategy: If you don't know the spelling and can't find out, use *ent, ence,* or *ency*. Before ending the session, be sure students clearly understand what the words mean.

## Talking Points

- If the related word spelling is *-ent* or *-ence*, use *-ency*; if the spelling is *-ant* or *-ance*, use *-ancy*; keep in mind that many words do not include all three forms.

*Did You Know?* The original meaning of *sign* was "mark" or "indication"; we see this meaning connection carried into the word **significant** when we consider that something significant shows signs or indications of being important or meaningful. *Sign* has served as a building block for many other words. What words related to *sign* can you brainstorm, and what meaning connection can you uncover? (There are many possibilities, including the following: *signal, signage, signature, signet, assignment, consignment, countersign, cosign, designee, insignia, sign language,* and *resignation.*)

## SORT 23. Examining Suffixes (*-ity*)

### Sorting by Pattern and Meaning

| No Change | E-Drop | Spelling Change |
|---|---|---|
| Base + *ity* | E-Drop + *ity* | *-ble* → *bil* + *ity* |
| **popular/popularity** | **creative/creativity** | **available/availability** |
| familiar/familiarity | mature/maturity | eligible/eligibility |
| original/originality | sensitive/sensitivity | possible/possibility |
| peculiar/peculiarity | | responsible/responsibility |
| personal/personality | | |

*Considerations:* This sort focuses on three ways to add *-ity* to base words: with no change, with *e*-drop, and with a spelling change. Ask students to begin by pairing base words with their derived forms. Then, with the headers as guides, tell them to work with a partner to categorize the pairs of words. As you discuss the results, ask students to look carefully at words in the spelling change category to determine what the change is. If needed, there are numerous additional examples, such as *accountable/accountability, adaptable/adaptability, capable/capability,* and *sustainable/sustainability.*

### Talking Points

- When *-ity* is added to base words ending in *-ble*, the spelling changes to *bil* before the ending is added: *responsible/responsibility.*

*Did You Know?* In ancient Athens and other Greek cities, once a year citizens gathered in the marketplace for a **popular** vote. The focus of the meeting was to determine who, if anyone, should be banished from the city in order to improve it. Though the banishment was not permanent, the act was still one of disgrace. Each voter was given an *ostrakon*, a shell or pottery shard, as a ballot and asked to write the name of a person on it. If 6,000 or more votes were cast and the majority of them listed the same man, that person was cast out, or *ostracized*. Common use of the word today is no longer literal—instead of being banished, a person who is ostracized by others is likely to be excluded from social activities.

## SORT 24. Examining Assimilated Prefixes (*in-*)

| Sorting by Pattern | | | |
|---|---|---|---|
| Not | | | |
| *in-* | *il-* | *im-* | *ir-* |
| **inexpensive** | **illegal** | **immature** | **irregular** |
| inappropriate | illegible | immeasurable | irrational |
| inconvenient | illiterate | immobile | irrefutable |
| indecisive | illogical | immortal | irrelevant |
| indefinite | | immovable | irresistible |
| indescribable | | | irresponsible |
| indispensable | | | |
| inequality | | | |
| inexperienced | | | |

*Considerations:* This is the first of two sorts on *assimilated prefixes*. As noted at the onset of this section, these are prefixes that are absorbed into the word or root to which they attach. What does this mean for reading and spelling? The altered spelling of the prefix, including the double consonants that usually result, obscures the identity of the prefix, making it difficult for readers and writers to understand and spell such words, especially when the prefix is attached to a root. Because roots and prefixes abound in the next section, in order to help students better understand assimilated prefixes, they are addressed here and in Sort 25 in the context of affixation to base words, which is more straightforward. Two awarenesses can make it easier for readers and writers to interpret assimilated prefixes. Being familiar with regular suffixes helps students understand the range of possibilities for interpreting the prefix. Also, being skeptical of words that include a double consonant toward the beginning of the word helps, especially if some of the initial letters in the word are those of a known prefix. Take the word *surrender*, for example. The double consonants and *su-* initial letters suggest that the prefix *sub-* might be involved. Indeed, the word does include the prefix *sub-*, plus the root *render*, and literally means to "deliver under."

Introduce the words as a pattern sort and ask students to use the headers as guides for sorting. When the sorts are completed, discuss the meaning of the words by applying "not" to the base word, as in *immeasurable* means "not measurable" or "you can't measure it." The same assimilations sometimes carry the other meaning of *in-*, namely, "into," as in *immigrate*.

### Talking Points

• The prefix *in-*, meaning "not," can also be spelled *il-* (*illegal*), *im-* (*immortal*), or *ir-* (*irregular*).

*Did You Know?* **Immature** is comprised of *im-*, an assimilation of the prefix *in-*, here meaning "not" rather than "into," plus *mature*, which means "fully grown or developed." Apples on a tree may be immature and not ready for picking, a person's behavior can be immature regardless of age, and animals and plants that are still growing and developing are also considered immature. Over time different words have evolved to designate a still-developing plant or animal; for example, *sapling* for a young tree and *seedling* for a young plant grown from a *seed*. Although the same word may be used to describe several different immature animals—such as *joey* for kangaroos, koalas, wallabies, and opossums—there tend to be different names for the young of different animals. For instance, young alligators are called *hatchlings*; young dogs are called *pups*, as are the young of bats; young bears and tigers are *cubs*; young cats are *kittens*, whereas young foxes, beavers, and ferrets are *kits*; young hares are *leverets*; young spiders are *spiderlings*, and young fish are *fry*. Young horses are *foals* and pigs are *piglets*; young swans are *cygnets*, young turkeys are *poults*, and young pigeons are *squabs*. There are also *lambs*, *fawns*, *calves*, *ducklings*, *goslings*, and *tadpoles*; and, of course, among others, *infants* for monkeys, *babies* for apes, and *kids* for goats. What other words describe immature plants or animals?

---

## SORT 25. Examining Assimilated Prefixes (*ad-, com-, ex-, ob-, sub-*)

### Sorting by Pattern and Meaning

| Toward | With | Out | To/Against | Under |
|---|---|---|---|---|
| *ad-* | *com-* | *ex-* | *ob-* | *sub-* |
| **adjoin** | **compliant** | **exchange** | **obligation** | **submarine** |
| accompany | colleague | emerge | oppress | subdivision |
| affix | commotion | enumerate | | suffix |
| allure | connote | | | suppliant |
| annotate | cooperate | | | surreal |
| appointment | correspond | | | |
| assure | | | | |
| attempt | | | | |

***Considerations:*** This sort extends students' knowledge of prefix assimilation. It is not so important for students to understand the specific meaning of the individual prefixes and bases as it is important that they begin to recognize the "look" of various types of assimilated prefixes. For that reason, although this list is not all inclusive, a wide variety of assimilations has been included for each prefix. Discuss the assimilations and word meanings. Also, for a few of the words with obvious connections, talk about the meaning of the prefix as it relates to the base word, as with *adjoin* (*ad-* meaning "to" + *join* = "join to"); *affix* (*ad-* meaning "to" + *fix* = "fix to," "attach"); *compliant* (*com-* meaning "with" + *pliant* = "flexible with"); *enumerate* (*ex-* meaning "out" + *numerate* = "number out"); and *subdivision* (*sub-* meaning "below" + *division* = "division below"), namely, not the main division, such as a town, but a smaller part. In the case of *ob-*, draw students' attention to the fact that the prefix has multiple meanings, two of which are nearly opposites, as in *obligation* (*ob-* meaning "to" + *ligation* = "bind to") and *oppress* (*ob-* meaning "against" + *press* = "press against"). Sentence context can help in determining which meaning to apply.

### Talking Points

• The prefixes *ad-*, *com-*, *ex-*, *ob-*, and *sub-* assimilate to base words and roots, often resulting in double letters and changed spellings, as in *appoint*, *commission*, and *effort*.

***Did You Know?*** **Accompany** means "to go with a companion." *Companion* derives from the Latin *com-*, "together," and *panin*, "bread." A companion is literally someone with whom you share bread. It is interesting to consider that *company*, which carries the same meaning connections, is, in the literal sense, a business made up of individuals who have the kind of close relationship that encourages them to sit down together to share their bread.

# SORT 19 Examining Suffixes (-*able* and -*ible*)

| -able | | -ible |
|---|---|---|
| acceptable | edible | remarkable |
| predictable | dependable | incredible |
| fashionable | indelible | questionable |
| compatible | avoidable | horrible |
| laughable | digestible | preferable |
| plausible | reasonable | favorable |
| comfortable | irascible | audible |
| feasible | perishable | ? |

# SORT 20 Taking a Closer Look (-able)

| Base + able | | E-Drop + able |
|---|---|---|
| agreeable | valuable | disposable |
| comparable | advisable | affordable |
| noticeable | recognizable | debatable |
| adorable | considerable | reusable |
| rechargeable | excusable | knowledgeable |
| accountable | desirable | admirable |
| believable | replaceable | amiable |
| manageable | commendable | ? |

# SORT 21 Examining Suffixes (-*ant*, -*ance*, -*ent*, -*ence*)

| -ant | -ance | -ent | -ence |
|------|-------|------|-------|
| attendant | attendance | | different |
| difference | tolerance | | independent |
| convenient | innocence | | reluctance |
| adolescent | negligent | | competent |
| negligence | important | | convenience |
| tolerant | adolescence | | obedience |
| innocent | competence | | reluctant |
| importance | obedient | | independence |

# SORT 22 Taking a Closer Look (*-ant, -ance, -ent, -ence*)

| -ant | -ance | -ent | -ence |
|------|-------|------|-------|
| relevant | relevance | | excellent |
| excellence | prominence | | insistent |
| diligent | efficient | | significance |
| abundant | insistence | | abundance |
| prominent | assistant | | equivalence |
| equivalent | efficiency | | persistence |
| diligence | persistent | | assistance |
| significant | relevancy | | ? |

# SORT 23 Examining Suffixes (*-ity*)

| No Change | E-Drop | Spelling Change |
|---|---|---|
| popular | popularity | creative |
| creativity | available | availability |
| familiar | personality | mature |
| originality | responsible | familiarity |
| possible | sensitivity | eligibility |
| peculiarity | eligible | peculiar |
| possibility | original | sensitive |
| maturity | responsibility | personal |

# SORT 24 Examining Assimilated Prefixes (*in-*)

| in- | il- | im- | ir- |
|---|---|---|---|

| | | |
|---|---|---|
| inexpensive | illegal | immature |
| irregular | immeasurable | irrelevant |
| indescribable | irrefutable | inappropriate |
| immortal | indispensable | illogical |
| indecisive | irresponsible | illegible |
| irrational | indefinite | irresistible |
| inequality | immobile | inexperienced |
| illiterate | inconvenient | immovable |

# SORT 25  Examining Assimilated Prefixes (*ad-*, *com-*, *ex-*, *ob-*, *sub-*)

| ad- | com- | ex- | ob- | sub- |
|-----|------|-----|-----|------|

| | | |
|---|---|---|
| adjoin | compliant | exchange |
| obligation | submarine | colleague |
| suffix | assure | affix |
| annotate | commotion | enumerate |
| emerge | subdivision | appointment |
| connote | allure | suppliant |
| surreal | oppress | correspond |
| accompany | cooperate | attempt |

# Greek and Latin Word Elements

This final section of word study for derivational constancy spellers explores words largely through the lens of meaning. By now, students should have a firm grasp of sound–pattern associations (*phonics*); realize how words divide into syllables (*syllabication*); and understand the structure of compounds, base words, and various prefixes and suffixes and how they work together (*morphology*). They have also explored meaning through such features as homophones and homographs. When it comes to understanding the meanings of words, particularly the sophisticated vocabulary of the academic language found in middle school and high school texts, learners will benefit from understanding the Greek and Latin roots (along with prefixes and suffixes) that make up the words. By understanding individual units of meaning, called *morphemes*, and considering them in relation to other meaning chunks in the word, readers can comprehend many otherwise unfamiliar words. Take, for example, the longest word in any English dictionary. Despite its rather intimidating 45-letter length, most readers of this book will probably be able to approximate a meaning for the word by considering one meaning chunk at a time. In fact, a seventh-grade teacher found her students quite up to the challenge after a brief introduction to the study of roots. The Fun with Words website (*www.fun-with-words.com*) reports that the word is included in several dictionaries; it was coined in the 1930s by the president of the National Puzzlers' League. Why? Just to create a new "longest" word. So whether you think of this as a "little-engine-that-could" sort of word or more simply a chunking challenge, give it a try. When finished, check the answer in the box on page 248.

What does the following word mean?

pneumonoultramicroscopicsilicovolcanoconiosis

This section on word roots includes 32 sorts. It begins with an exploration of common Greek and Latin prefixes and a study of basic Greek roots, also known as *combining forms*. These elements are examined first because words generated from them tend to be semantically more transparent and because many of the words occur with relative frequency beginning in the upper elementary grades and continuing on through middle school and high school. Common Latin roots are then introduced, with a thorough look at the way meaning changes when prefixes are combined with the root. Following the study of common Greek and Latin roots, the focus shifts to less common roots. In these sorts, the roots may be all Greek, all Latin, or a combination of the two. Some sorts include two different roots with the same meaning. Because English includes borrowings from both Greek and Latin, we sometimes have roots for the same concept from each language. For example, we have *pod*, which comes from Greek, meaning "foot" (as in *tripod, gastropod, podium*), but we also have *ped* from Latin, which means "foot" (as in *pedal, pedestrian, pedestal*). At times this has the potential to confuse readers, because the same spelling used for a root in one language may be used for a root with an entirely different meaning in the other language; as, for example, *ped*, which in Latin means "foot," but which in Greek means "child," as in *pediatrics*. The context of the sentence and the combining parts used with the word can help readers to determine the appropriate meaning.

Word elements for the 32 sorts in this section were selected and sequenced on the bases of utility or frequency, clarity of meaning, combinability with other word elements, interest, and topic. Each sort focuses on a theme, and the roots chosen for the sort reflect that particular theme. Examples of themes include numbers, size and amount, senses, actions, body parts, ruling and governing, and others. In most cases I have refrained from including words with as-yet-unstudied roots. Although this was not always possible, it does help students to focus on a more limited number of

> *It is a lung disease caused by breathing in particles of volcanic dust.*

new word parts, and it provides opportunity to review roots when students encounter words in later studies with roots they already know. Despite the progression laid out for the sorts in this section, most can be used flexibly to fit with a particular content area or literature study. If they are going to be used out of order, I suggest that you first help students to build a foundation of knowledge through Sorts 26, 27, 29, 31, and 32, then identify particular themed sorts of interest for study. As students study Greek and Latin word elements, they will undoubtedly encounter words with which they are not familiar. Learning to unravel the meanings of such words and expanding vocabulary knowledge is really what this section is all about, with the hope that, along the way, students will learn to savor the language as well.

Because the focus for studying Greek and Latin word elements is on building vocabulary, definitions and meaning connections replace the how-to information of earlier "Considerations" discussions. Also, instead of a separate "Talking Points" section for each sort, important information for students to understand and remember related to roots and their meanings is incorporated into the answer key for each sort.

The sorts can be introduced in various ways. One possibility is to ask students to categorize the words according to elements listed in the headers. Allow time for them to consider and talk about meaning connections among the words, as well as any unfamiliar words. If one aim is for them to try to determine the meanings of the various roots or prefixes, retain the headers until the discussion. Be sure that students have access to a good unabridged dictionary so that they can investigate meanings and explore the etymologies of some of the words. Any unabridged dictionary will include etymological information, as well as definitions. Definitions in this section come from *The American Heritage College Dictionary* (4th ed., 2004), and from the larger *American Heritage Dictionary of the English Language* (3rd ed., 1996). If students are not already recording word study work in a notebook, this is an excellent time to start.

## SORT 26. Greek and Latin Prefixes: Numbers (*mono-, bi-, tri-*)

| One | Two | Three |
|-----|-----|-------|
| *mono-* | *bi-* | *tri-* |
| **monotone** | **bicycle** | **triangle** |
| monolingual | biceps | triad |
| monolith | bicuspid | triathlon |
| monologue | biennial | trigonometry |
| monopoly | bifocals | trilogy |
| monorail | bimonthly | trio |
| monotonous | binary | triplets |
| | biweekly | triptych |
| | | trivial |

*Considerations:* This sort sets the stage for future discussions of word elements. The meaning of each word in the sort is made transparent by linking the meaning of the prefix to the meaning of the word root. This type of process can be applied to other sorts in this section, but **keep the idea-sharing conversational**; it should not be a recitation of the meanings of prefixes and roots.

Ask students to categorize the words, using the headers as guides. Then suggest that they consider how the prefixes affect the meanings of the words in each category and share their ideas. They should realize some of the following connections and you should draw others to their attention: *Monotone* means "one tone," in other words a tone with no variation; *monolingual* means "one language" (students may be familiar with *bilingual*, but not *monolingual*); a *monologue* is "a (long) speech by one person," whereas a dialogue involves two or more persons. You might ask students what they think *-logue* means. In *monopoly*, the prefix meaning "one" combines with a root that means "to sell." Whether in the game or in real life, a monopoly exists when a person or group has total control over selling or producing services and goods. A *monorail* is a system of transportation that relies on one rail instead of two. For a discussion of *monolith*, see "Did You Know?" for this sort.

*Bicycle* has a clear connection to *bi-* with its two wheels; *bifocals* are lenses that are corrected for two different types of seeing or focusing. *Bimonthly* and *biweekly* have multiple meanings that can be confusing; lexicographers urge writers to use the words to mean "happening every 2 months" or "2 weeks," respectively (not twice monthly or weekly; *semi-* is the prefix of choice for these meanings). *Bisect* means "cut into two parts." *Biceps* are muscles that attach in two places, what must *triceps* be? *Bicuspids* are teeth with two sharp points, or cusps, located midway on each side of your mouth, top and bottom. *Biennial* stems from a root meaning "year," as does *annual;* it means "happening every other year" or "lasting for 2 years." *Binary* refers to something composed of two parts. For example, a binary number system uses just the numbers 0 and 1, rather than 0–9, as does our base-10 number system. Instead of counting 0, 1, 2, 3, 4, 5, . . . counting goes 0, 1, 10, 11, 100, 101, and so on.

The meaning connection to "three" is clear in *triangle, triplets,* and *trio* but may not be in some of the words. A *triathlon* is an athletic competition that involves three events: swimming, bicycling, and running. *Trigonometry* is the study of triangles. A *triad* is a group of three (students may sometimes work in triads), and a *trilogy* is a group of three literary works that are united by a theme. (You might ask students if they have read any *trilogies.*) What about the word *triptych,* which may be unfamiliar to teachers and students? Invite students to guess possible meanings for the word before telling them "three folds." In ancient Rome, a triptych (**trĭp•**tĭk) was a hinged writing tablet with three leaves. It is also a piece of artwork consisting of three painted or carved panels that are hinged together. Most museums of art have examples on display. The last *tri-* word, *trivial,* stems from a word meaning "three roads" (*tri-* + *via*). Places where three roads met were sometimes very public. The "public" sense of the word evolved into "commonplace" and eventually to the modern meaning of something insignificant.

***Did You Know?* Monolith** is derived from *mono-,* meaning "one," and *lith,* meaning "stone." It refers to a geological feature that is a single massive stone, as well as to something made of a large block of stone, such as a monument or sculpture. *Monolithic* rock formations are found on all of the continents, including Antarctica. *Trilithons* (trī•**lĭth•**ŏn), as the name suggests, have something to do with three stones. Trilithons, or *triliths,* are a type of prehistoric structure made of two large upright stones with a third placed across the top. The most famous trilithons are part of Stonehenge in England. The standing stones were placed in a circle more than 4,000 years ago, with an embankment and ditch surrounding the stones that is even older. Based on the circular design, archeologists believe that Stonehenge was used as a religious center and as an astronomical observatory.

**SORT 27.** Greek and Latin Prefixes: More Numbers (*quadr-, pent-, oct-, dec-, cent-*)

| Four | Five | Eight | Ten | Hundred |
|------|------|-------|-----|---------|
| *quadr-* | *pent-* | *oct-* | *dec-* | *cent-* |
| **quadruple** | **pentagon** | **octopus** | **decade** | **century** |
| quadrangle | pentathlon | octagon | decathlon | bicentennial |
| quadrant | pentad | octave | December | centenarian |
| quadruplets | | octet | decimal | centigrade |
| | | October | decimeter | centimeter |
| | | octogenarian | | percent |

*Considerations:* Students may or may not make a connection between words with *quadr-* and words with *quart-* (not included in this sort), which have a related but different meaning. Words of the latter type (*quarter, quart, quarterly*) also have to do with the number four, but mean "one-fourth." A *pentad* is a group of five (providing opportunities for students to work in triads and pentads will help to reinforce the meanings of these two words). *Pentagon* is a shape with five sides and five angles, but when capitalized it refers to a building in which the U.S. Department of Defense is located. It takes its name from the shape of the building. A *pentathlon*, like the *triathlon* of the previous sort, is an athletic competition, in this case with five events. What, then, is a *decathlon*? What events make up each competition? An *octave* refers to a tone that is eight steps higher or lower than another tone, as well as to eight lines of poetry, and an *octet* usually refers to a group of eight singers. The *gen* in *octogenarian* means "ten times." If students apply their prior understanding of *-ian*, as well as knowledge of *gen* and *oct-*, they may deduce that an *octogenarian* is a person in his or her 80s (10 × 8 = 80). Then how old is a *centenarian*? Ask students what they think *bicentennial* means (happening every 200 years). See "Did You Know?" for discussions of *octopus*, *October*, and *December*.

*Did You Know?* **Octopuses** or octopi are marine mollusks with round, soft bodies and eight tentacles, often called "arms." A close look at the word *octopus* gives rise to a question: Octo- = "eight," but what about *pus*? Rather than meaning "arm," this root is a variation of the Greek root for "foot" (see "Considerations" for Sort 39), probably so called because the creature moves around on these, which is something we do not do with our arms.

You might be wondering: If *octo-* means "eight" and *dec-* means "ten," why is our tenth month called **October**, and why is **December**, with its meaning of "ten," used for the twelfth month? To understand how this came about, we must know more about the calendar. The first Roman calendar probably came into existence more than 2,700 years ago. At that time the year had 10 months, or 304 days. A month went from one full moon to the next. The calendar started with the spring equinox in March, ignoring 2 months of winter altogether. The names of the months fit that early calendar. Some 700 years after the calendar was initiated, Julius Caesar, a famous Roman leader, hired an astronomer to identify ways to improve the calendar. Instead of a lunar-based calendar, the astronomer suggested one based on the sun. He allowed for leap year and moved the beginning of the year from March 1 to January 1. It is still the calendar we use today.

## SORT 28. Greek and Latin Prefixes: Size and Amount (*semi-, poly-, multi-, micro-, mega-*)

| Half, Partly | Many | Many | Small | Large |
|---|---|---|---|---|
| *semi-* | *poly-* | *multi-* | *micro-* | *mega-* |
| **semisweet** | **polysyllabic** | **multicultural** | **microphone** | **megaphone** |
| semicircle | polydactyl | multimedia | microbe | megabyte |
| semicolon | polygon | multinational | microchip | megalopolis |
| semifinals | polygraph | multiplication | microcosm | |
| semiskilled | | multipurpose | microfilm | |
| semisolid | | | microscope | |

*Considerations:* Most of the meaning connections for this sort are straightforward. *Polydactyl* is an unusual word. Though uncommon, *dactyl* is a word meaning "finger" or "toe"; it is derived from the Greek word for "finger." So *polydactyl* means "many fingered" or "many toed"; it refers to a person or animal having more than the usual number of fingers or toes. A *polygraph* is an instrument that can keep track of several bodily processes, such as blood pressure and breathing, at the same time. It is often used as a lie detector. A *microbe* is a microscopic organism. The word comes from *microscopic* and *bios* and literally means "small life." *Microcosm*, which comes from *micro-* and *cosm*, literally means "small world." A *megabyte* is a unit of computer memory equal to 1,000,000 bytes. So how much is a *byte*? It is the amount of computer memory it takes to store one character (the word *character* is composed of nine characters, so imagine how many characters there are in this book!). *Megalopolis* is discussed in the "Did You Know?" section for this sort.

*Did You Know?* Although the *mega-* in **megalopolis** stems from the same Greek word as the other listed words and means "large" or "great," its meaning is slightly different, referring to something of *abnormal* size or greatness. The root *-polis* means "city." When we combine it with *megal-*, we have "a city of abnormal size." A *megalopolis* is not a typical city. In fact, it is not an actual city at all; it is a "region made up of several large cities sufficiently close to be considered a single urban complex." In other words, people commute between the cities and may live in suburbs that are residential areas of more than one of the cities. For example, in the United States, the Boston to Washington, D.C., corridor is sometimes referred to as the "BosWash" megalopolis that includes the cities of Boston and Washington and also Hartford, Connecticut; New York City; Philadelphia, Pennsylvania; Baltimore, Maryland; and all of their surrounding areas, such as New Jersey, Delaware, and other areas. The biggest megalopolis is in Japan, but other parts of Asia, as well as Europe and Africa, also have megalopolises. By looking at a map you might be able to tell where they are located.

## SORT 29. Common Greek Elements (*auto-*, *bio-*, *geo-*, *graph*, *-meter/metr*, *therm*)

| Self | Life | Earth | Write | Measure | Warm, Hot |
|------|------|-------|-------|---------|-----------|
| *auto-* | *bio-* | *geo-* | *graph* | *-meter/metr* | *therm* |
| automatic | biology | geology | graphite | speedometer | thermostat |
| (autobiography) | antibiotics | geode | (autograph) | barometer | (geothermal) |
| (autograph) | (autobiography) | (geography) | (autobiography) | (geometry) | (thermometer) |
| automobile | biodegradable | (geometry) | (biography) | odometer | |
| | (biography) | (geothermal) | cartographer | (thermometer) | |
| | bionic | | epigraph | | |
| | biosphere | | (geography) | | |
| | | | homograph | | |

*Considerations:* Numerous words in this sort include elements from other words in the sort. For example, *autobiography* includes the prefixes *auto-* and *bio-* and the root *graph*. Such words are designated in the answer key by parentheses, and they are listed with each applicable word element. As you guide students through the sort, placement of these words into a particular category is not important; what is important is that students recognize that some of the words include multiple elements from the sort. Ask them to consider why all of this duplication exists. If they do not mention the possibility that the word elements are common and therefore found in lots of words, bring this to their attention. Encourage students to generate additional words for one of the roots; *graph*, in particular, is in many words, often as *-graphy*. Because *auto-* occurs at the beginning of words, a dictionary can easily be used to help generate words for that word element. With word roots this is more difficult, because roots often have prefixes and suffixes attached. Go over any unfamiliar words as you discuss meaning connections. You might invite students to speculate on the meaning of *automaton*. It derives from a word that means "self-acting" and refers to a robot. (See Part 2, Sort 21.) *Epigraph* and several words sometimes confused with it are discussed in the "Did You Know?" section.

*Did You Know?* The prefix *epi-* has several meanings, including "over," "around," "beside," "near," "after," and "on," as in the epicenter of an earthquake, which is on or at the center of an earthquake. There are several writing-related words with the prefix *epi-* that can be confusing: **epigraph** (included in this sort), *epigram*, *epithet*, and *epitaph*. *Epigraph* refers to the inscription on a statue and to a short saying at the beginning of a literary work related to the theme. *Epigrams* are short and often witty sayings. Samuel Taylor Coleridge, a poet, captured the meaning of *epigram* in the following epigram: "*What is an epigram? A dwarfish whole; its body brevity, and wit its soul.*" An *epithet*, meaning literally "attributed to," is a term used to characterize a person or thing. Homer, an ancient Greek poet, for example, often called Vulcan (Sort 13) "the famous craftsman" and Poseidon, thought to be the god of water, earthquakes, and horses, "earth-shaker." An *epitaph*, which literally means "on tomb," is an inscription on a tomb written in memory of someone buried there. Two examples follow. The first was written about the deceased, Stanley Laurel, a famous English-born comedian who, with Oliver Hardy, was a Hollywood star between the 1930s and 1950s: "*A master of comedy; his genius in the art of humour brought gladness to the world he loved.*" The second epitaph was written by Benjamin Franklin in anticipation of his death:

The body of Benjamin Franklin, Printer,
Like the covering of an old book
Its contents torn out and
Stript of its lettering and gilding
Lies here, food for worms;
Yet the work shall not be lost.
For it will (as he believed) appear once more
In a new and beautiful edition,
Corrected and amended by the author.

## SORT 30. Common Greek and Latin Elements (*aud, phon, vis, -scope, tele-*)

| Hear | Sound | See | See | Distance |
|---|---|---|---|---|
| *aud* | *phon* | *vis* | *-scope* | *tele-* |
| **audience** | **homophone** | **supervise** | **kaleidoscope** | **telegraph** |
| inaudible | phonics | (audiovisual) | periscope | telecommunications |
| (audiovisual) | phonograph | envision | stethoscope | telemarketing |
| audition | symphony | (television) | (telescope) | (telephone) |
| auditorium | (telephone) | visibility | | (telescope) |
| | | vista | | telethon |
| | | | | (television) |

*Considerations:* Some students may be unfamiliar with the meaning of *phonograph*, a device on which "written sound" can be heard by means of a stylus and record or rotating disk. *Symphony* literally means "sound together"; a *vista* is a view, or "what you see"; and *kaleidoscope*, an apt name given the beautiful patterns created by the device, literally means "see beautiful." *Stethoscope*, a device used by a doctor to listen to a person's heart and lungs, quite literally means "see chest"; here viewing is used figuratively and refers to being able to take in information. A discussion of *television* and *telethon* follows.

*Did You Know?* The **television**, a more recent invention, was first revealed at the Chicago 1933 Century Progress Exposition. How long do you suppose it was before the first TV dinner was created? Or before the first TV **telethon** was held? In *telethon*, the prefix *tele-* has been combined with a portion of *marathon*, which is a prolonged activity or event that usually involves endurance. *Telethon* first came into use in 1952, but before that there was *walkathon* (1932) and *talkathon* (1948). Since the early 1970s numerous *-thon* words have appeared: *bikeathon, hikeathon, readathon, singathon, workathon*. Words of this type with limited use have not yet made into the dictionary and would be considered nonsense words. If you were going to coin a *-thon* word, what would it be?

**SORT 31.** Applying Prefix Knowledge to Common Latin Roots (*ject* and *tract*)

| Throw | Draw, Pull |
|-------|------------|
| *ject* | *tract* |
| **projector** | **tractor** |
| abject | abstract |
| adjective | attract |
| conjecture | contraction |
| dejected | detract |
| eject | distracted |
| injection | extract |
| interject | intractable |
| objection | protracted |
| projectile | retraction |
| rejection | subtract |
| subjects | traction |

*Considerations:* Prefixes play a critical role throughout the word studies in this section: Many of the words generated with a particular root involve no other word roots, just the addition of a prefix and/or suffix. Again and again, you find the same prefixes being attached to different roots. Although by now students have considerable experience affixing prefixes to base words, in this sort and the one that follows, attention turns to combining prefixes with word roots. By considering the meaning of the root and an attached prefix, students can approximate the meaning of an unfamiliar word. The table that follows illustrates this. It shows the word, the literal meaning of the prefix and root combined, and the actual meaning of the word. Because of the strong recurrence of these prefixes, take the time to discuss the meaning relationships, literal and actual. Making comparisons across the two roots, which rely on many of the same prefixes, can help to make the connections clear. Invite students to think of sentence examples for the words; share and talk about these.

Begin by asking students to speculate on the literal meanings of *projector* and *tractor*. Explain that a projector is literally something that "throws forward," in this case light and an image, and a tractor is "something that pulls or draws." Ask what part of each word carries the meaning of "throw" or "pull." After talking about the roots, ask students to sort the word cards into two categories, using the headers as guides. Distribute copies of the blank chart "Applying Prefix Knowledge to Common Latin Roots," found in Appendix H. Explain to students that you will be taking a close look at how prefixes affect the meaning of a root. Talk about the meaning of words in the sort categories that have prefixes. As you do so, ask students to add the word and its meaning to the table. (Although the literal or actual meaning listed in the following table may be used for recording, it will likely be more valuable to students to use a meaning that they articulate after discussing the word.) Continue the process for each word. If time is limited, continue the discussion at a later time. The "Understanding Prefixes" table from Appendix G may be helpful for this activity and other word studies in this section. After discussing information from the table, you might ask students to brainstorm additional words that could have been included but were not.

| | ject *(throw)* | | | tract *(draw, pull)* | |
|---|---|---|---|---|---|
| **Word** | Literal meaning | *Actual meaning* | **Word** | Literal meaning | *Actual meaning* |
| **abject** | throw away, as in "outcast" | *wretched, contemptible* | **abstract** | draw away | *consider apart from* |
| **adjective** | throw to, as in "add to" | *added to (a noun)* | **attract\*** | pull to | *draw interest to* |
| **conjecture\*** | throw together | *infer or guess* | **contraction\*** | draw together | *a pulling together* |
| **dejected** | throw down | *downcast* | **detract** | pull away | *divert attention, draw away* |
| — | | | **distracted** | draw apart | *diverted attention* |
| **eject\*** | throw out | *force to leave* | **extract** | draw away from | *pull away, remove, derive* |
| **injection** | throw into | *something put in, as a shot* | **intractable** | not able to be pulled | *stubborn* |
| **interject** | throw between | *insert between* | — | | |
| **projectile** | throw forth | *something that can be thrown* | **protracted** | draw forth | *drawn out* |
| **rejection** | throw back | *refusal* | **retraction** | draw back | *something taken back* |
| **subjects** | throw under | *persons under the power of another* | **subtract** | draw under | *take away* |
| — | | | **traction** | pull, draw | *act of pulling* |

*Prefix is assimilated.

*Did You Know?* **Tractors,** as the name suggests, are vehicles used to pull. They come in various sizes suited to the job: from small garden tractors for mowing lawns and tilling gardens to large tractors used in agriculture to plow fields, harvest crops, and pull heavy equipment. Work performed by the latter type of tractor was carried out by horses before the tractor's invention. In mid-1800 when horses pulled the farming machines, farmers would often boast about the strength of their horses. Horse pulling contests were held to test the strength and stamina of the animals. A sled was attached to the horse and weight added to see if the horse could pull it. If the horse moved the load, more weight was added. Sometimes the pulling was done by teams of horses. Although it has been suggested that this event gave rise to the term *horsepower,* the word actually was coined by James Watt, an inventor. Pulling events are still held, but now the boasting and comparing is done with tractors.

## SORT 32. Applying Prefix Knowledge to More Common Latin Roots (*mis/mit, port*)

| Send<br>*mis/mit* | Carry<br>*port* | Oddball |
|---|---|---|
| **mission** | **portfolio** | **?** |
| admittance | comport | transatlantic |
| commission | deport | transit |
| dismiss | export | transplant |
| emissions | import | |
| intermittent | rapport | |
| missile | reporter | |
| omitted | supportive | |
| promise | transportation | |
| remittance | | |
| submissive | | |
| transmission | | |

*Considerations:* Like the previous sort, this one builds knowledge of meaning connections between specific prefixes and two word roots, in this case *mis* or *mit* and *port*. In addition, students are introduced to *trans-*, a prefix that is used in two of the words. Discuss the meaning of *trans-* in relation to the words *transit*, *transplant*, and *transatlantic*, then talk about the two roots. The same process used in the previous sort can be used here. The time spent familiarizing students with prefixes and how they affect the meaning of roots will benefit them throughout their study of roots. Begin with *mission*, *missile*, and *portfolio*, which do not include prefixes, and talk about their meaning connection to the root, *mis/mit* or *port*. Students should understand that *mis* and *mit* are the same root but just have different spellings to fit different endings that may be attached to them. They may wonder about rapport and its prefix. This word, which is of French and Latin origins, actually reveals remnants of two prefixes (*re-* and *ad-*) plus the root *port*. As you discuss the words, watch for signs of carryover from the previous sort. Are students able to suggest meanings for some of the prefixes? Are they able to use their knowledge to make sense of the word?

| | **mit/mis** *(send)* | | | **port** *(carry)* | |
|---|---|---|---|---|---|
| **Word** | Literal<br>meaning | *Actual*<br>*meaning* | **Word** | Literal<br>meaning | *Actual*<br>*meaning* |
| **admittance** | send toward | *permission to*<br>*enter* | — | | |
| **commission** | send with | *persons*<br>*allowed to*<br>*perform*<br>*certain duties* | **comport** | carry together | *behave*<br>*oneself, agree*<br>*with* |
| — | | | **deport** | carry away | *expel from a*<br>*country; also,*<br>*comport* |

| | mit/mis *(send)* | | | port *(carry)* | |
| | Literal meaning | Actual meaning | | Literal meaning | Actual meaning |
| **Word** | | | **Word** | | |
| --- | --- | --- | --- | --- | --- |
| **dismiss** | send apart | direct or allow to leave | — | | |
| **emissions*** | send out | substances released into the air | **export** | carry out | send out goods, cause an idea to spread |
| — | | | **import** | carry in | bring or carry in from an outside source |
| **intermittent** | send between | stopping and starting | — | | |
| **omitted*** | send away | left out | — | | |
| **promise** | send forth | a vow or pledge to do something | — | | |
| — | | | **rapport** | bring (carry) back toward | relationship of mutual trust |
| **remittance** | send back | sending of money to someone at a distance | **reporter** | carry back | one who carries back and repeats to another |
| **submissive** | send under | inclined to yield to the will or power of another | **supportive*** | carry below | give assistance to |
| **transmission** | send across | something sent from one place to another | **transportation** | carry across | means of carrying goods/ people from one place to another |

---

*Prefix is assimilated.

***Did You Know?** **Portmanteau** is another word that could be added to the *port* category. In one sense it is a large suitcase with two compartments. This meaning is evident in the literal meaning of the roots of the word: *port* ("carry") and *manteau* ("cloak" or "coat"), which stem from French. However, in the latter half of the 19th century, Lewis Carroll (author of *Alice in Wonderland*, *Through the Looking Glass*, and other works) gave new meaning to *portmanteau* when he applied it to words. In *Through the Looking Glass* Humpty Dumpty explains to Alice words from the poem "Jabberwocky." "Well, '*slithy*' means 'lithe and slimy.' . . . You see it's like a portmanteau—there are two meanings packed up into one word" (1971, p. 164). Additional examples from the poem include *chortle* (*chuckle* + *snort*), *mimsy* (*flimsy* + *miserable*), and *galumphing* (*gallop* + *triumphantly*). Other common examples of *portmanteau words* include *smog* (*smoke* + *fog*), *guesstimate* (*guess* + *estimate*), *Spanglish* (*Spanish* + *English*) and *infomercial* (*information* + *commercial*). Portmanteau words are *neologisms*, new words. They are sometimes called *frankenwords*, which is itself a portmanteau word, composed of *Frankenstein* (named after the monster Frankenstein) + *words*. Do you know of other portmanteau words?

---

## SORT 33. Latin Roots: Senses (*dict, spect/spic, spir, tact/tag/tang*)

| Speak | Look | Breathe | Touch |
|-------|------|---------|-------|
| *dict* | *spect/spic* | *spir* | *tact/tag/tang* |
| **contradict** | **spectator** | **spirited** | **contact** |
| dictate | aspect | aspiration | contagious |
| dictionary | inspector | conspire | tactful |
| dictator | perspective | expire | tactile |
| edict | perspicacious | inspiration | tangent |
| | spectacle | respiratory | tangible |
| | specter | | |

*Considerations:* After the words have been categorized by root, discuss the meaning connections of several words. An *edict* ("speak out") is a proclamation or command issued by an authority and often enforceable by law. *Aspect*, which is made up of the prefix *ad-* (here assimilated), meaning "to," plus *spect*, literally means "to look to"; it refers to the appearance of something to the eye—a person might have a pleasing aspect, for instance. *Per-* warrants discussion. It means "through" or "thoroughly." *Perspective* literally means to "look through," as when you consider your perspective from a hilltop or on an issue. Before talking about the meaning of *perspicacious*, you might ask students if they consider themselves to be perspicacious. This will allow them to attempt to apply knowledge of the prefix *per-* and the root. The word literally means having the quality of being able to "look through" and actually means "clear-sighted," as having acute mental discernment. When discussing the meaning connections for *tact*, caution students that *tact* can have a different meaning, namely "to arrange," as in *tactics* or *tactical*.

*Did You Know?* The first American dictionary of the English language was published in 1806 by Noah Webster, who was, among other things, a *lexicographer* ("one who compiles dictionaries") and a spelling reformer. He used his role as a lexicographer to institute changes in spelling; for example, he changed the spelling of words ending in *-re* to *-er*, as in *centre* to *center*, and those ending in *-our*, such as *colour* and *honour*, to *color* and *honor*. Rather than prescribe changes to the language as Noah Webster's dictionary did, most dictionaries describe the language as it exists at the time. Today there are many different kinds of dictionaries, and they appear in electronic, as well as printed, forms. An online Wikipedia search for **dictionary** brings up an article on dictionaries, which at the end provides links to several online dictionaries, including links for searching etymologies, translating words, and creating and submitting new words or pseudowords.

## SORT 34. Latin Roots: Actions Set 1 (*fract/frag, rupt, flect/flex, vers/vert*)

| Break | Break | Bend | Turn |
|---|---|---|---|
| *fract/frag* | *rupt* | *flect/flex* | *vers/vert* |
| **fracture** | **eruption** | **flexible** | **avert** |
| fraction | abrupt | deflect | adversity |
| fragile | bankrupt | reflex | advertise |
| fragment | disrupt | reflection | anniversary |
| infraction | interrupt | | controversy |
| | rupture | | invert |
| | | | versatile |
| | | | versus |
| | | | vertigo |

**Considerations:** This is the first of four sorts (one follows and two are presented later) that focus on roots pertaining to actions. Most of the meaning connections for the first three roots are straightforward. *Bankrupt,* which has obscure connections, is discussed under "Did You Know?" The meaning connection of "turn toward" in *adversity* seems unexpected considering that the word means "misfortune." Perhaps the connection has more to do with a person's reaction to times of adversity, namely to turn toward assistance. *Anniversary* literally means "turn year." Before talking about *vertigo* ("dizziness"), you might tell students that people sometimes suffer from vertigo and ask what they think it means. Although not included in the sort, you might also ask students to consider the meaning connection in the word *vertebrate.*

**Did You Know?** Most of the *rupt* words show an obvious meaning connection to "break"—for example, *eruption,* "a breaking out"; *interrupt,* "break between"; and *disrupt,* "break apart." But what about the word **bankrupt**? More than one person has mistakenly speculated that when you're bankrupt, you're "breaking the bank." Although the finances of a person who is bankrupt are "broken," one person's bankruptcy is unlikely to lead to the fall of an entire bank. So what is the story? Origins of the word take us back to Italian medieval times, when moneylenders, the precursors of our bankers, carried out their business on a small bench (*banca*) in the marketplace. If their business failed, they were obligated to break up their benches. This *banca rupta* evolved into English *bankrupt.*

## SORT 35. Latin Roots: Actions Set 2 (*fac/fact, fer, mot, struct, ven/vent*)

| Make | Carry/Bear | Move | Build | Come |
|---|---|---|---|---|
| *fac/fact* | *fer* | *mot* | *struct* | *ven/vent* |
| **factory** | **ferry** | **promote** | **construction** | **convention** |
| artifact | conifer | demoted | destruction | adventure |
| facilitate | inference | emotion | infrastructure | avenue |
| facsimile | transfer | motivate | instruct | intervene |
| satisfaction | | motorist | obstruction | prevention |

*Considerations:* This is the second set of roots whose meanings relate to actions. An *artifact* refers to something that is made or shaped by human abilities, as, for example, a tool used in ancient times. *Satisfaction* is the noun form of *satisfy*, meaning "make sufficient." *Facsimile*, which means to "make the same," is discussed under "Did You Know?", as is *infrastructure*. You might ask students to speculate on the connection between *conifer* and "carry." They may or may not recognize *coni* as meaning "cone"; the word literally means "carry cone" or "cone bearing." Meaning connections for several of the *ven* words are straightforward. However, students may wonder about *avenue*. This word and *adventure* are related to *advent* ("to come to"), and their literal meanings all have to do with arriving. What might the connection be? *Obstruction* refers to the result of "piling up or building against" (*struct* "build" + *ob-* "against").

*Did You Know?*  Two words in this sort that may be somewhat unfamiliar are *infrastructure* and *facsimile*, though both are an integral part of our everyday living. The *infra-* in **infrastructure** means "under," so the word's literal meaning is "structure below." Just what this refers to differs depending on the context, but usually the word refers to roads, bridges, airports, and utilities, the underlying structure of a city or other area, sometimes called *public works*. The *infrastructure* is something people do not tend to think much about until a disaster occurs that disrupts the workings of the infrastructure, as with such happenings as a tornado, hurricane, earthquake, or war.

A **facsimile** is an exact copy (*fac*, meaning "make" + *simile*, meaning "same"). It is often called a *fax* and refers to a printed copy sent electronically to someone. We find this same meaning of "like" or "same" in other words such as *similar*, *simile*, and *simulate* or *simulation*.

---

## SORT 36. Greek and Latin Elements: Air, Land, Water, and Light (*aero-*, *aster*, *hydr*, *naut/nav*, *photo-*, *terra*)

| Air | Star | Water | Ship | Light | Earth |
|---|---|---|---|---|---|
| *aero-* | *aster* | *hydr* | *naut/nav* | *photo-* | *terra* |
| **aerobic** | **astronomy** | **hydrant** | **navigate** | **photograph** | **terrain** |
| aerial | asterisk | dehydrated | (aeronautics) | photosynthesis | Mediterranean |
| aerodynamic | asteroid | hydroelectric | nautical | telephoto | subterranean |
| (aeronautics) | astronaut | hydroplane | navigable | | terrace |
| | disaster | | | | territory |

*Considerations:* An asterisk (*) resembles a star, but what about *disaster*? If the sun, our star, fell apart or even moved apart from Earth, it would mean the end of our planet. The word *disaster* literally means "star apart" or "star asunder." *Asunder* means "in separate pieces." It is not surprising that when disaster strikes, we often say that things are falling to pieces. *Photograph* is sometimes mistakenly thought to literally mean "picture writing." However, it is light that is causing the image, so the literal translation is actually "light writing." You might ask students if they are familiar with any other words with *terra*, as for example, *terra cotta* ("baked earth"); *terra firma* ("solid earth"), *terrestrial*, and *extraterrestrial*. What is the meaning connection to earth for each? *Nausea* is another word that is actually related to the *nav/naut* words in this sort. For a discussion of the connection, see Part 2, Sort 46, "Did You Know?"

***Did You Know?*** Important civilizations, such as ancient Greece and Rome, flourished in the area around the **Mediterranean** Sea, which is nearly enclosed by land: Europe on the north, Africa on the south, and Asia on the east. It connects to the Atlantic Ocean on the west by way of a narrow strait (the Strait of Gibraltar is just 9 miles wide). The Mediterranean Sea covers nearly a million square miles. Its name literally means "middle of" or "heart of" "land." Although the Mediterranean is situated far inland, the name probably carried more of the connotation of "center of" rather than "surrounded by" land. It was the center of the world to those who lived there.

## SORT 37. Greek and Latin Elements: Round and Around (*circum-*, *peri-*, *centr*, *circ*, *vol[v]*)

| Around | Near, around | Center | Circle | Roll |
|---|---|---|---|---|
| *circum-* | *peri-* | *centr* | *circ* | *vol(v)* |
| **circumference** | **perimeter** | **central** | **circular** | **revolving** |
| circumnavigate | perihelion | concentration | circa | convoluted |
| circumspect | periodic | concentric | circuit | evolve |
| circumvent | periodical | egocentric | circuitous | involvement |
| | periphery | | circulation | revolution |
| | | | | volume |

***Considerations:*** This sort examines two prefixes, *circum-* and *peri-*, and three roots with related meanings, *centr*, *circ*, and *volv*. Roots from previous studies are found in several of the words, as in *circumference*, *circumnavigate*, *circumspect*, *circumvent*, and *perimeter*. Students are likely to be unfamiliar with several of the words in this sort, including some of those just listed. Provide an opportunity for them to work in dyads or triads to try to figure out the meanings of some of the more difficult ones. Discuss their ideas, and demonstrate the meaning connection for any words that are still unknown. For example, *circumvent* literally means to "come, or go, around." When you go around something, you avoid it, which is one of the meanings of *circumvent*. It often carries the sense of doing so artfully, as in "He tried to circumvent the review process but found he could not." *Peri-* also means "around" or "near." Its meaning should be familiar in *perimeter*. *Perihelion* literally means "near the sun"; it refers to the point at which the earth (or any other orbiting planet or celestial body) is closest to the sun. How do the other words in that category relate to "near" or "around"? As an extra challenge, students might ponder whether the name Cyclops, a mythological figure, has any connection to *cycle*, and if so, what? (The name actually comes from *cycl*, meaning "circle," and *op*, meaning "eye." For more *opt* words, see Sort 40.) *Convoluted* literally means "with rolls or coils." Seashells are sometimes described as convoluted, with their many overlapping spirals. A complicated argument might also be said to be convoluted.

***Did You Know?*** The first books used by the ancients of Egypt, Greece, and Rome were actually rolls made from the papyrus plant. The Greeks called the plant *biblos* after the city of Byblos, which exported papyrus. By contrast, the Romans named their rolls after the word for the action of rolling, *volumen*. The books or **volumes** were made by pasting sheets of papyrus together, edge to edge, and then rolling the lengthy strip around a cylinder with projecting ends. Text was written on only one side of the material due to its thinness, and it was written from left to right in columns. To read such a book you had to hold the roll in the right hand, read a column, and then roll up what was read with the left hand while unrolling a new portion with the right. When finished reading, instead of merely closing a cover, the reader had to reroll the entire *volumen*. This form of book fell from use in the 400s when parchment (made from the skins of animals) replaced papyrus. The new material had several advantages: It was stronger, could be used on both sides, and could be folded and bound.

### Literature Link

Fritz, J. (1994). *Around the world in a hundred years*. New York: Putnam & Grosset. Read about explorers who tried to circumnavigate the world.

## SORT 38. Greek and Latin Roots: Reading and Writing (*gram, leg, lit, scrib/script*)

| Write, Letter, Line | Read | Letter | Write |
|---|---|---|---|
| *gram* | *leg* | *lit* | *scrib/script* |
| **monogram** | **legend** | **literate** | **scribble** |
| anagram | legendary | alliteration | ascribe |
| cryptogram | legible | literal | circumscribe |
| diagram | | literature | inscription |
| epigram | | obliterate | nondescript |
| grammar | | | prescription |
| parallelogram | | | Scripture |
| telegram | | | subscribe |

*Considerations:* The words listed for *gram* all derive from the same root, but because the root existed before the Greek language, several Greek words derived from it, each with related but different meanings, such as "write," "letter," "line," and even "draw." The words listed in the sort derived from the various Greek words. Because spelling of the root is identical and the meanings are somewhat related, they are examined as a group. An *anagram* is a word or phrase formed of reordered letters, as in *read → dear*. It comes from the prefix *ana-*, meaning "up" and "back" (see also Sort 52), and *gram*, which here means "letter." The letters of anagrams are sometimes in scrambled order, as in *here come the dots* for "the Morse code." An *epigram*, it may be recalled, is a short, witty poem or saying (see Sort 29), as in the following by Benjamin Franklin: *Little strokes fell big oaks*. What is the message of this epigram? *Crypto-* is a Greek prefix that means "hidden" or "secret." A cryptogram is writing that is in code. When you obliterate something you get rid of it completely, so that there is no trace. The word literally means "over letter," as when you rub or wipe over letters to erase them. *Nondescript* is often used to refer to animals and places that lack distinctive qualities, as in "A nondescript dog has been frequenting our backyard." *Scripture* refers to a sacred writing or book, or a passage from such a book.

*Did You Know?* **Aliteracy** is a relatively new term that refers to people who *can* read but choose not to (prefix *a-*, meaning "without" + *literacy*). Many people view aliteracy as a problem. Why? The following quote by Mark Twain provides a clue: "*The man who does not read good books has no advantage over the man who cannot read them.*" Mark Twain may be thinking about the fact that people can gain knowledge through reading, develop their vocabularies, and enjoy themselves. Do you agree or disagree with his quote? Why, or why not? What might be reasons that some people lack motivation for reading? What could be tried to motivate them?

---

## SORT 39. Greek and Latin Roots: Body Language (*man, ped, pod, ped*)

| Hand | Foot | Foot | Child |
|------|------|------|-------|
| *man* | *ped* | *pod* | *ped* |
| **manual** | **centipede** | **tripod** | **pediatric** |
| manacle | expedite | antipodes | encyclopedia |
| management | expedition | podiatrist | pedagogue |
| maneuver | impede | podium | pedagogy |
| manipulate | pedestal | | pedantic |
| manufacture | pedestrian | | pediatrician |
| manure | quadruped | | |

*Considerations:* This is the first of two sorts to highlight body language. In this sort the focus is on "hand," *man*, and "foot," which, as pointed out in the introduction to this section, can be either *ped* or *pod*, depending on its origins, Latin or Greek. Because there is also a Greek root spelled *ped*, meaning "child," it too is included in this sort. Students can often use context to determine which *ped* is being referred to; if not, they should consult a dictionary. Because many of the words in this sort have clear meaning connections but may be unfamiliar words, it is worthwhile to go over them. *Manacles*, which are metal rings attached to a chain, were often used to restrain prisoners or slaves. *Expedite* literally means "out foot," or in other words, "free from entanglements," a situation that would indeed expedite an action. As you discuss *quadruped*, you might ask students "If a horse is a quadruped, what are humans?" (bipeds). *Antipodes* (ăn•tĭp′•ə•dēz′) is literally "opposite feet"; it refers to any two things that are exact opposites, such as the North and South Poles. *Encyclopedia* is composed of *en-*, meaning "in," *cyclo*, meaning "circle," and *ped*, meaning "child." Together, *encyclo-* means "circular" or, more loosely, "general," and *-pedia* means "education." By reading the encyclopedia, you can gain a general education. *Pedagogue* is made up of *ped* plus *gogue*, which comes from a root meaning to "lead." "Child leader" refers to a "teacher." As sometimes happens, this word has come to have a negative connotation, one associated with a narrow concern for rules and book learning, as in the word *pedantic*. By contrast, *pedagogy* simply refers to the "art or profession of teaching."

*Did You Know?* Although we associate manufacturing with industry, machines, and other mechanical devices, **manufacture** literally means "hand made." Actually, manufactured articles can be made by hand or machine. Even ideas and excuses can be manufactured, as in "They manufactured an excuse to avoid being grounded." **Manure** is a relative, though perhaps not an obvious one. The word first meant "to work with the hands"; in other words, to do manual labor, such as tilling the soil, with various tools. When a more polite word was needed for *dung*, which was often worked into the soil as fertilizer, *manuere*, the verb for the act of cultivating, was applied as a euphemism or polite substitution for excrement.

## SORT 40. Greek and Latin Roots: More Body Language (*cap, cord, corp, dent/don, derm, ocu/opt*)

| Head | Heart | Body | Tooth | Skin | Eye, Vision |
|------|-------|------|-------|------|-------------|
| *cap* | *cord* | *corp* | *dent/don* | *derm* | *ocu/opt* |
| **captain** | **accord** | **corpse** | **dentures** | **epidermis** | **optical** |
| capitalize | concord | corps | dentils | dermatology | binoculars |
| capitol | discord | corpulent | dentist | pachyderm | optometry |
| decapitate | cordially | corporation | orthodontist | | |
| per capita | | incorporate | | | |

*Considerations:* Most of the meaning connections in this sort are straightforward. *Per capita*, like the previously discussed *terra firma* and *terra cotta* (Sort 36), is a Latin phrase and literally means "per head." Per capita refers to something figured per person; it is a phrase often used in discussions about expenditures. Although *cap* often means "head," it can also mean "seize," as in *capture*. *Corpulent* means "with body" and is used to describe someone who is obese. The "body" in *corporation* refers to a body or group of people. *Pachyderm* refers to animals such as the *elephant, rhinoceros,* and *hippopotamus*. It is the "thick" (*pachy*) "skin" (*derm*) of these animals that affords them entry to the group. You might ask students to share their ideas on *pachyderm* before delving into the meaning of individual parts.

*Did You Know?* We have the French to thank for **dentist** and *dandelion*, both of which relate to "tooth." The meaning connection of the former is clear, but what about *dandelion*? Lions do have big teeth, but that is not the connection. In French, the word is *dent de lion* ("tooth of lion") and refers to the deeply serrated leaf edges of the plant. Although both of these words can be traced to Latin origins, the Greek root for "tooth," *don*, is also represented in English words related to teeth, as in *orthodontist*, in which *ortho* means "straight" or "correct," as it also does in *orthography*, a rather sophisticated word for spelling ("straight" or "correct" + "writing"). What about *dentils*? you might be wondering. Dentils are a type of molding or trim sometimes found in architecture, including homes. The molding is made up of a series of small, rectangular blocks that resemble teeth. It is sometimes used under the rooflines of houses, as well as under the mantels of fireplaces. There are other architectural features whose names are also associated with the body, as, for example, *capital* and *oculus*. The former, not surprisingly, given its root meaning "head," is the name for the top part of a pillar or column. The latter is the term for a round window in a wall or at the top of a dome. Have you ever seen an oculus, or "eye" window?

## SORT 41. Greek and Latin Roots: People (*dem, greg, pol/polis, pop/pub, civ*)

| People | Flock, Herd | City | People | Citizen |
|--------|-------------|------|--------|---------|
| *dem* | *greg* | *pol/polis* | *pop/pub* | *civ* |
| **democratic** | **congregation** | **metropolis** | **population** | **civics** |
| demographics | desegregate | cosmopolitan | populace | civil |
| endemic | egregious | police | publication | civilian |
| epidemic | gregarious | policy | publicize | civility |
| | segregation | politician | | civilization |
| | | | | uncivilized |

*Considerations:* *Endemic* ("in people") is used to describe something that is common or peculiar to a particular group of people or to a region, as in a disease that is endemic to the tropics. *Epidemic* ("on people") usually refers to a disease or infection that spreads rapidly among people. A person who is *gregarious* "belongs to the herd," is sociable. *Segregation* literally means "apart from the flock," as when people are separated from the main body or group. The word element *se-* often means "apart," as it does in *segregation* and also in *separate, secret,* and *seclusion. Congregation* means "together herd," as when people assemble. See "Did You Know?" for a discussion of *egregious. Cosmopolitan* is made up of the root *cosm,* meaning "universe" or "world," and *poli,* which means "city." English is sometimes said to be a *cosmopolitan language,* meaning that it is common around the world. A *cosmopolitan problem* would be one with worldwide relevance. The root *polis* is often combined in the names of cities, as in *Annapolis, Indianapolis,* and *Minneapolis.* Ask students if they know of any other cities with the root.

*Did You Know?* **Egregious** stems from a Latin word meaning "outstanding" The assimilated prefix, *e(x)* + the root *greg* literally means "out of the flock." A person or act characterized by exceptionally good qualities, namely, characteristics that make her or it stand out from others, was considered *egregious.* However, today the word has a completely opposite meaning and denotes something "conspicuously bad or offensive." How did such a turnaround in meanings come about? The change may be the result of an ironic use of the original meaning, as occurred in one of Shakespeare's plays, which then became popular. Whatever the case, the negative meaning that was first recorded in mid-1500 is still used today.

## SORT 42. Greek and Latin Elements: Ruling and Governing (-*archy*, -*cracy*, *dom*, *reg*)

| Rule, Government | Government, Rule | Lord | Rule |
|---|---|---|---|
| -*archy* | -*cracy* | *dom* | *reg* |
| **monarchy** | **democracy** | **dominate** | **regulation** |
| anarchy | aristocracy | domain | regime |
| hierarchy | autocracy | dominant | regimen |
| matriarchy | bureaucracy | domineering | regiment |
| oligarchy | plutocracy | dominion | region |
| patriarchy | technocracy | predominate | |
| | theocracy | | |

*Considerations:* Many of the words in the first two categories of this sort are likely to be unfamiliar to students, though they may have heard of some of them. To introduce the sort, ask students to turn to a partner and identify words they think they know by noting the meaning on the back of the word card. Then discuss the words and verify or clarify the meanings with dictionaries. The literal meanings follow:

-*cracy:* aristocracy, "best rule"; autocracy, "self-rule"; bureaucracy, "office rule"; democracy, "people rule"; plutocracy, "wealth rule"; technocracy, "skill rule" (technical); theocracy, "God rule."

-*archy:* anarchy, "without ruler"; hierarchy, "high priest (rank) rule"; matriarchy, "mother (women) rule"; monarchy, "one rule"; oligarchy, "few rule"; patriarchy, "father (men) rule." (Other words with *matr-* and *patr-* are highlighted in Sort 52.) Dictionaries also include the word *mobocracy*. You might ask students to speculate on the word's meaning, or consider other possible *-cracy* or *-archy* words that might one day be coined. Words with *dom* require caution when interpreting; this spelling pattern can also mean "house," as in *domicile* and *domesticate*. *Reg* also has another meaning, "regal."

*Did You Know?* As other stories have illustrated, word meanings change over time. **Hierarchy** is an example of the gradual and sometimes surprising changes that occasionally occur. *Hierarchy* was first used to describe the ranks of angels. This earliest meaning is evident in the word elements: *hier-*, which stems from the Greek word for "holy, powerful" and *-archy*, which means "leader, rule." From the angel-related meaning evolved reference to rule by an authoritarian group. The political meaning developed into the sense of classifying the populace according to wealth, social standing, or ability, a meaning that seems unrelated to the earlier political sense. One explanation put forth for the change is that because *hier-* sounded like *higher*, people confused the two meanings (Barnhart, 2005). Eventually, the meaning came to encompass ordered classification of a group of elements or objects, as when scores are listed in hierarchical series from strongest to weakest.

## SORT 43. Greek and Latin Roots: Truth or Consequences (*jud, mon, ques/quir/quis, leg, ver*)

| Judge | Warn | Seek | Law | True |
|---|---|---|---|---|
| *jud* | *mon* | *ques/quir/quis* | *leg* | *ver* |
| **judicial** | **admonish** | **inquiry** | **legality** | **verdict** |
| adjudge | monitor | acquire | legitimate | verification |
| injudicious | monster | inquisitive | legislation | verify |
| judgmental | monstrosity | questionnaire | privilege | very |
| | premonition | requirement | | |
| | remonstrate | | | |
| | summon | | | |

*Considerations: Adjudge* means to "rule" or "decide" a case, as in *He adjudged the man not guilty of the charges. Adjudicate*, a word not included in the sort, is related; it means to "hear and settle a case by judicial procedure." *Privilege* comes from *privi*, meaning "single," and *leg*, which means "law"; in effect, the word means "a law affecting one person." *Private* shares the same meaning of "single" and the same root. To *admonish* someone is literally to "warn toward," as when someone is scolded for something or reminded of a forgotten item. In turn, the scolded person might *remonstrate* or "warn back" by presenting an objection. *Premonition* means "warn before"; it is a forewarning of something to happen. *Monstrosity* and *monster* stem from an early meaning of *monster*, which meant a "warning" or "portent"; in other words, an indication of something terrible about to occur. *Monstrosity* has a somewhat softened meaning today, referring to something frightful, ugly, or exceptionally large, as in *The vase we received is truly a monstrosity.* Caution is needed when interpreting words with *leg*, as there are different meanings for this spelling, for example, "gather" (*legion*), "dispute" (*legacy, allegations, college*), and "read" (*legend, legible*).

***Did You Know?*** In Saxon England (England before 1066) trials were often used to determine a person's innocence or guilt, but they were trials of a different sort than those we associate with the modern-day judicial system. Instead of being presumed innocent until proven guilty, the accused individual often had to undergo an ordeal involving a physical test. For instance, the person might be plunged into water, be expected to place a bare arm in boiling water, or be required to handle a very hot object. If the accused could perform the test without getting hurt, he was ***adjudged*** innocent; if not, he was found guilty. Sometimes trials were decided by jury. In this process, an accused person could be freed if enough people came forward to swear that they believed the person to be innocent. In 1066 Saxon England was conquered by French-speaking Normans, who made French the official language for more than a century. The French influence brought many legal terms into the language. One example is ***verdict***, which means "truly said" (*ver* + *dict*).

## SORT 44. Greek and Latin Word Elements: Opposites (*ante-, post-, bene, mal, hyper-, hypo-*)

| Before | After | Good | Bad | Over, Beyond | Under, Below |
|---|---|---|---|---|---|
| *ante-* | *post-* | *bene* | *mal* | *hyper-* | *hypo-* |
| **anterior** | **posterior** | **benefit** | **malfunction** | **hypersensitive** | **hypothermia** |
| ante meridiem | posterity | benefactor | dismal | hyperbole | hypochondriac |
| anteroom | posthumous | beneficial | malaria | hypercritical | hypocrite |
| | post meridiem | | malnutrition | hyperventilate | hypodermic |
| | postscript | | malpractice | | |

***Considerations:*** Because this sort includes three different pairs of words, you may want to stagger their introduction, discussing one pair each day for a series of days. Several words in this sort include roots from previous word studies: *script, fac, derm,* and *therm.* As they are discussed, notice which students seem to recall their meanings. You might ask students to search the dictionary for additional words to add to the discussion. *Bene* and *mal* mean "good" and "bad," respectively. A *benefactor,* then, is literally one who "makes or does good." Though it is not included in the sort, ask students to consider what a *malefactor* is. The literal meaning of *malaria* is "bad air," and of *dismal,* "bad day." *Dis* looks like a prefix in this word and may fool students, but it actually comes from the Latin word for day, *dies.* Though students have probably heard of *hyperbole,* they may not have a clear understanding of its meaning. It is a figure of speech that uses exaggeration for emphasis, as in *I'm so hungry I could eat a horse.*

Several of the *ante-* and *post-* words may be unfamiliar to most students. *Anterior* refers to "before" in the sense of either time or location, just as *posterior* refers to "after" in relation to time or place. An *anteroom* is an outer room, such as a waiting room. *Ante meridiem* is the phrase behind the abbreviation A.M., just as *post meridiem* is for P.M. The two Latin phrases literally mean "before midday" and "after midday," *midday* referring to "noon." *Postscript* is another Latin word; it is synonymous with P.S. *Posthumous* refers to something occurring after a person's death, such as the posthumous publication of a person's memoir. Its origins are a little unclear; *humous* stems either from the Latin word for to "bury" (*humare*) or from a word meaning "earth, ground" (*humus*). Other words derived from the latter include *exhume,* meaning to "remove from a grave," and *humus,* a type of rich soil.

*Did You Know?* **Hypocrite** stems from the Greek word *hypocrites*, referring to an onstage actor. Over time the word evolved to mean a different sort of actor, a pretender, such as one who claims to have certain beliefs, opinions, or virtues but does not. This meaning of "falseness" was first recorded in the 1200s, though with a slightly different spelling—*ypocrite*.

---

**SORT 45.** Latin Roots: Conflicts (*bell, cede/cess, pug, vinc/vict, val*)

| War | Go, Yield | Fight | Conquer | Be Strong |
|---|---|---|---|---|
| *bell* | *cede/cess* | *pug* | *vinc/vict* | *val* |
| **rebellion** | **concede** | **pugnacious** | **victory** | **valiant** |
| antebellum | excessive | impugn | conviction | convalesce |
| bellicose | intercede | pugnacity | convince | evaluate |
| belligerent | recede | repugnant | evict | invalid |
| | secede | | invincible | prevalent |
| | secession | | | |

*Considerations:* Several of the *bell* words are likely to be unfamiliar to students. Begin with *rebellion*, a known word, and apply the meaning of the root "war," then add on the prefix until you have the literal meaning of "war back." Ask students how this meaning relates to the actual meaning of *rebellion*. *Antebellum* ("before war") refers to something belonging to the period before a war, usually the American Civil War, as in *antebellum slavery* or *antebellum architecture*. *Belligerent* literally means to "make war"; it describes someone who is hostile and aggressive. Words stemming from *cede/cess* and *vinc/vict* have fairly straightforward meaning connections but still should be discussed. The *se-* in *secede* and *secession* means "apart." *Pugnacious* is synonymous with *belligerent*. It stems from a Latin word meaning "fist." *Impugn* (ĭm•pūn) means to "challenge in argument," as to impugn the record of a political candidate. Something repugnant might be so repulsive that you would "fight against" it.

*Did You Know?* "Strong" is evident in all of the *val* words included in this sort—**valiant** means "courageous," **convalesce** means to "become strong," **evaluate** means "to bring out the strength or value of something," **invalid** (both senses of this homograph) means "without strength," and **prevalent** means "stronger," though the literal sum of its parts do not lead to this whole. Several other words not included in this sort are related; for example, *valedictorian*, meaning "one who gives a farewell speech" (in other words, a speech in which strength and worth are highlighted); *valid*, meaning "something strongly grounded, with legal force"; *valor*, meaning "boldness"; and *value*, meaning "worth, strength." When considering words with a *val* spelling, it is important to think carefully about the meaning and context. Some words that include the spelling pattern stem from other sources and have different meaning connections, as in *valentine*, *valet*, and *valley*.

## SORT 46. Latin Roots: Actions Set 3 (*clud/clus, duc/duct, pend, scend, tend*)

| Close | Lead | Hang | Climb | Stretch |
|---|---|---|---|---|
| *clud/clus* | *duc/duct* | *pend* | *scend* | *tend* |
| **exclude** | **conductor** | **pendulum** | **ascend** | **tendon** |
| inclusive | abduct | appendage | condescend | distend |
| preclude | aqueduct | appendix | descend | extensive |
| recluse | deduction | impending | transcend | intensify |
| secluded | induction | pendant | | superintendent |

*Considerations:* Most of the meaning connections in this sort are apparent when the meaning of the prefix is applied to the root meaning. A few warrant discussion. In *secluded*, as in *secession* from the previous sort, the *se-* means "apart." Something that is secluded is shut off or apart from other things. Ask students what a *recluse* might be. *Aqueduct* may be unfamiliar to students. Ask what they think this means. Although *aqueducts* were devised earlier in other parts of the world, the most famous ones are the Roman aqueducts, some of which were built as early as the 7th century B.C. They formed an extensive network for carrying water, not only in Rome but also in other parts of the Roman Empire, from Germany to Africa. They were an amazing feat of engineering. After discussing *aqueduct*, ask students what they think a *viaduct* is.

*Did You Know?* **Appendix** refers to a collection of supplementary material that is sometimes placed at the end of a book in a separate section, such as the appendices in this book. It also describes a part of the human anatomy that no longer serves a real purpose but which sometimes becomes inflamed and must be removed (see Sort 51 for *appendicitis*). Although the word *appendicitis* was in use in 1885, it was not included in the *Oxford English Dictionary* of the times because lexicographers were uncertain about including scientific words of recent origin, so they omitted it. In 1902, the soon-to-be-crowned Edward VII had to have his appendix removed, and, in fact, the operation delayed his coronation. The incident was much talked about and brought the word into widespread use. As is usually the case, if a word is used enough by enough people, whether or not to include it in a dictionary is no longer a question.

## SORT 47. Latin Roots: Actions Set 4 (*flu, junct, mod, press, sect*)

| Flow | Join | Measure | Press | Cut |
|---|---|---|---|---|
| *flu* | *junct* | *mod* | *press* | *sect* |
| **fluid** | **conjunction** | **modular** | **pressure** | **dissect** |
| confluence | adjunct | accommodate | compression | bisect |
| fluctuate | junction | commodious | irrepressible | insect |
| fluent | juncture | moderate | oppression | intersection |
| influence | | modify | | |
| influenza | | | | |
| superfluous | | | | |

*Considerations:* Students have considerable experience with roots and prefix combinations at this point; they should be able to grasp at least a literal meaning for most of the words that may be unfamiliar. You might ask them to speculate on the meaning connection to *influenza* before explaining that this word for an acute, infectious illness was borrowed from an Italian word with the same spelling, meaning "epidemic." Epidemics were originally thought to be due to the influence of the stars. When talking about the *mod* words, caution students that this spelling can also mean "manner," as it does in *modern*. As you discuss the root *sect*, you might ask students to brainstorm other words with the root (as *section* and *sector*), as well as words with *cis*, another Latin root that means "to cut," as in *incision*, *decision*, *incisor*, *incisive*, and so forth). The Greeks also have a word for "cut," which we see reflected in the suffix *-tomy*, meaning "act of cutting," as in the surgical procedures *tonsillectomy* and *appendectomy*.

*Did You Know?* **Superfluous** and **accommodate** are often misspelled, even by literate adults. In the former case, the *l* and *u* are often reversed in order (*superfulous*), and in the latter instance an *m* is often omitted (*accomodate*). A careful look at the spelling–meaning connections of these two words can make spelling them easier. *Super-* (see Sort 7) means "over" and *flu* means "flowing," so something that is *superfluous* is "beyond what is needed." To understand how *accommodate* works, we can also look at its parts: the assimilated prefix *ad* + *commodus*. The latter is really our word **commodious**, which means "spacious enough" or "suitable" (*com-*, meaning "with" + *mod*, meaning "measure"). When we *accommodate* someone, we make the situation "suitable" or "fitting" for them.

## SORT 48. Latin Roots: Peace and Goodwill (*fid, grac/grat, pac, sens/sent, sol*)

| Faith, Trust | Pleasing | Peace | Feel | Alone |
|---|---|---|---|---|
| *fid* | *grac/grat* | *pac* | *sens/sent* | *sol* |
| **fidelity** | **gratifying** | **pacify** | **sensible** | **solitude** |
| affidavit | congratulate | Pacific Ocean | consensus | desolate |
| bona fide | gracious | pacifier | sensational | solitaire |
| confident | gratitude | pacifist | sensibility | solitary |
| confidential | ingratiate | | sentimental | |
| perfidious | | | | |

*Considerations:* Although all of the words should be discussed, a few of the words in the *fid* column may be unfamiliar to students. Though most will have heard of *fidelity*, their understanding of the meaning may be somewhat vague. You might ask them why banks sometimes include the word in their name. What message does this send to potential patrons? An *affidavit* is a written pledge made under oath in the presence of an authorized person. *Bona fide* is another direct borrowing from Latin (like *per capita*). It literally means "good faith" and refers to something said or done with sincerity, something genuine, as in *She made a bona fide attempt to complete the project on time*. *Perfidious* literally means "through faith," but in the sense of wronging someone, as a deliberate breach of faith. *Ingratiate* may also need explanation. Although its meaning is indeed "to bring oneself into favor," it is important for students to realize that the act is often deliberate and therefore the connotation negative. Though not in the sort, *ingrate* is another related word, but here the *in-* bears the meaning of "not." An ingrate is an ungrateful person.

***Did You Know?*** The **Pacific Ocean** was named by Ferdinand Magellan when much of the world was being explored. Why did Magellan call the world's largest ocean *Pacificum*? At the time of his voyage, the ocean was relatively calm and free of violent storms, so the name seemed appropriate. This same meaning of "peaceful" is obvious in the word *pacifier*, an object that babies like to suck on that generally has a calming influence. The word *appease* ("to bring peace or quiet") is descended from the same root, *pax*, as is *pay*. In the latter instance, the connection to peace is not readily apparent. It stems from the practice of paying debts in order to pacify creditors.

On a related note, the Atlantic Ocean takes its name from Mount Atlas, a mountain in West Africa, on which, according to Greek mythology, the heavens were thought to rest. Actually, a Greek Titan or giant was believed to be responsible for holding them up. By the 1500s *Atlas* was synonymous in English with "someone who bears a heavy burden." Mercator, a 16th-century cartographer, included a picture of Atlas holding up the heavens on the title page of a book of maps and called the book *Atlas*, a name that is still used today to designate a collection of maps.

## SORT 49. Latin Roots: Speaking (*lingu, loc/loq, voc/vok, verb*)

| Tongue | Speak | Call | Word |
|---|---|---|---|
| *lingu* | *loc/loq* | *voc/vok* | *verb* |
| **bilingual** | **eloquent** | **vocalize** | **verbalize** |
| lingo | circumlocution | advocate | adverb |
| linguini | colloquial | provoke | verbatim |
| linguistics | elocution | revoke | verbiage |
| multilingual | loquacious | vocabulary | verbose |
| sociolinguist | soliloquy | vociferous | |
| | | vocation | |

***Considerations:*** Though students may initially be unfamiliar with several of the words, the meanings of most become transparent when the meanings of the prefixes and roots are applied. Because we use our tongues to speak, the connection of "tongue" to the various language-related words is clear. *Linguini* requires more thought; this pasta takes its name form its tongue-like shape. *Lingo* may require explanation; it refers to the specialized vocabulary of a particular field—baseball lingo, technology lingo, medical lingo, and so forth. Meaning connections with the *loc/loq* words include *eloquent* ("speak out"); *circumlocution* ("speak around," sometimes with the meaning of "wordiness"); *colloquial* ("speak with," as in informal speech); *elocution* ("speak out," in the sense of public speaking and the qualities associated with it—gesture, production, delivery), *loquacious* ("talkative"); and *soliloquy* ("speak alone"; although this word can mean to talk to oneself, it usually refers to a character's revealing of his or her thoughts during a dramatic production). You might invite students to speculate on the meaning of *vociferous* ("voice carry"; namely, "loud and noisy") before discussing it.

***Did You Know?*** **Vocabulary** derives from a Latin word with the same meaning. The word was first recorded in the early 1500s. You may be wondering how many words there are in English. It's difficult to say because new words are coined and old ones fall out of use on a constant basis. Although an average person uses only about 3,000 words in everyday communication, research has shown that about 90,000 different words are used in school texts in grades 3 through 9. Robert Hendrickson's *Facts on File Encyclopedia* (2004) suggests that with "words from many other disciplines, jargons of professions and trades, and slang expressions from England and America, the total must come to at least between 15 and 20 million" (p. 703).

---

## SORT 50. Greek and Latin Roots: Wisdom and Wonder (*anima, cogn, mem, mir/marv, sci, soph*)

| Mind, Soul | Know, Learn | Mindful | Wonderful | Know | Wise |
|---|---|---|---|---|---|
| *anima* | *cogn* | *mem* | *mir/marv* | *sci* | *soph* |
| **unanimous** | **recognize** | **memorize** | **miracle** | **conscience** | **philosophy** |
| inanimate | cognition | immemorial | marvelous | conscientious | sophisticated |
| animated | cognizant | memento | miraculous | prescience | sophomore |
|  | incognito | memorandum | mirage | subconsciously |  |
|  |  | memoir |  |  |  |
|  |  | remember |  |  |  |

*Considerations:* Be sure that students understand that the *un-* in *unanimous* means "one" rather than "not." Ask them to brainstorm other words with this prefix and inquire whether they recall another prefix with the same meaning (*mono-*). *Prescience*, which means "foresight," is similar in meaning to the previously studied *premonition* (Part 3, Sort 43). Talk about the nuances of their meanings. The word *science* was discussed at the syllable juncture stage (Part 2, Sort 18); how does it fit with the other words in this category? As students analyze the meanings of words in this sort, you might discuss other related words, such as *commemorate* and *admirable*.

*Did You Know?* **Philosophy**, which means "love of wisdom," is composed of two roots: *phil*, meaning "love," and *soph*, meaning "wisdom." We have the Greeks to thank for this word. It was borrowed in 1340. Numerous other words relate to *phil*, as for example, *Philadelphia* ("city of brotherly love"), *philharmonic* ("love of music"), *audiophile* ("one who loves sound"), *bibliophile* ("one who loves books"), *philanthropy* ("love of mankind"), *philodendron* ("love of trees," said because of the plant's tendency to twine around branches), and, perhaps in the future, *logophile* (one who loves words). On a final note, the *soph* in *philosophy* is also found in *sophomore*, in which it means "wise." However, the *more* refers to "foolish"; this creates an interesting contradiction—"wise" and "foolish." What might be the connection?

### Literature Connections

Madden, D. (1989). *Incognito mosquito: Private insective.* New York: Random House Books for Young Readers. Other books in this series include *Incognito Mosquito: Flies* and *Incognito Mosquito Makes History* (Ages 9–12).

## SORT 51. Greek and Latin Elements: Care and Illness (*cur, path, -phobia, -itis, vol*)

| Care | Suffer, feel | Fear | Inflammation | Will, willing |
|------|--------------|------|--------------|---------------|
| *cur* | *path* | *-phobia* | *-itis* | *vol* |
| **manicure** | **empathy** | **claustrophobia** | **arthritis** | **volunteer** |
| pedicure | antipathy | acrophobia | appendicitis | benevolent |
| security | apathetic | agoraphobia | bronchitis | malevolent |
| | pathetic | xenophobia | laryngitis | volition |
| | pathology | | tonsillitis | voluntary |
| | sympathetic | | | |
| | telepathy | | | |

*Considerations:* Students should be able to identify the meanings of these words, although a dictionary will likely be needed for the *-phobia* group. Thinking of *acrobat* may help to determine the meaning of *acrophobia* ("fear of heights"). Other *-phobia* words include *agoraphobia* ("fear of open, public spaces"), *claustrophobia* ("fear of closed spaces"), and *xenophobia* ("fear of strangers"). Encourage students to brainstorm other illness-related endings besides *-phobia* and *-itis*. The former word part is discussed further under "Did You Know?" Students may already know *manicure* and *pedicure*. If not, their knowledge from earlier word studies can be applied to figure out the words. *Security* ("without care") is less transparent; students may need to consult the etymology section of a dictionary. As with *segregation* (Part 3, Sort 41), the *se-* element carries meaning, here "without." Though several of the words with *path* may be new, with the exception of *pathology*, the meanings are clear. *Pathology* extends the sense of "suffering" to a cause; *pathology* is the study of diseases. The *vol* words are fairly easy to grasp. If you do something of your own *volition*, you do it willingly, voluntarily. As students consider *benevolent* and *malevolent*, they should recall the meanings of *bene* and *mal* (Part 3, Sort 44) and be able to apply them to *vol* to realize that the words mean characterized by "good will" and "bad will." Students may wonder about the meaning connection between "mother" and *matrix* or *matriculate*. *Matrix* refers to "a situation or surrounding substance in which something else originates, develops, or is contained." A sense of beginning is also associated with *matriculate*: "to be admitted to a group." If you have not already done so, you might present students with the "longest word" from the introductory matter of this section to see whether they can decipher its meaning.

*Did You Know?* A *phobia* is a strong fear of or aversion to something; the fear can have a legitimate source but can also be irrational, as when it causes a person to avoid something despite awareness that the "something" is harmless. Because we all tend to have our own fears, it is not surprising that many names for phobias have been coined. A collection found at *www.phobialist.com* requires that a listed word be referenced in some text in order to be included, and it identifies 530 different phobias! Unless you suffer from technophobia, it is a list well worth browsing. Although *-phobia* is derived from Greek, contributions to the list from the medical profession, which relies heavily on Latin for its terminology, have led to the inclusion of many words with Latin roots affixed to the Greek suffix.

**SORT 52.** Greek and Latin Roots: Time and Family (*chron, mat/matr, pat/patr, onym, doc*)

| Time | Mother | Father | Name | Teach |
|------|--------|--------|------|-------|
| *chron* | *mat/matr* | *pat/patr* | *onym* | *doc* |
| **chronic** | **maternal** | **paternal** | **pseudonym** | **doctor** |
| anachronism | matriarch | patriarch | acronym | docent |
| chronicle | matriculate | patriotic | anonymous | documentary |
| chronology | matrimony | patronize | antonym | indoctrinate |
| synchronize | matrix | (patronymic) | eponym | |
| | | | (patronymic) | |

*Considerations: Anachronism* like *anagram* (Part 3, Sort 38), includes the prefix *ana-*, which here means "out of," as in "out of time." Including a cell phone in a story about medieval times would be an anachronism. Students should be familiar with several members of the *onym* family: *homonym* ("same name"); *synonym* ("similar name"); *antonym* ("opposite name"); *acronym* ("beginning name"), such as UNICEF for United Nations International Children's Emergency Fund; *eponym* (*epi-*, meaning "after" + *onym*, meaning "name"), as a place or word derived from a person's name, such as *pasteurize* after Louis Pasteur; and *pseudonym* ("false name"). *Patronymic* ("father name") may be new. It refers to a name derived from one's father, as, for example, a person's surname in the United States.

*Did You Know?* Another interesting *onym* word besides those included in this sort was coined by Franklin Pierce Adams, an early 20th-century American columnist. *Aptronym*, a term meaning "label name," refers to names that writers sometimes give to their characters to reveal something about their personality or occupation. Writers have long engaged in the practice. John Bunyan's *Pilgrim's Progress*, written in the 1600s, includes two such characters: Mr. Worldly Wiseman and Mr. Talkative. The works of Charles Dickens abound with examples. Children's authors also make use of aptronyms. For example, there is little doubt that Joan Aiken's "Miss Slighcarp" is an unlikable character in the *Wolves of Willoughby Chase*, and can you tell which school person to side with in Roald Dahl's *Matilda*—"Miss Honey" or "Miss Trunchbull"? Have you used aptronyms in your writing?

**SORT 53.** Latin Roots: Beginnings and Endings (*nov, sen, mort, nat, gen*)

| New | Old | Death | Be born | Birth |
|-----|-----|-------|---------|-------|
| *nov* | *sen* | *mort* | *nat* | *gen* |
| **novelty** | **senator** | **mortal** | **native** | **genetic** |
| innovation | senile | mortality | cognate | generation |
| novice | senility | mortgage | innate | engender |
| renovation | seniority | mortuary | national | indigenous |
| | | mortified | nativity | progeny |
| | | | natural | |

***Considerations:*** Most of the words in this sort have obvious meaning connections to their root. *Mortgage*, which does not, is discussed in "Did You Know?" The concept of *cognate*, which was first introduced in Part 3, Sort 20, should be reviewed. The word literally means "born with"; it is the name for words from different languages that are descended from the same ancestral root, such as the Indo-European roots that many languages share. The roots *matr* and *patr* from Part 3, Sort 52, are examples of words that have cognates in other languages. *Gen* is a root that can also mean "kind," as in *general*, *generalize*, and *genre*. *Progeny*, literally "forward birth," means "offspring." *Indigenous* is synonymous with "native" (literally "born in"). It should not be confused with a similarly spelled word, *indigent*, which stems from a different root with the meaning of "lacking." *Indigent* is used to describe someone who is impoverished.

***Did You Know?*** Few people have enough money to pay for property (such as a house, land, business) outright. Instead, they usually have to take out a **mortgage**, an agreement in which the borrower promises to complete payment by a certain date (sometimes as long into the future as 30 years) or otherwise forfeit the property and all money paid toward purchasing it. Sometimes property that is already owned is used as security for another debt. In either case, the mortgage is literally a "dead pledge." It is called this because the debt is "dead" or void when the pledge is paid off. The words *engage* and *engagement* also include a pledge or promise in their meanings, as evident from the *gage* root.

## SORT 54. Greek and Latin Elements: Order (*equa/equi, medi, prim, proto-, secu/sequ*)

| Equal | Middle | First | First | Follow |
|---|---|---|---|---|
| *equa/equi* | *medi* | *prim* | *proto-* | *secu/sequ* |
| **equator** | **medium** | **primary** | **prototype** | **sequential** |
| equality | intermediary | primate | protocol | consecutive |
| equanimity | intermediate | primer | protozoan | consequence |
| equilibrium | median | primeval | | prosecute |
| equinox | mediocre | primitive | | subsequent |
| equivocate | | | | |

***Considerations:*** Of the roots presented in this sort, *equa/equi* may present the most difficulties for students in terms of unfamiliar words. As you discuss this category, ask students what known roots they see in the words. They should notice *anim* ("mind") in *equanimity*, which literally means "equal mind," a meaning that is close to the actual meaning of "even-tempered, composed." They should also notice *voc* in *equivocate*. Ask students to speculate on the meaning of this word before checking in a dictionary. *Equilibrium* literally means "equal balance," as in *When nature is in balance there is equilibrium*. *Nox* in *equinox* means "night"; *equinox* refers to 1 of 2 days a year when there are approximately equal hours of daylight and darkness; there is a spring equinox and a fall equinox. *Nox* can also mean "harm," as in a *noxious* substance or *obnoxious* behavior. (Other words related to night with a different spelling, *noc*, are discussed in Sort 56.) The two elements in this sort with the meaning of "first" have different sources: *prim* stems from Latin, whereas *proto-* comes from Greek. Thinking of *zoo* or *zoology* may help students to understand the meaning of *protozoan*.

*Did You Know?* **Medium** is by no means a mediocre word, despite its ancestral relationship with the word *mediocre*. Instead, it is a word rich in meanings. When *medium* became part of the English language in the 1500s, it referred to the middle placement of an object or person. Since then it has acquired diverse other meanings, including among others a "conveyance" (as in a *medium of transportation*), a "situation or environment in which something can thrive" (*potting soil is a perfect medium for a violet*), an "artistic technique" (*oil paints are his favorite medium*), a "way of communication" (often used as a plural, as in *newspapers, radio, and television are part of the mass media*), and a "person used to communicate with the dead" (*a medium was used to try to communicate with her dead friend*).

---

## SORT 55. Greek and Latin Elements: All or Nothing (*nihil/nil/null, omni-, pan-, plen/plet, vac*)

| Zero, Nothing | All | All | Full | Empty |
|---|---|---|---|---|
| *nihil/nil/null* | *omni-* | *pan-* | *plen/plet* | *vac* |
| **nil** | **omnipresent** | **pandemic** | **plentiful** | **evacuate** |
| annihilate | omnipotence | panacea | completed | vacancy |
| nullify | omniscient | pandemonium | depletion | vacation |
|  | omnivore | pangram | plethora | vacuous |
|  |  | panoply | replenish | vacuum |
|  |  | panorama |  |  |
|  |  | pantomime |  |  |

*Considerations:* The word *nil* is actually a contraction of the root *nihil*, meaning "nothing," as in *What did I do today? Nil.* Students will likely be familiar with *omniscient* as a narrator who is "all knowing." Remind them that it is the *sci* root that carries the meaning of "knowing" and that *omni-* means "all" in the word. In *omnipotent*, which means "having unlimited power or ability," *pot* is a root meaning to "be able to." The same root is found in words such as *potent* and *potential* and even *possible* and *possibility*. *Omnivore* also includes a root that is likely unfamiliar, *vor*. It is discussed in the "Did You Know?" section for this sort. Most of the meaning connections for *pan-* are straightforward; *panacea* is not. It literally means "cure-all," as in a remedy to fix anything and everything. A *pangram* is a "sentence that uses all letters of the alphabet." You might invite students to create their own pangrams or to search the Web for examples. A *panoply* is literally a "complete suit of armor" but now also "a splendid or striking array." Also as part of the discussion of the *plen* words, you might ask students to guess the meaning of *plenipotentiary* ("full power," as in the case of a deputy or dignitary).

*Did You Know?* **Omnivore** literally means "devour all" (*omni-*, meaning "all," + *vor*, "devour"). Omnivores, including humans, have a distinct advantage over animals that are carnivores ("meat eaters") or herbivores ("plant eaters") in that they can live on plants *and* animals. If one food supply is limited, they can turn to the other. There are many different types of omnivores, including some fish and various mammals and birds. Some creatures are insectivores and feed mainly at night. Others, such as earthworms, feed on decomposed matter. What do you suppose they are called? As a final thought about *vor*, have you ever had a voracious appetite? What was it like?

**SORT 56.** Latin Roots: Light and Dark; Day and Night (*cand/chand, jour, luc/lum, noc, omb/umbr*)

| Shine | Day | Light | Night | Shade |
|---|---|---|---|---|
| *cand/chand* | *jour* | *luc/lum* | *noc* | *omb/umbr* |
| **candlelight** | **journal** | **lucid** | **nocturnal** | **umbrella** |
| candelabra | adjourned | elucidate | nocturne | adumbrate |
| candid | journey | illuminated | | somber |
| candidate | photojournalism | luminary | | sombrero |
| candor | sojourner | luminosity | | umbrage |
| chandelier | | translucent | | |

*Considerations:* The only word likely to need additional explanation, besides those discussed in "Did You Know?" is *sojourner*. The word takes its name from *sub-*, perhaps here meaning to "subdivide," and *jour*, meaning "day." It literally means one who "daily rations," something you would have to think about if you made a sojourn, a word that means a "temporary stay."

*Did You Know?* Although we think of an **umbrella** as protection from rain, it was first used to protect people from the sun's hot rays. It comes from the Latin word for shade (*umbra*) and, when considered with its ending, means a "little shade." Although the umbrella has long been used in England to provide shade, it has been keeping people dry for only about 250 years. *Sombrero* is a related word; it comes from the Spanish word for "shade," *sombra*.

   *Candidate* was borrowed from a Latin word that originally meant "clothed in white." During ancient Roman times, a candidate seeking office wore a white toga to suggest that his character and reputation were unstained and that he was worthy of the office for which he was campaigning.

**SORT 57.** Latin Roots: Odds and Ends (*loc, pos, mut, magn, min*)

| Place | Put | Change | Great | Lessen |
|---|---|---|---|---|
| *loc* | *pos* | *mut* | *magn* | *min* |
| **dislocated** | **disposal** | **mutation** | **magnify** | **minimize** |
| allocate | composite | commuter | magnanimous | diminish |
| locality | compost | immutable | magnate | mince |
| locomotive | exposure | permutation | magnificent | minimum |
| | imposition | | magnitude | minuscule |
| | | | | minutia |

*Considerations:* Note that *miniscule* is an alternative spelling for *minuscule*. Minutia (mĭ•noo•shē•ə) refers to a small or trivial detail. The plural is minutiae, as in "people sometimes have to deal with minutiae as part of their work." Students should be able to identify the meanings of each word in this sort by considering the meaning of the word elements involved. If they have doubts as you discuss them, suggest that they consult a dictionary.

*Did You Know?* The phenomenon of someone shuttling back and forth between home and work every day is American. Although most people probably associate **commuters** with the 20th and 21st centuries, the word originated in 1865. Railroads made commuting possible, and the 1840s invention of the multiple-ride ticket, called the *commutation ticket*, made commuting easier and less expensive. The word *commuter* evolved from the commutation ticket: Riders involved in exchanging individual tickets for a less expensive, collective one were called *commuters*. Multiple ride tickets remain the preference of commuters for the same reasons they were desirable in the 1800s.

---

**SORT 58.** Latin Roots: "Stand," Alone (*sist, stab, stan, stat, stit*)

| | | | Stand | | |
|---|---|---|---|---|---|
| *sist* | *stab* | *stan* | *stat* | *stit* | *?* |
| **consistent** | **establish** | **stance** | **statue** | **institution** | **obstacle** |
| resistance | destabilize | circumstances | statistics | constitution | obstinate |
| subsist | instability | instant | stature | destitute | stamina |
| | | standard | status | restitution | |
| | | substance | | substitute | |

*Considerations:* Depending on the group, engage students in an open sort, or ask them to sort the words using the headers. In the latter case, explain that there may be oddballs despite the absence of a "?" card. After the sorting, discuss the categories and the relationship of each of the words to "stand." In some cases a dictionary may be of help; in others, it may require a guess. Incorporate the following "Did You Know?" into the discussion.

*Did You Know?* All of the words in this sort share a common ancestor, the root *sta*, meaning "to stand." However, unlike nearly all of the other roots discussed in Part 3, *sta* is much older. It is an Indo-European root and goes back to a language that was spoken about 7,000 years ago in an area somewhere between the eastern part of Europe and western Asia. The Indo-European language gave rise to many other languages. English and most of the languages of Europe and South, Southeast, and Central Asia descended from it. Because many languages arose from a common ancestor, certain words across languages descended from the same root; as previously noted, these words are called **cognates**. For example, consider "mother," for which there are numerous cognates: Spanish and Italian, *madre*; German, *mutter*; Swedish, *moder*; Greek, *meter*; Russian, *mat*; and Dutch, *moeder*. Knowing the word in one language can sometimes help with understanding the word in another. For example, though you may not know Spanish, you can probably guess the English word for all or nearly all of the following cognates: *automóvil, teléfono, octubre, miniature, importante, familia, foto,* and *vegetales*. Can you think of other cognates?

Greek and Latin Prefixes: Numbers (*mono-*, *bi-*, *tri-*)

| mono- | bi- | tri- |
|---|---|---|
| monotone | bicycle | triangle |
| biennial | trivial | biceps |
| triathlon | biweekly | trigonometry |
| monolingual | trio | bifocals |
| triad | bimonthly | monopoly |
| binary | monotonous | triptych |
| monologue | triplets | monolith |
| bicuspid | monorail | trilogy |

# SORT 27

Greek and Latin Prefixes: More Numbers
(*quadr-, pent-, oct-, dec-, cent-*)

| quadr- | pent- | oct- | dec- | cent- |
|---|---|---|---|---|
| quadruple | pentagon | octopus | | |
| decade | century | decimal | | |
| octogenarian | decathlon | octagon | | |
| percent | quadrant | centenarian | | |
| octave | pentathlon | October | | |
| December | centimeter | quadruplets | | |
| quadrangle | decimeter | pentad | | |
| bicentennial | octet | centigrade | | |

# SORT 28 Greek and Latin Prefixes: Size and Amount
(*semi-, poly-, multi-, micro-, mega-*)

| semi- | poly- | multi- | micro- | mega- |
|-------|-------|--------|--------|-------|

| semisweet | polysyllabic | multicultural |
|-----------|--------------|---------------|
| microphone | megaphone | polygon |
| semicolon | multipurpose | microchip |
| microfilm | megabyte | polygraph |
| multiplication | semicircle | multinational |
| polydactyl | microscope | semiskilled |
| semisolid | megalopolis | microbe |
| microcosm | multimedia | semifinals |

# SORT 29

Common Greek Elements
(*auto-, bio-, geo-, graph, -meter/metr, therm*)

| auto- | bio- | geo- | graph | -meter/ metr | therm |
|-------|------|------|-------|--------------|-------|

| | | |
|---|---|---|
| automatic | biology | geology |
| graphite | speedometer | thermostat |
| biosphere | geothermal | geode |
| homograph | bionic | odometer |
| geometry | cartographer | epigraph |
| biodegradable | barometer | autobiography |
| thermometer | automobile | biography |
| autograph | antibiotics | geography |

# SORT 30 Common Greek and Latin Elements (*aud, phon, vis, -scope, tele-*)

| aud | phon | vis | -scope | tele- |
|---|---|---|---|---|

| | | |
|---|---|---|
| audience | homophone | supervise |
| kaleidoscope | telegraph | periscope |
| phonics | visibility | audiovisual |
| audition | telescope | symphony |
| telethon | inaudible | telephone |
| envision | stethoscope | auditorium |
| phonograph | television | vista |

| | |
|---|---|
| telecommunications | telemarketing |

# SORT 31
**Applying Prefix Knowledge to Common Latin Roots** (*ject* and *tract*)

| ject | tract |
|------|-------|

| | | |
|------|------|------|
| projector | tractor | protracted |
| extract | subjects | conjecture |
| dejected | traction | projectile |
| subtract | interject | detract |
| injection | attract | abject |
| distracted | rejection | retraction |
| adjective | intractable | eject |
| contraction | objection | abstract |

Applying Prefix Knowledge to More Common Latin Roots
*(mis/mit, port)*

| mis/mit | port | ? |
|---|---|---|
| mission | portfolio | transplant |
| transportation | omitted | reporter |
| deport | transit | dismiss |
| commission | remittance | submissive |
| export | rapport | intermittent |
| missile | admittance | transatlantic |
| supportive | transmission | comport |
| emissions | import | promise |

# SORT 33 Latin Roots: Senses (*dict, spect/spic, spir, tact/tag/tang*)

| dict | spect/ spic | spir | tact/tag/ tang |
|------|-------------|------|----------------|
| contradict | spectator | | spirited |
| contact | respiratory | | tactile |
| inspector | conspire | | dictionary |
| edict | tangent | | perspicacious |
| inspiration | dictate | | expire |
| perspective | specter | | spectacle |
| tactful | contagious | | aspect |
| dictator | aspiration | | tangible |

# SORT 34
Latin Roots: Actions Set 1 (*fract/frag, rupt, flect/flex, vers/vert*)

| fract/ frag | rupt | flect/ flex | vers/ vert |
|---|---|---|---|
| fracture | eruption | | flexible |
| avert | reflex | | interrupt |
| fragile | rupture | | adversity |
| bankrupt | advertise | | abrupt |
| versatile | fragment | | vertigo |
| infraction | versus | | anniversary |
| controversy | fraction | | reflection |
| disrupt | deflect | | invert |

# SORT 35

Latin Roots: Actions Set 2 (*fac/fact, fer, mot, struct, ven/vent*)

| fac/ fact | fer | mot | struct | ven/ vent |
|-----------|-----|-----|--------|-----------|
| factory | | ferry | | promote |
| construction | | convention | | conifer |
| instruct | | emotion | | adventure |
| prevention | | facsimile | | demoted |
| inference | | transfer | | destruction |
| satisfaction | | motorist | | facilitate |
| motivate | | intervene | | avenue |
| infrastructure | | artifact | | obstruction |

# SORT 36 Greek and Latin Elements: Air, Land, Water, and Light
*(aero-, aster, hydr, naut/nav, photo-, terra)*

| aero- | aster | hydr | naut/nav | photo- | terra |
|---|---|---|---|---|---|
| aerobic | | astronomy | | hydrant | |
| navigate | | photograph | | terrain | |
| subterranean | | hydroplane | | asterisk | |
| nautical | | aerodynamic | | Mediterranean | |
| asteroid | | territory | | telephoto | |
| hydroelectric | | disaster | | aeronautics | |
| aerial | | navigable | | terrace | |
| photosynthesis | | astronaut | | dehydrated | |

# SORT 37
### Greek and Latin Elements: Round and Around
(*circum-, peri-, centr, circ, vol[v]*)

| circum- | peri- | centr | circ | vol(v) |
|---------|-------|-------|------|--------|
| circumference | | perimeter | | central |
| circular | | revolving | | periodical |
| circuit | | periphery | | circa |
| concentric | | involvement | | circumnavigate |
| perihelion | | evolve | | circulation |
| convoluted | | circumspect | | egocentric |
| revolution | | volume | | periodic |
| circumvent | | concentration | | circuitous |

# SORT 38

Greek and Latin Roots: Reading and Writing
(*gram, leg, lit, scrib/script*)

| gram | leg | lit | scrib/ script |
|------|-----|-----|---------------|
| monogram | legend | | literate |
| scribble | literal | | epigram |
| parallelogram | inscription | | legible |
| subscribe | telegram | | Scripture |
| legendary | prescription | | diagram |
| ascribe | cryptogram | | alliteration |
| grammar | circumscribe | | nondescript |
| obliterate | anagram | | literature |

# SORT 39
Greek and Latin Roots: Body Language (*man, ped, pod, ped*)

| man | ped | pod | ped |
|---|---|---|---|
| manual | centipede | | tripod |
| pediatric | quadruped | | expedition |
| pedagogue | expedite | | maneuver |
| management | podiatrist | | pediatrician |
| pedestal | manure | | podium |
| manufacture | encyclopedia | | pedantic |
| impede | pedestrian | | manacle |
| manipulate | antipodes | | pedagogy |

# SORT 40  Greek and Latin Roots: More Body Language
*(cap, cord, corp, dent/don, derm, ocu/opt)*

| cap | cord | corp | dent/don | derm | ocu/opt |
|---|---|---|---|---|---|
| captain | | accord | | | corpse |
| dentures | | epidermis | | | optical |
| cordially | | capitalize | | | dentist |
| dentils | | corporation | | | decapitate |
| capitol | | pachyderm | | | corpulent |
| dermatology | | discord | | | optometry |
| incorporate | | binoculars | | | concord |
| per capita | | corps | | | orthodontist |

# SORT 41 Greek and Latin Roots: People (*dem, greg, pol/polis, pop/pub, civ*)

| dem | greg | pol/polis | pop/pub | civ |
|---|---|---|---|---|
| democratic | congregation | | metropolis | |
| population | civics | | publicize | |
| civilization | policy | | desegregate | |
| egregious | civility | | cosmopolitan | |
| populace | endemic | | epidemic | |
| segregation | police | | uncivilized | |
| civil | gregarious | | politician | |
| demographics | publication | | civilian | |

# SORT 42

Greek and Latin Elements: Ruling and Governing
(-archy, -cracy, dom, reg)

| -archy | -cracy | dom | reg |
|---|---|---|---|
| monarchy | democracy | dominate | |
| regulation | regimen | aristocracy | |
| theocracy | technocracy | domineering | |
| oligarchy | regime | hierarchy | |
| autocracy | domain | bureaucracy | |
| regiment | anarchy | region | |
| dominion | plutocracy | predominate | |
| matriarchy | dominant | patriarchy | |

# SORT 43

Greek and Latin Roots: Truth or Consequences
(*jud, mon, ques/quir/quis, leg, ver*)

| jud | mon | ques/quir/quis | leg | ver |
|---|---|---|---|---|
| judicial | | admonish | | inquiry |
| legality | | verdict | | privilege |
| inquisitive | | requirement | | premonition |
| monstrosity | | very | | injudicious |
| legislation | | questionnaire | | summon |
| verify | | monster | | judgmental |
| legitimate | | acquire | | remonstrate |
| monitor | | adjudge | | verification |

# SORT 44

Greek and Latin Word Elements: Opposites
(*ante-, post-, bene, mal, hyper-, hypo-*)

| ante- | post- | bene | mal | hyper- | hypo- |
|-------|-------|------|-----|--------|-------|
| anterior | | posterior | | benefit | |
| malfunction | | hypersensitive | | hypothermia | |
| posthumous | | hypocrite | | dismal | |
| hypercritical | | anteroom | | malpractice | |
| beneficial | | hyperbole | | post meridiem | |
| malnutrition | | benefactor | | hypochondriac | |
| ante meridiem | | hypodermic | | postscript | |
| hyperventilate | | posterity | | malaria | |

# SORT 45 Latin Roots: Conflicts (*bell, cede/cess, pug, vinc/vict, val*)

| bell | cede/cess | pug | vinc/vict | val |
|------|-----------|-----|-----------|-----|
| rebellion | | concede | | pugnacious |
| victory | | valiant | | excessive |
| prevalent | | impugn | | convince |
| intercede | | evaluate | | bellicose |
| conviction | | secede | | repugnant |
| antebellum | | invincible | | recede |
| invalid | | pugnacity | | convalesce |
| secession | | belligerent | | evict |

# SORT 46 Latin Roots: Actions Set 3 (*clud/clus, duc/duct, pend, scend, tend*)

| clud/ clus | duc/ duct | pend | scend | tend |
|---|---|---|---|---|
| exclude | | conductor | | pendulum |
| ascend | | tendon | | abduct |
| appendix | | descend | | superintendent |
| recluse | | pendant | | inclusive |
| intensify | | aqueduct | | extensive |
| condescend | | distend | | impending |
| deduction | | transcend | | preclude |
| secluded | | appendage | | induction |

# SORT 47

Latin Roots: Actions Set 4 (*flu, junct, mod, press, sect*)

| flu | junct | mod | press | sect |
|-----|-------|-----|-------|------|

| | | |
|---|---|---|
| fluid | conjunction | modular |
| pressure | dissect | fluent |
| superfluous | junction | intersection |
| juncture | commodious | fluctuate |
| modify | adjunct | compression |
| irrepressible | influenza | bisect |
| insect | accommodate | confluence |
| moderate | influence | oppression |

# SORT 48 Latin Roots: Peace and Goodwill
*(fid, grac/grat, pac, sens/sent, sol)*

| fid | grac/ grat | pac | sens/ sent | sol |
|---|---|---|---|---|
| fidelity | gratifying | | pacify | |
| sensible | solitude | | sensational | |
| confident | desolate | | gratitude | |
| pacifist | congratulate | | bona fide | |
| ingratiate | sensibility | | solitary | |
| consensus | affidavit | | pacifier | |
| solitaire | gracious | | perfidious | |
| confidential | Pacific Ocean | | sentimental | |

# SORT 49 Latin Roots: Speaking (*lingu, loc/loq, voc/vok, verb*)

| lingu | loc/<br>loq | voc/<br>vok | verb |
|---|---|---|---|
| bilingual | eloquent | | vocalize |
| verbalize | soliloquy | | linguini |
| loquacious | verbatim | | colloquial |
| adverb | sociolinguist | | provoke |
| circumlocution | verbose | | vocabulary |
| vocation | lingo | | advocate |
| linguistics | vociferous | | verbiage |
| multilingual | revoke | | elocution |

# SORT 50

Greek and Latin Roots: Wisdom and Wonder
(*anima, cogn, mem, mir/marv, sci, soph*)

| anima | cogn | mem | mir/marv | sci | soph |
|-------|------|-----|----------|-----|------|
| unanimous | | recognize | | memorize | |
| miracle | | conscience | | philosophy | |
| incognito | | marvelous | | memento | |
| mirage | | cognizant | | subconsciously | |
| memorandum | | sophomore | | animated | |
| prescience | | immemorial | | conscientious | |
| inanimate | | miraculous | | memoir | |
| remember | | cognition | | sophisticated | |

# SORT 51

Greek and Latin Elements: Care and Illness
(*cur, path, -phobia, -itis, vol*)

| cur | path | -phobia | -itis | vol |
|---|---|---|---|---|

| | | | |
|---|---|---|
| manicure | empathy | claustrophobia |
| arthritis | volunteer | pathetic |
| volition | pedicure | antipathy |
| security | appendicitis | benevolent |
| acrophobia | pathology | agoraphobia |
| tonsillitis | malevolent | sympathetic |
| apathetic | bronchitis | voluntary |
| xenophobia | telepathy | laryngitis |

# SORT 52
### Greek and Latin Roots: Time and Family
(*chron, mat/matr, pat/patr, onym, doc*)

| chron | mat/<br>matr | pat/<br>patr | onym | doc |
|-------|--------------|--------------|------|-----|
| chronic | | maternal | | paternal |
| pseudonym | | doctor | | matrimony |
| patronize | | antonym | | synchronize |
| anachronism | | matrix | | indoctrinate |
| patriarch | | chronology | | acronym |
| docent | | eponym | | matriculate |
| anonymous | | documentary | | patriotic |
| matriarch | | patronymic | | chronicle |

# SORT 53 Latin Roots: Beginnings and Endings (*nov, sen, mort, nat, gen*)

| nov | sen | mort | nat | gen |
|-----|-----|------|-----|-----|
| novelty | senator | mortal |  |  |
| native | genetic | natural |  |  |
| mortgage | senility | progeny |  |  |
| engender | seniority | mortality |  |  |
| mortuary | innate | renovation |  |  |
| nativity | indigenous | national |  |  |
| senile | novice | generation |  |  |
| cognate | mortified | innovation |  |  |

# SORT 54 Greek and Latin Elements: Order
*(equa/equi, medi, prim, proto-, secu/sequ)*

| equa/ equi | medi | prim | proto- | secu/ sequ |
|---|---|---|---|---|
| equator | | medium | | primary |
| prototype | | sequential | | prosecute |
| consequence | | equilibrium | | median |
| equivocate | | primate | | protozoan |
| primeval | | consecutive | | equanimity |
| intermediate | | equinox | | subsequent |
| protocol | | mediocre | | primer |
| equality | | primitive | | intermediary |

# SORT 55 Greek and Latin Elements: All or Nothing
### (nihil/nil/null, omni-, pan-, plen/plet, vac)

| nihil/ nil/null | omni- | pan- | plen/ plet | vac |
|---|---|---|---|---|
| nil | | omnipresent | | pandemic |
| plentiful | | evacuate | | completed |
| replenish | | panoply | | vacuum |
| panacea | | vacancy | | omniscient |
| vacuous | | depletion | | pandemonium |
| omnipotence | | plethora | | nullify |
| pantomime | | vacation | | panorama |
| annihilate | | pangram | | omnivore |

# SORT 56

Latin Roots: Light and Dark; Day and Night
(cand/chand, jour, luc/lum, noc, omb/umbr)

| cand/chand | jour | luc/lum | noc | omb/umbr |
|---|---|---|---|---|
| candlelight | | journal | | lucid |
| nocturnal | | umbrella | | adumbrate |
| sojourner | | candidate | | translucent |
| somber | | luminary | | candid |
| candelabra | | journey | | elucidate |
| umbrage | | luminosity | | chandelier |
| adjourned | | sombrero | | nocturne |
| illuminated | | candor | | photojournalism |

# SORT 57  Latin Roots: Odds and Ends (*loc, pos, mut, magn, min*)

| loc | pos | mut | magn | min |
|-----|-----|-----|------|-----|

| | | |
|-----|-----|-----|
| dislocated | disposal | mutation |
| magnify | minimize | exposure |
| minuscule | locality | magnate |
| magnitude | commuter | mince |
| diminish | locomotive | permutation |
| compost | magnificent | minutia |
| magnanimous | composite | allocate |
| imposition | minimum | immutable |

# SORT 58  Latin Roots: "Stand," Alone (*sist, stab, stan, stat, stit*)

| sist | stab | stan | stat | stit |
|------|------|------|------|------|

| | | |
|---|---|---|
| consistent | establish | stance |
| statue | institution | substance |
| destitute | status | instability |
| establish | stamina | restitution |
| stature | resistance | statistics |
| circumstances | instant | standard |
| obstinate | destabilize | substitute |
| constitution | obstacle | subsist |

# Appendices

# Appendix A   Performance Records

| Category | # | Skill |
|---|---|---|
| **Compounds and inflectional endings** | 1 | Introducing compound words |
| | 2 | *ing:* No change and e-drop |
| | 3 | *ed:* No change and e-drop |
| | 4 | *ing:* No change, e-drop, and double |
| | 5 | *ed:* No change, e-drop, and double |
| | 6 | *ed: r*-controlled, no change, e-drop, and double |
| | 7 | *ed* and *ing:* No change, e-drop, and double |
| | 8 | Plurals: *s* and *es* |
| | 9 | More plurals |
| | 10 | *er* and *est:* No change, e-drop, double, and *y* to *i* |
| **Open and closed syllables** (Syllable juncture) | 11 | VCV and VCCV (doublet) |
| | 12 | VCV and VCCV (doublet or different) |
| | 13 | VCV, VCCV (doublet or different), and VV |
| | 14 | More VCV, VCCV (doublet or different) |
| | 15 | VCV (long and short), VCCV (doublet or different) |
| **Vowel patterns in stressed syllables** (Syllable juncture) | 16 | Long and short *a* |
| | 17 | Long and short *e* |
| | 18 | More long and short *e* |
| | 19 | Long and short *i* |
| | 20 | More long and short *i* |
| | 21 | Long and short *o* |
| | 22 | Long and short *u* |
| | 23 | *r*-controlled Vre |
| | 24 | *r*-controlled *o* |
| | 25 | *r*-controlled *a* |
| | 26 | *r*-controlled /ûr/ |
| | 27 | *r*-controlled *e* |
| | 28 | Abstract vowels with *o* |
| | 29 | Abstract vowels with *a* |
| **Unstressed syllables** (Syllable juncture) | 30 | Final syllables with aCe and *ai* |
| | 31 | Final syllables with /ən/ |
| | 32 | Final syllables with /ər/ |
| | 33 | More final syllables with /ər/ |
| | 34 | Final syllables with /chər/ and /zhər/ |
| | 35 | Final syllables with /əl/ |
| | 36 | Initial syllables |
| **Consonant extensions** | 37 | Hard and soft *c* and *g* |
| | 38 | Final /k/ |
| | 39 | *ch* and *ph* |
| | 40 | *gu(e)* and *qu(e)* |
| | 41 | Vowel *i* |

Name: _____

**Derivational constancy**

Vowel alternations

| # | Category |
|---|----------|
| 18 | Vowel, consonant, and stress changes with c |
| 17 | Changes in stress |
| 16 | With predictable spelling changes |
| 15 | Long and short to schwa |
| 14 | Long to schwa |
| 13 | Long to short |

Consonant alternations

| # | Category |
|---|----------|
| 12 | Adding ion: Predictable spelling changes |
| 11 | Adding ion: e-drop |
| 10 | Adding ion or ian: No spelling change |
| 9 | Adding ion: No spelling change |
| 8 | Silent and sounded consonants |

Revisiting prefixes and suffixes

| # | Category |
|---|----------|
| 7 | Prefixes (inter, mid, sub, super) |
| 6 | Prefixes (mis, en, de, anti) |
| 5 | Prefixes (un, dis, in) |
| 4 | Suffixes with final -y (ier, iness, ious, ily, ied) |
| 3 | Various suffixes with no change and double |
| 2 | ed and ing: No change and double |
| 1 | ed and ing: e-drop and no change |

**Syllable juncture**

Additional sorts

| # | Category |
|---|----------|
| 63 | States stress break |
| 62 | Hyphenated compounds with repeated elements |
| 61 | Hyphenated compounds |
| 60 | Color compounds |
| 59 | Food compounds |
| 58 | Weather compounds |
| 57 | Position compounds |
| 56 | Around-the-home compounds |
| 55 | Opposite compounds |
| 54 | Space compounds |
| 53 | Substance compounds |
| 52 | Homographs set 2 |
| 51 | Homographs set 1 |
| 50 | Homophones set 3 |
| 49 | Homophones set 2 |
| 48 | Homophones set 1 |

Prefixes and suffixes

| # | Category |
|---|----------|
| 47 | Putting it all together |
| 46 | Suffix y: No change, e-drop, and double |
| 45 | Suffixes: ful, less, ly, and ness |
| 44 | Prefixes: in, in, non, and pre |
| 43 | Prefixes: dis, fore, and mis |
| 42 | Prefixes: un and re |

Name

315

From *Mindful of Words* by Kathy Ganske. Copyright 2008 by The Guilford Press. Permission to photocopy this form is granted to purchasers of this book for personal use only (see copyright page for details). Enlarge 135% to fill page.

## Derivational constancy

| # | Category | Description |
|---|----------|-------------|
| 19 | A further look at suffixes and prefixes | Suffixes (able and ible) |
| 20 | | Taking a closer look (able) |
| 21 | | Suffixes (ant, ance, ent) |
| 22 | | Taking a closer look (ant, ance, ent, ence) |
| 23 | | Suffixes (ity) |
| 24 | | Assimilated prefixes (in) |
| 25 | | Assimilated prefixes (ad, com, ex, ob, sub) |
| 26 | Greek and Latin word elements | Numbers (mono, bi, tri) |
| 27 | | More numbers (quad, pent, oct, dec, cent) |
| 28 | | Size and amount (semi, poly, multi, micro, mega) |
| 29 | | Common elements: (auto, bio, geo, graph, meter/metr, therm) |
| 30 | | Common elements (aud, phon, vis, scope, tele) |
| 31 | | Applying prefixes to roots (ject, tract) |
| 32 | | Applying prefixes to roots (mis/mit, port) |
| 33 | | Senses (dict, spect/spic, spir, tact/tag/tang) |
| 34 | | Actions set 1 (fract/frag, rupt, flect/flex, vers/vert) |
| 35 | | Actions set 2 (fac/fact, fer, mot, struct, ven/vent) |
| 36 | | Air, land, water, and light (aero, aster, hydr, naut/nav, photo, terr) |
| 37 | | Round and around (circum, peri, centr, circ, volv) |
| 38 | | Reading and writing (gram, leg, lit, scrib/script) |
| 39 | | Body language (man, ped, pod, ped) |
| 40 | | More body language (cap, cord, corp, dent/don, derm, ocu/opt) |
| 41 | | People (demo, greg, pol/polis, pop/pub, civ) |
| 42 | | Ruling and governing (archy, cracy, dom, reg) |
| 43 | | Truth or consequences (jud, mon, ques/quir/quis, leg, ver) |
| 44 | | Opposites (ante, post, bene, mal, hyper, hypo) |
| 45 | | Conflicts (bell, cede/cess, pug, vinc/vict, val) |
| 46 | | Actions set 3 (clud/clus, duc/duct, pend, scend, tend) |
| 47 | | Actions set 4 (flu, junct, mod, press, sect) |
| 48 | | Peace and good will (fid, grac/grat, pac, sens/sent, sol) |
| 49 | | Speaking (lingu, loc/log, voc/vok, verb) |
| 50 | | Wisdom and wonder (anima, cogn, mem, mir/marv, sci, soph) |
| 51 | | Care and illness (cur, path, phobia, itis, vol) |
| 52 | | Time and family (chron, mat/matr, pat/ped, onym, doc) |
| 53 | | Beginnings and endings (nov, sen, mort, nat, gen) |
| 54 | | Order (equa/equi, medi, prim, proto, secu/sequ) |
| 55 | | All or nothing (nihil/nil/nul, omni, pan, plet, vac) |
| 56 | | Light/dark, day/night (cand, jour, luc/lum, noc, omb/umbr) |
| 57 | | Odds and ends (loc, pos, mut, magn, min) |
| 58 | | "Stand" alone (sist, stab, stan, stat, stit) |

Name: _____

Sampling of 100+ Important Math Words

### 3-D figures

cone
cube
cylinder
faces
hexagon
pentagon
plane
polygon
prism
pyramid
rhombus
sphere
three-dimensional
trapezoid
triangle

### Numbers

data
decimal
denominator
digit
equivalent
estimation
even
formula
fraction
numeral
numerator
odd
percent
pi
prime
probability
random
rounding
simplify
solve
variable

### 2-D figures

circle
circumference*
congruent
diameter*
intersecting
obtuse
parallel
perpendicular
quadrilateral
radius*
ray
rectangle
symmetry
two-dimensional

### Other

array
axis
bisect
coordinates
grid
horizontal
interval
matrix
mean
median
mode
probability
proportion
range
scale
segment
ratio
vertical

### Operations

addend
addition
computation
difference
divide
dividend
divisor
equation
minus
multiple
multiply
product
quotient
subtraction
sum
total

### Measurement

acre
area
capacity
centimeter
distance
gallon
gram
foot
height
kilometer
length
liter
mass
measure
meter
mile
millimeter
minute
perimeter
pint
pound
quart
second
temperature
volume
weight
width
yard

*Applicable to 3-D figures also.

Sampling of 100+ Important Science Words

| Biology | Astronomy | Physical science | Earth science | Other |
|---|---|---|---|---|
| adaptation | asteroid | acids | cloud | classification |
| amphibians | celestial | bases | conservation | environment |
| birds | constellation | circuit | core | extinct |
| cell | eclipse | compound | crust | magnify |
| decompose | galaxy | concave lens | earthquake | observation |
| diversity | lunar | conductor | erosion | properties |
| ecosystem | meteor | convex lens | evaporation | prehistoric |
| edible | meteorite | dissolving | force | reasoning |
| endangered | moon | elements | fossils | renewable |
| fish | nebula | friction | gravity | scientist |
| habitat | planet | gas | igneous | vibration |
| inherit | orbit | liquid | metamorphic | |
| invertebrates | phases | machine | mantle | |
| life cycle | radiation | magnet | ocean | |
| mammals | reflection | matter | plate tectonics | |
| metamorphosis | revolution | mixture | pollution | |
| offspring | rotation | molecule | precipitation | |
| organism | solar system | nucleus | seasons | |
| osmosis | space | plasma | sedimentary | |
| photosynthesis | universe | solid | thermometer | |
| predatory | wavelength | solution | volcano | |
| prey | | velocity | water cycle | |
| reptiles | | | weather | |
| respiration | | | | |
| shelter | | | | |
| species | | | | |
| threatened | | | | |
| thriving | | | | |
| traits | | | | |
| vertebrates | | | | |

# Sampling of 100+ Important Social Studies Words

| Families/ communities | Geography | Government | History | Economy |
|---|---|---|---|---|
| ancestors | borders | amendments | ancient | agriculture |
| community | boundary | Bill of Rights | civilization | boycott |
| cooperate | climate | census | colonial | consumer |
| culture | coast | citizen | Civil Rights | economy |
| custom | compass rose | city | Civil War | export |
| neighborhood | continent | Congress | expansion | famine |
| population | desert | Constitution | expedition | global |
| respect | equator | country | explorers | goods |
| responsibility | geography | Declaration of Independence | Great Depression | import |
| rural | globe | democracy | immigration | industry |
| settlement | hemisphere | document | independence | monopoly |
| suburban | latitude | election | Louisiana Purchase | produce |
| tradition | longitude | executive branch | migration | product |
| urban | map legend (key) | government | Native American | resources |
| volunteer | mountains | governor | pioneer | tariff |
|  | mouth | judicial branch | religion |  |
|  | ocean | justice | republic |  |
|  | plains | laws | Revolutionary War |  |
|  | plateau | legislative branch | segregation |  |
|  | prime meridian | mayor | settlers |  |
|  | region | President | slavery |  |
|  | source | Representative | suffrage |  |
|  | tidal basin | rights | treaty |  |
|  | tributary | Senator | World War |  |
|  | valleys | state |  |  |
|  | vegetation | Supreme Court |  |  |

From *Mindful of Words* by Kathy Ganske. Copyright 2008 by The Guilford Press. Permission to photocopy this form is granted to purchasers of this book for personal use only (see copyright page for details). Enlarge 135% to fill page.

| | |
|---|---|
| accept | I plan to **accept** their invitation to the party. |
| addition | **Addition** is used to find the sum of numbers. The family put an **addition** on their house after the baby was born. |
| affect | Will the change in schedule **affect** you? |
| allowed | We're **allowed** to stay up as long as we want on Friday nights. |
| aloud | The teacher read the story **aloud** to the class. |
| ascent | His **ascent** to the top of the mountain made him famous. |
| assent | Dad finally gave his **assent**, so I can go to the game. |
| bazaar | There were lots of interesting things to buy for cheap prices at the church **bazaar**. |
| berry | My favorite **berry** is the strawberry. |
| bizarre | That was one of the most **bizarre** movies I've ever seen, strange . . . really strange. |
| boarder | The **boarder** paid his rent and left. |
| border | There was a **border** around the bulletin board. Mexico **borders** the United States. |
| borough | A **borough** is another name for a town in some states, such as New Jersey. |
| burrow | Animals such as gophers, prairie dogs, woodchucks, moles, and rabbits dig underground tunnels called **burrows** for shelter. |
| bury | We will **bury** the dead bird. |
| capital | Begin the sentence with a **capital** letter. Washington, D.C., is the **capital** of the United States. To start a business you need **capital**, in other words, money. |
| capitol | The state government meets in the **capitol**. The U.S. Congress meets in the **Capitol** in Washington, D.C. |
| carat | **Carat** is the unit of measure used for diamonds and gold. |
| caret | When I revise my work, I use a **caret** (^) to show that I want to insert more information. |
| carrot | Do you want me to put a **carrot** in the stew? |
| ceiling | They looked up to see how high the **ceiling** was. |
| cellar | The **cellar** was used as an underground shelter from storms and to store items; it had an outside entrance. |
| cent | A penny is worth one **cent**. |
| cereal | I have **cereal** for breakfast every morning. |
| choral | For the **choral** reading, everyone read the same piece aloud at once. |

| | |
|---|---|
| colonel | He is a **colonel** in the army and hopes to become a general one day. |
| complement | This angle is a **complement** to that one; together they equal 90°. I have new shelves in my room; now all I need is a **complement** of books to fill them. |
| compliment | I appreciated the **compliment** about my work. |
| coral | **Coral** are marine creatures that produce rocklike deposits that are pinkish or red-orange in color. |
| council | The student **council** met to discuss the problem. |
| counsel | My brother's always trying to **counsel** me on how to improve my game. |
| currant | There's a **currant** bush behind my grandmother's house; she uses the berries to make great jelly. |
| current | I listen or read about the news every day to know about **current** events. Water in the river's **current** was fast-moving. |
| cymbal | I love to hear the crash of the **cymbals** when the percussion instruments play. |
| desert | After the battle was lost, the soldier decided to **desert** the army. To go to jail is a just **desert** for breaking certain laws. |
| dessert | The chocolate **dessert** was unbelievably tasty. |
| dual | I have a **dual** role in the play: Dr. Jekyll and Mr. Hyde. |
| duel | In olden times, two people sometimes fought a **duel** to preserve their honor. |
| edition | That company puts out both a morning and evening **edition** of the newspaper. |
| effect | Being able to read independently in school had a positive **effect** on their reading interest. The special lighting **effects** surprised everyone. |
| except | I'd go **except** that I have to watch my brother and sister. Everyone is going **except** me. |
| fairy | Which **fairy** tale is your favorite? |
| ferry | They crossed the wide river on a **ferry**. |
| flew | A bird suddenly **flew** out of the tree. |
| flu | They had to close the school because so many people were sick with the **flu**. |
| flue | We need to get a chimney sweep to come and clean the **flue** before a fire starts in it. |
| frees | Having no class tomorrow **frees** me to work on my project. |
| freeze | Water will **freeze** at temperatures of 32° Fahrenheit or 0° Celsius. |
| frieze | A **frieze** is an architectural decoration located above columns on a building or wall. |
| hangar | The airplane **hangar** held six planes. |
| hanger | Please hang your suit on a **hanger**. |
| kernel | Corn on the cob is delicious, but I have a **kernel** of corn stuck between my teeth. |

| | |
|---|---|
| lessen | An ice pack might **lessen** the swelling from your bump. |
| lesson | The **lesson** on plate tectonics was fascinating. |
| manner | His **manner** of speaking was clear and relaxed. |
| manor | The **manor** house on the plantation was a mansion. |
| marry | The man and woman decided to **marry**. |
| medal | The soldier was awarded a **medal** for his bravery. |
| meddle | Some people love to **meddle** in other people's business. |
| merry | If you have a **merry** time, it's a fun time. |
| metal | There's a lot of **metal** in an automobile. |
| miner | The **miner** put on his hard hat and headed down the deep shaft with a pick and shovel. |
| minor | He was released from the hospital after his **minor** accident. You are considered a **minor** until you reach full legal age. |
| morning | We'll leave in the **morning**, sometime before noon. |
| mourning | They were **mourning** the death of their old dog. |
| muscle | She exercises every day to keep her **muscles** toned. |
| mussel | Clams are a kind of **mussel**. |
| palate | She doesn't like bread that sticks to your **palate,** you know, the roof of your mouth, when you eat it. |
| pallet | Cargo from the ship was unloaded onto wooden **pallets**. |
| palette | The artist spread paint on the **palette**. |
| patience | I hate waiting for things, but I guess **patience** is something we all have to learn. |
| patients | Six **patients** were ahead of me in the doctor's waiting room. |
| peak | The climber made it to the top of the mountain **peak**. Most athletes reach their **peak** at an early age. |
| pedal | It can be difficult to **pedal** a bike uphill. |
| peddle | It used to be very common for people to **peddle** or sell goods door to door. |
| peek | Let's take a **peek** at the next chapter. Spring flowers were beginning to **peek** through the snow. |
| petal | The flower **petal** was ruffled around the edge. |
| pique | The odors drifting from the restaurant **pique** my interest; let's check it out. |
| principal | The **principal** starts the day with announcements. She is the **principal** dancer in her organization. |
| principle | Do you understand the **principles** we discussed in class? |
| profit | Businesses have to make a **profit** or they can't afford to stay in business. |

| | |
|---|---|
| prophet | The words of the **prophet** inspired the people. |
| rain | The **rain** poured for three days. |
| raise | I need to **raise** the height of this shelf. My boss gave me a **raise**. |
| rays | The **rays** of the sun streamed across the sky. |
| raze | I didn't know what the newsperson meant by "They will **raze** the old building on Monday," but then my friend told me that that kind of **raze** means *to demolish.* |
| reign | The **reign** of King Henry VI started when he was an infant and lasted for nearly 40 years. |
| rein | The rider controlled the horse by pulling on the **reins**. (*Reindeer* includes the same spelling but is unrelated in meaning.) |
| roomer | Because they had extra space, the family decided to take in a **roomer**. |
| rumor | A **rumor** is just hearsay and may or may not be true. |
| scent | Bears have a very keen or strong **scent**. |
| sealing | We are **sealing** this package in order to mail it. |
| seas | The stormy **seas** were rough and choppy. |
| sees | He **sees** my point but still won't let me go. With her new glasses she **sees** better than ever. |
| seize | He **seized** his backpack and raced to the bus stop. |
| seller | The **seller** had just about every product you could imagine. |
| sent | I **sent** her a postcard on my vacation. |
| serial | I like **serial** novels the best, because after the first one you can read another and another and so on. |
| stationary | You can't move the birdhouse because it's **stationary**. |
| stationery | When I write a thank-you note I like to use **stationery**. |
| symbol | Lots of **symbols** are used in math, such as +, −, $, %, >, and <, to name a few. |
| tidal | The storm created a huge **tidal** wave. |
| title | I need a **title** for my story that will grab the reader's interest. |
| vain | Your efforts to complete the project before tomorrow when you haven't even started it will be in **vain**. My sister's **vain** about her looks; she's always admiring herself in the mirror. |
| vane | The weather **vane** on top of the shed turned in the wind. |
| vein | The **veins** of a person carry blood to the heart; the lines on the leaf are also called **veins**; and streaks of gold or other ore in rock are **veins**, too. |
| weather | The **weather** today is supposed to be sunny and breezy. |
| whether | I don't know **whether** we'll go with them or not. |

## Appendix G  Understanding Prefixes

| Prefix | Meaning | Prefix | Meaning |
|--------|---------|--------|---------|
| ab- | away from | mis- | badly, wrongly |
| acro- | top, height, beginning (acr-) | mono- | one (mon-) |
| ad- | to, toward (ac-, af-, ag-, al-, ap-, as-, at-) | multi- | many |
| | | neo- | new |
| anti- | opposing, against (ant-) | non- | not |
| ante- | before | ob- | against, away, over, (toward) (oc-, of-, op-, o-) |
| auto- | self (aut-) | | |
| bi- | two | omni- | all |
| centi- | hundred | pan- | all |
| com- | together, with (co-, col-, con-, cor-) | para- | beside, beyond, similar to (par-) |
| | | penta- | five (pent-) |
| contra- | against | per- | through, thoroughly |
| de- | out, off, apart, away, down (des-) | peri- | around, near |
| di- | two | pre- | before |
| dia- | through, across (di-) | poly- | many |
| dis- | not, opposite of, apart (dif-, dis-, di-) | post- | after |
| | | pro- | before, in front of, forth |
| en- | put into, cause to (em-) | proto- | first, earliest (prot-) |
| epi- | on, over, near, after (ep-) | pseudo- | false (pseudo-) |
| eu- | good, well | quadri- | four, square (quadru-, quadr-) |
| ex- | out, away from (ec-, ef-, e-) | re- | back, again |
| fore- | before | retro- | backward, back |
| homo- | same | semi- | half, partial |
| hyper- | over, beyond | sub- | below, under (suc-, suf-, sug-, sum-, sup-, sur-, sus-) |
| hypo- | below, under (hyp-) | | |
| in- | not (il-, im-, ir-) | super- | above, over |
| in- | into (il-, im-, ir-) | syn- | together, with, similar (sym-, syl-) |
| inter- | between, within, mutual | tele- | distant, from afar (tel-) |
| kilo- | thousand | trans- | across, beyond, through |
| mega- | large | tri- | three |
| micro- | small (micr-) | un- | not, opposite of |
| mid- | middle | uni- | one, single |
| milli- | thousand | | |

Applying Prefix Knowledge to Common Latin Roots

| Root: | | |
|---|---|---|
| **Word** | **Literal Meaning** | **Actual Meaning** |
| | | |
| | | |
| | | |
| | | |
| | | |
| | | |
| | | |
| | | |
| | | |
| | | |
| | | |
| | | |
| | | |

# References

## Professional Literature

Adams, M. J. (2004). Modeling the connections between word recognition and reading. In R. B. Ruddell & N. J. Unrau (Eds.), *Theoretical models and processes of reading* (5th ed., pp. 1219–1243). Newark, DE: International Reading Association.

Allen, J. (1999). *Words, words, words*. York, ME: Stenhouse.

*American Heritage college dictionary* (4th ed.). (2004). Boston: Houghton Mifflin.

*American Heritage dictionary of the English language* (3rd ed.). (1996). Boston: Houghton Mifflin.

Ammer, C. (1997). *American Heritage dictionary of idioms*. Boston: Houghton Mifflin.

Barnhart, R. K. (Ed.). (2005). *Chambers dictionary of etymology*. New York: Chambers.

Bear, D., Invernizzi, M., Templeton, S., & Johnston, F. (2000). *Words their way: Word study for phonics, spelling, and vocabulary instruction*. Columbus, OH: Merrill/Macmillan.

Beck, I. L., McKeown, M. G., & Kucan, L. (2002). *Bringing words to life: Robust vocabulary instruction*. New York: Guilford Press.

Blachowicz, C. L. Z. (1986). Making connections: Alternatives to the vocabulary notebook. *Journal of Reading, 29*, 643–649.

Blevins, W. (2001). *Teaching phonics and word study in the intermediate grades*. New York: Scholastic.

Block, C. C., & Mangieri, J. N. (2003). *Exemplary literacy teachers: Promoting success for all children in grades K–5*. New York: Guilford Press.

Bruner, J., Goodnow, J., & Austin, G. A. (1956). *A study of thinking*. New York: Wiley.

Carroll, L. (1971). *Alice in Wonderland and Through the looking glass*. New York: Norton.

Cary, S. (2000). *Working with second language learners: Answers to teachers' top ten questions*. Portsmouth, NH: Heinemann.

Chomsky, N., & Halle, M. (1968). *The sound pattern of English*. New York: Harper & Row.

Copland, M. A. (2004). Distributed leadership for instructional improvement: The principal's role. In D. S. Strickland & M. Kamil (Eds.), *Improving reading achievement through professional development*. Norwood, MA: Christopher-Gordon.

Cotton, K. (2003). *Principals and student achievement: What the research says*. Alexandria, VA: Association for Supervision and Curriculum Development.

Dale, E. (1965). Vocabulary measurement: Techniques and major findings. *Elementary English, 42*, 82–88.

Ehri, L. C., & Rosenthal, J. (2007). Spelling of words: A neglected facilitator of vocabulary learning. *Journal of Literacy Research 39*(4), 389–409.

Ganske, K. (1999). The developmental spelling analysis: A measure of orthographic knowledge. *Educational Assessment, 6*(1), 41–70.

Ganske, K. (2000). *Word journeys: Assessment-guided phonics, spelling, and vocabulary instruction*. New York: Guilford Press.

Ganske, K. (2006). *Word sorts and more: Sound, pattern, and meaning explorations K–3*. New York: Guilford Press.

Harris, T. L., & Hodges, R. E. (1995). *The literacy dictionary: The vocabulary of reading and writing*. Newark, DE: International Reading Association.

Heaney, S. (2000). *Beowulf: A new verse translation* (bilingual ed.). New York: Farrar, Straus, & Giroux.

Henderson, E. H. (1981). *Learning to read and spell: The child's knowledge of words*. Dekalb, IL: Northern Illinois Press.

Henderson, E. H. (1990). *Teaching spelling* (2nd ed.). Boston: Houghton Mifflin.

Hendrickson, R. (2004). *Facts on file encyclopedia: Word and phrase origins*. New York: Checkmark Books.

McDermott, P. C., & Rothenberg, J. J. (1999, April). *Teaching in high poverty urban schools: Learning from practitioners and students*. Paper presented at the annual meeting of the American Educational Research Association, Montreal, Quebec, Canada.

*Merriam-Webster new book of word histories.* (1991). Springfield, MA: Merriam-Webster.

Moats, L. (2005/2006, Winter). How spelling supports reading: And why it is more regular and predictable than you may think. *American Educator,* 12–16, 20–22, 42–43.

Nagy, W. E., & Scott, J. A. (2000). Vocabulary processes. In M. Kamil, P. Mosenthal, P. D. Pearson, & R. Barr (Eds.), *The handbook of reading research* (Vol. 3, pp. 269–284). New York: Longman.

National Institute of Child Health and Human Development. (2000). *Report of the National Reading Panel: Teaching children to read: An evidence-based assessment of the scientific research literature on reading and its implications for reading instruction.* Washington, DC: U.S. Government Printing Office.

Oldfather, P. (1995). Commentary: What's needed to maintain and extend motivation for literacy in the middle grades. *Journal of Reading, 38,* 420–422.

Rutherford, P. (2002). *Why didn't I learn this in college?* Alexandria, VA: Just ASK.

Snow, C.E., Burns, S., & Griffin, P. (1998). *Preventing reading difficulties in young children.* Washington, DC: National Academy Press.

Spears, R. A. (2000). *NTC's American idioms dictionary* (3rd ed.). New York: McGraw-Hill.

Stanovich, K. E. (2000). *Progress in understanding reading: Scientific foundations and new frontiers.* New York: Guilford Press.

Templeton, S. (1983). Using the spelling/meaning connection to develop word knowledge in older students. *Journal of Reading, 27,* 8–14.

Zeno, S. M., Ivens, S. H., Millard, R. T., & Duvvuri, R. (1995). *The educator's word frequency guide.* Brewster, NY: Touchstone Applied Science.

## Children's Literature

Aiken, J. (2000). *The wolves of Willoughby Chase.* New York: Delacorte Press.

Barrett, J. (1978). *Cloudy with a chance of meatballs.* New York: Scholastic.

Clements, A. (1997). *Double trouble in Walla Walla.* Brookfield, CT: Millbrook Press.

Dahl, R. (1990). *Matilda.* New York: Puffin Books.

D'Aulaire, I., & D'Aulaire, E. P. (1967). *D'Aulaires' book of Norse myths.* New York: Doubleday.

D'Aulaire, I., & D'Aulaire, E. P. (1992). *D'Aulaires' book of Greek myths.* New York: Delacorte Books for Young Readers.

Editors of Time for Kids. (2006). *Butterflies!* New York: HarperCollins.

Fifth Grade Students of St. Joseph Montessori School in Columbus, Ohio. (2006). *What do you call a rhyming riddle? A hinky pinky!* New York: Scholastic.

Fritz, J. (1994). *Around the world in a hundred years.* New York: Putnam & Grosset.

Lawrence, J. (Illustrator). (1995). *The great migration: An American story.* New York: Harper Trophy.

Libbrecht, K. (2007). *The art of the snowflake: A photographic album.* St. Paul, MN: Voyageur Press.

Madden, D. (1989). *Incognito mosquito: Private insective.* New York: Random House Books for Young Readers.

Martin, J. B. (1998). *Snowflake Bentley.* Boston: Houghton Mifflin.

National Geographic Society. (2007, Spring). Body beasts. *Extreme Explorer,* 2–9.

Palatini, M. (1995). *Piggie Pie!* New York: Clarion.

Sczieska, J. (1992). *The stinky cheese man and other fairly stupid tales.* New York: Viking.

Still, J. (1991). *Amazing butterflies and moths.* New York: Knopf.

Terban, M. (1988). *Guppies in tuxedos: Funny eponyms.* New York: Clarion.

Terban, M. (2006). *Scholastic dictionary of idioms.* New York: Scholastic.

Truss, L. (2006). *Eats, shoots and leaves: Why commas really do make a difference.* New York: G. P. Putnam's Sons.

Vinge, J. P. (1999). *The Random House book of Greek myths.* New York: Random House for Young Readers.

## Websites

Discovery Education: *www.puzzle-maker.com* (retrieved April 8, 2008).

Between the Lions: PBS for Kids: *pbskids.org/lions/videos/homophones.html* (retrieved April 8, 2008).

edHelper.com's United States Theme Unit—50 States: *www.edhelper.com/geography/Fifty_States.htm* (retrieved April 8, 2008).

Ethnologue: Languages of the World: *www.ethnologue.com* (retrieved April 8, 2008).

Fun with Words: *www.fun-with-words.com* (retrieved April 8, 2008).

Miss Spelling's Spelling Center: *www.alphadictionary.com/articles/misspelling.html* (retrieved April 8, 2008).

Phobia List: *www.phobialist.com* (retrieved April 8, 2008).

Rick Walton's Compound Word Riddles: *www.rickwalton.com/curricul/comprid.htm* (retrieved April 8, 2008).

Southern Poverty Law Center's Site for Teaching Tolerance. *www.teachingtolerance.org* (retrieved April 8, 2008).

U.S. Census Bureau's U.S. and World Population Clocks: *www.census.gov/main/www/popclock.html* (retrieved April 8, 2008).

Webster's Online Dictionary: *www.websters-online-dictionary.org/definition/laughter* (retrieved April 8, 2008).

# Index of Words Used in the Sorts

Italic page numbers indicate where the word can be found in a sort template; *i* stands for the "Integrating Idioms" section; *d* stands for the "Did You Know?" section.